HIMALAYAN BARBARY

By the same author

THE NAKED NAGAS
  Second Edition (revised and enlarged) Calcutta 1946

THE ABORIGINAL TRIBES OF HYDERABAD. 3 Vols.
  Vol. I. THE CHENCHUS
  Vol. II. THE REDDIS OF THE BISON HILLS
  Vol. III. THE RAJ GONDS OF ADILABAD

CHRISTOPH VON FÜRER-HAIMENDORF

HIMALAYAN BARBARY

★

LONDON
JOHN MURRAY
ALBEMARLE STREET, W

First Published . . . 1955

Printed in Great Britain by Butler & Tanner Ltd., Frome and London
and Published by John Murray (Publishers) Ltd.

CONTENTS

1990

ILLUSTRATIONS

Illustrations

AUTHOR'S NOTE

THE EXPEDITION described in this book was intended to prepare the ground for the extension of administrative control over a group of little known tribes in the Indo-Tibetan borderlands. One of the most important aspects of this task was the study of the people's economy and social organization, but in an account of a mission which was basically exploratory a systematic analysis of the anthropological data gathered in the course of my travels would be out of place. Some of these data, moreover, have already been published and the student of anthropology interested in the Himalayan region, may find it useful to consult my reports and articles which are listed on page 238.

I am deeply indebted to the Government of India for affording me the unusual opportunity of working in an area whose inhabitants had never been subject to any form of external administration. To thank individually all the officials responsible would not be possible, nor do I think it proper to violate the traditional anonymity of Political Officers either here or in the following chapters. But I cannot suppress the name of my old friend J. P. Mills, who at the end of a distinguished career in the Indian Civil Service was in direct control of the programme of exploration in the hill regions of the Indo-Tibetan borderlands. His encouragement and support were invaluable and have added to the debt of gratitude which I owe him from the days when he was Deputy Commissioner of the Naga hills and I a young anthropologist on my first field trip. I would also like to thank Mr. and Mrs. Farmer of the Joyhing Tea Estate for help with many practical arrangements and for the hospitality of their house which my wife and I enjoyed whenever we passed through Joyhing.

Of our companions in the hills of the Subansiri area, I should like to mention four : Rajoni Gogoi, Ajitkumar Bhattachariya, Kop Temi and Siraj-ud-Dhin. They shared our discomforts and our achievements and each in his own way made a vital contribution to the success of the expedition. How they did this is told in the pages that follow, but

Author's Note

here I wish to record our lasting appreciation of their friendship and
loyal co-operation.

There is little to say about the equipment of the expedition ; it was
conspicuous by its absence rather than by its excellence. The only
exception was my Zeiss Contax III camera with which I took all the
photographs reproduced in this book. To field anthropologists it may
be of interest that the lense used for the portraits was a Sonnar 1 : 4 of
13·5 cm. focal length.

CHRISTOPH VON FÜRER-HAIMENDORF.

School of Oriental and African Studies,
University of London,
January 1955.

INTRODUCTION

On new year's day 1944 nothing was further from my mind than the thought of leaving the Deccan and the Gond village in which Betty and I had lived for the past two years. Yet, a month later, we found ourselves on our way to Assam heading for an obscure part of the borderlands between India and Tibet. This sudden change of plans was due to the unexpected offer of an appointment on the North-East Frontier, where the Government of India had launched an ambitious programme of exploration and development under the direction of J. P. Mills, then Adviser to the Governor of Assam for Tribal Areas and States. From him I learnt that I would be assigned to the Balipara Frontier Tract, where I was to 'establish friendly relations with the unadministered hill-tribes, collect data on general conditions and tribal customs, and ultimately explore the upper reaches of the Subansiri River'.

To accept this proposal meant to disrupt my anthropological work among the Gonds of Hyderabad and abandon for an indefinite period of time the experiment in tribal education which I was then directing. To decline was out of the question. No anthropologist could have forgone the chance of working in so tempting a field, and for me the project was especially attractive as it promised the fulfilment of an early ambition.

When I worked in the Naga hills in 1936 and 1937 I had often looked with longing at the line of blue mountains and glittering snow peaks which on fine days were clearly visible on the northern horizon. In between lay the broad trough of the Brahmaputra valley, and I wondered whether the little known tribes inhabiting those mysterious hills might have any affinities with the Nagas whom I was studying. My only experience of any of the 'North Assam tribes', as—failing a more apposite collective term—they are sometimes called, was a brief stay in several Abor villages of the Sadiya Frontier Tract. To penetrate beyond the foothills, whose inhabitants had been brought under a loose form of administration, was at that time out of the question, and the

x

vast hill-region extending west of the Abor hills between Assam and the borders of Tibet remained *terra incognita*, a country closed to both traveller and anthropologist.

The headquarters of the Adviser for Tribal Areas and States were at Shillong, and early in February Betty and I arrived there, bringing with us the camp kit which we had been using in the Deccan. In vain had we tried to supplement it with equipment more suitable to Himalayan conditions, but after four and a half years of war and import restrictions the Calcutta stores were practically empty and we were unable to buy either sleeping sacks or warm clothing, not to speak of tents or waterproof bags.

On my first day in Shillong, Mills explained how it was that at a time when the Japanese invasion of Burma had brought the war to the frontiers of Assam, the Government of India were nevertheless embarking on an ambitious programme of exploration in the Eastern Himalayas. The sudden realization that India's eastern borders were vulnerable had convinced Government of the need to fill the political and administrative vacuum which had been allowed to persist between Assam and Tibet ever since the establishment of British rule. Mills pointed out that my work in the eastern part of the Balipara Frontier Tract, henceforth to be called the Subansiri Sub-Agency, was to be part of a larger plan which embraced the whole frontier.

The ordinary small-scale maps of Northern India showed the international frontier boldly marked along the main range of the Himalayas, but the quarter-inch maps, which I now saw for the first time, reflected a very different position.

From these it appeared that between the 93rd and the 97th degrees eastern longitude, the frontier was undefined and much of the country through which it was presumed to run was unsurveyed. In the area of the Subansiri River, lying south and south-east of the Tsari region of Tibet, the Himalayan main range had never been reached from the Indian side ; and the Tibetans who came up to, and were believed at times to cross the passes from the north, seldom ventured southwards into the region of tropical rain forest which was inhabited by 'wild and independent' tribes, known in Tibet as Lobas and in Assam as Daflas and Miris.

This mountain country, enclosed for the most part within the great bend of the Subansiri, and lying between the foothills bordering on the Assam valley and the Tibetan districts to the north of the Himalayan main range, had always remained a political no man's land. In 1914 there had been negotiations with Tibet and China aimed at defining the Indo-Tibetan boundary east of Bhutan. They resulted in a convention drawn up by Sir Henry McMahon and initialled by the delegates of Tibet and China, which recognized the ridge line of the Great Himalayan Range as the international frontier, implying thereby that the entire sub-montane tract lying to the south of it belonged to India. The convention, however, was never ratified ; and though official Indian documents had ever since referred to the proposed border as the McMahon Line, no attempt had been made to demarcate the frontier or to administer any part of the Subansiri area. While Tibet took no steps either to implement or to repudiate the convention, China never renounced her claim to the sub-montane tract. Indeed on a recently published Chinese map the whole of the region through which we travelled in 1944 and 1945 is included within the borders of China. According to this map, China's frontier with India runs along the edge of the Assam plain, skirting the tea-gardens, and incorporating even those villages in the Abor hills which have long been administered by the Government of Assam.

While in 1914 Chinese claims were not likely to cause the Government of India any great anxiety, the Japanese thrust into the Naga hills in 1941 and the tragic fate of those refugees from Burma, who had tried to reach India through such unadministered areas as the Hukwang valley, had discredited the policy of leaving vast stretches of no man's land at India's back door.

The first step towards the extension of political influence over the country recognized as belonging to India in the convention of 1914 was to be the collection of data on local conditions and the establishment of friendly contacts with the inhabitants. The information at the disposal of the Government of India was at that time patchy and of very uneven quality. While a part of the Abor hills comprised within the Sadiya Frontier Tract had been brought under political control and military outposts in the Lohit valley and the Sela Agency guarded some of the trade-routes to Tibet, the Subansiri area had remained entirely un-administered. Knowledge of this part of the Balipara Frontier Tract was based almost entirely on the report of a semi-military expedition, which in the winter of 1911–12 had attempted to explore the upper reaches of the Subansiri River. This expedition, officially known as the Miri Mission, had succeeded in surveying a considerable area, but, meeting armed resistance in the valley of the Kamla river, had turned back before reaching the snow ranges.

Political Officers in charge of the Balipara Frontier Tract had subsequently made some minor tours through the country of the outer ranges, but such brief visits at widely spaced intervals had added little of importance to Government's knowledge of the tribesmen. They served, however, to uphold a belief in the treacherous and fierce character of both Daflas and Miris, and to perpetuate the tradition that in tribal country it was only safe to travel with a substantial armed escort. These beliefs and traditions still persisted, and I was told that an escort of Assam Rifles, Gurkha units organized as military police, would be assembled to accompany me on my tours.

Though at that time I did not fully realize the enormous difficulties of transport and supply involved in travelling with an escort in unadministered country, I was opposed to making my first contacts with the tribesmen under the eyes of an armed force. Such an approach, I pointed out, would jeopardize the chances of establishing relations based on mutual trust. Against this view stood the weighty opinion of the Political Officer of the Balipara Frontier Tract, who maintained that fifty Rifles were the minimum force that could secure the safety of any Government officer entering the Subansiri area. This appeared to be the view of all those who had had anything to do with the Daflas and Miris and it took a great deal of argument with officials many years senior to myself before I won my point. It was Mills' support which finally enabled me to set out, at least on that first season's tour, unescorted, and it was his recommendation that secured me permission to take Betty with me. Needless to say, the proposal that a woman should enter the Subansiri area met with the strongest disapproval of both officials and non-officials. But on this point I had equally strong views ; apart from personal considerations, I felt that, far from adding to my difficulties, the presence of a woman would greatly help to create confidence, and allay any suspicions the arrival of strangers might arouse among the tribesmen. Betty had lived among aboriginals for four years and I had no doubt that she would enjoy life among the Himalayan hillmen.

Having settled these problems and secured the financial provision for the porters' wages and other expenditure we proceeded to plan our first tour. The best approach seemed to be to concentrate on one community in a compact area and, after making friends, expand our relations to neighbouring regions as occasion offered. Mills suggested that the Apa Tanis, a large tribe which thirty years before had impressed the Miri Mission by its comparatively advanced civilization, offered the best opportunities for a first encounter. In the populous and apparently fertile country in which they lived I was to establish a forward base whence, in the following autumn, an expedition could set out towards the upper course of the Subansiri and the main range of the Himalayas.

We left Shillong with this aim incorported in official instructions in which I was designated Special Officer, Subansiri, directly responsible to the Adviser for Tribal Areas and States. My base was to be North Lakhimpur, a small town on the north bank of the Brahmaputra, and I was to draw on the resources of the Political Officer, Balipara Frontier Tract, for supplies and equipment. How sterile this source of supplies would prove I was only to learn later.

We travelled by car from Shillong to Gauhati. The station and the ferry-boats were crowded with troops on their way to the defence of Kohima, and after crossing the Brahmaputra, we boarded a narrow-gauge train for Charduar, the headquarters of the Balipara Frontier Tract. The Political Officer was away on tour, but we were met by his head clerk, a charming, elderly man who had spent a life-time on the North-East Frontier and appeared to know more than anyone else at that time about Daflas and their way of life.

Next morning we set out for North Lakhimpur. The road runs eastwards through the plain of the Brahmaputra valley, traversing great expanses of irrigated rice-fields, stretches of high tropical forest and acres of well tended tea-estates. During the rains and immediately afterwards the way is long and tedious, but in the cold weather the 199 miles are easily covered in a day ; at this season the tributaries of the Brahmaputra, which meander through the Assam plains, are bridged by temporary bamboo structures and only the Bareli river has to be crossed by motor-ferry. We made the journey in the Political Officer's station-wagon. The brilliance of the landscape, so refreshingly green after the browns and the greys of the Deccan, and an occasional glimpse of snow-mountains that rose in majestic splendour from behind the barrier of the outer ranges, conspired to heighten the spirit of adventure in which we approached the straggling bazaars of North Lakhimpur.

1

THE GREEN BARRIER

WHEN I look back on the two weeks we spent in North Lakhimpur preparing for that first season's tour, I wonder how we ever got into the hills. Mills had impressed me with the need for haste, and I was myself anxious to reach the Apa Tani country, so that I should have a fair stretch of consecutive work before the onset of the monsoon. But in this hinterland of war a civil expedition could claim no official priorities nor any stamp of urgency.

The problem of collecting equipment, supplies and transport—in ordinary circumstances a mere routine task—seemed here to meet with insuperable difficulties. Little was to be had in North Lakhimpur, and after the first few days I felt like a fisherman who casts his net again and again into a sea empty of fish. Amidst all these frustrations there were two things that encouraged us and spurred us on to further endeavour; the constant invitation of the blue mountains stretching out across the northern horizon, and the resourcefulness and level-headedness of Rajoni Gogoi, the local representative of the Political Officer, Balipara, who had been attached to my staff.

Rajoni's home was in North Lakhimpur and, like other Assamese of high caste, he claimed descent from the Ahoms, a people of eastern affinities related to the Shans of Burma that had ruled Upper Assam from the eleventh to the early nineteenth century. A man in his forties, Rajoni had had many years' experience of the hillmen, and he knew personally every shopkeeper, tea-garden manager and Government official in the district. His local knowledge of personalities and conditions stood me in good stead, and between us we wheedled and, where necessary, browbeat the inhabitants of North Lakhimpur into providing the bare necessities for our journey. On the open market one could at that time buy only such necessaries of the Indian kitchen as ghee, dhal, spices and onions; adequate quantities of the basic supplies we required,

I

such as rice, salt, sugar and kerosene, were obtainable only by circumventing ration regulations, a tedious and troublesome business that entailed enormous expenditure of time and energy.

Neither did the small shops of North Lakhimpur have stocks of goods normally required for an expedition into unknown and possibly inhospitable country—no tinned stores, no powdered milk, no butter and no jam or cheese. But I was able to buy a reasonable assortment of barter goods with which to pay for services in the hills where, I was told, Indian currency was not acceptable. Rajoni's experience of the hillman's needs was in this matter also of great value, and on his advice we packed into ten fifty-pound packages large quantities of matches, cheap cigarettes, dried country tobacco, brass bowls and cups and strings of beads of every colour. In Shillong I had bought some knives and a few red and green blankets as presents for important personages, but Rajoni did not think much of these. He said, and in this he was right, that what the local hillmen most valued were the handspun and handwoven silk cloths known as *endi*. They are manufactured in the homesteads of the Assam plains and with great difficulty we procured a few of these costly cloths to add to our 'political' presents.

The only other member of the staff was at that time a Brahmin clerk called Manik, who had been detailed from the Political Officer's office in Charduar. He was to remain in North Lakhimpur and supervise the dispatch of supplies once we were in the hills. After a long search we found him a poky little room in the Assam Rifles lines and there he set up an office.

Towards the end of the first week twenty-five porters arrived from Sadiya. They were Gallong Abors, recruited by the Political Officer, Sadiya Frontier Tract, from areas already under administration. A sturdy, smiling band in coiled cane pot hats and tufted cotton coats, they adjusted themselves quickly to local conditions and often delighted us with their haunting chants. They tackled the difficult journeyings in the Subansiri hills with energy and courage, and working in two parties successfully maintained my lines of communication until the beginning of the rains.

Our outstanding piece of good fortune was the arrival in the plains about that time of three Apa Tanis who carried news of some importance, and one morning Rajoni brought them to the Rest House with a Dafla to interpret. Compared to the tribesmen from foothill villages whom we had seen stalking through the bazaar loaded with bead neck-

2

laces of cornelian, turquoise and conch shell, these Apa Tanis seemed
a poor lot. They were dirty and ragged, and the only thing about them
which caught the eye were their red tails. These tails, one of the characteristic features of Apa Tani dress, are a constant source of mirth to
all who are not Apa Tanis, but they themselves are inordinately proud
of their brilliant appendage. Unlike the Naga who wears his decorative
tail only on ceremonial occasions, the Apa Tani is never without this tail ;
it is moulded to his body, an extension of his broad tight belt, and is
made of many strands of spliced cane. Curving down over the buttocks
and thighs to within a few inches of the hollow of the knee, it is dyed
a vivid red. Rich men and youths, particularly those careful of their
appearance, wear their tails broad and long, but the tails of poor men
and slaves are often short and skimpy and can only just be seen under
the body cloth. Below the knees the three men wore multiple rings
of the same red-dyed cane, but their only ornaments were small feathers
in their hats and brass pins stuck horizontally through their hair-knots.

I asked the men their names. The elderly gentleman with the greying
hair was Nada Rika, the handsome cheerful youth Koj Karu, and he
of the sullen face, who never lifted his eyes from the ground, Nada Pila.

So little was known of the Apa Tanis that neither Rajoni nor anyone
else was able to assess the status of the three emissaries and the importance
of their mission. What emerged from that first conversation was only
that they had come from the village of Haja, which was marked on the
map compiled by the Miri Mission in 1912. They claimed to have been
sent by two of the village headmen, referred to by the interpreter as
‘ rajas ’, to complain of the continuous raids made on the Apa Tanis by
the Daflas of Licha, raids which did not take the form of open attacks
but aimed at the capture of cattle and often also of men. It was not
clear whether the Apa Tanis had come to beg Government to take direct
action against the Licha Daflas or whether they thought that friendly
relations with the powers ruling in the plains would have a deterrent
effect on their troublesome neighbours.

They greeted my assurance that we would visit their valley with
enthusiasm and promised to act as guides and to render us every possible
assistance. Such an offer had, as we immediately saw, its advantages
as well as its drawbacks. To arrive in the Apa Tani country as the
friends and guests of Haja village would ensure us a good reception from
the Apa Tanis, but if the news spread that we had come in response
to the Apa Tanis’ complaints against their Dafla neighbours, we were

likely to become involved in tribal politics. Yet, we had little choice. Here were three Apa Tanis ready and indeed anxious to guide us to their country ; to enter the Apa Tani country under such favourable auspices was too good an opportunity to be missed.

But we were not yet ready to start. Our immediate problem was not only how to get our party, consisting of myself, Betty, Rajoni, interpreters and servants, up to the Apa Tani country with basic provisions for at least one month, but to find, and if necessary improve, a route which could be kept open until the middle of June. With the onset of the monsoon some of the unbridged streams to be crossed on the way to the Apa Tani valley would become unfordable. When I discussed the position with Rajoni, he suggested that Daflas experienced in building cane and bamboo bridges could be employed to bridge those streams which were likely to block our route.

Local politics helped us to enlist the co-operation of several villages in the foothills ; in recent times they had suffered from the raids of Daflas from the interior, and they hoped that the appearance of a Government party in the hills would enable them to recover some of their captured kinsmen. I spoke to some of the elders who came down to see me and they promised their co-operation in building temporary bridges on contract. Among the Daflas of the foothills the power of Government was well known, and in past years more than one Political Officer had taken action against villages that had raided across the so-called Inner Line, the boundary between the provincially administered plains districts and the unadministered highlands over which the Government of India claimed, but did not exercise, political control. The Inner Line was, indeed, the effective frontier of India, and various groups of Daflas, consisting partly of the survivors of villages defeated in war and partly of escaped slaves, had long been settled in the plains where they enjoyed the full protection of the law. Raids against them were punished, if necessary, by armed expeditions into tribal territory.

It was from among the Plains Daflas, the only section of Daflas over whom Government had at that time administrative authority, that we hoped to recruit most of the porters required to take us up to the Apa Tani valley. With this aim in view Rajoni and I visited several of their villages, but the results were disappointing. At a time when the United States Air Force was offering most attractive wages for building work on aerodromes, needed both for operational use against the Japanese and for the air-lift to China across ' the hump ', few Plains Daflas were pre-

4

pared to carry luggage at Government rates on a difficult trek into the high hills. In some of the plains villages I met a few Hill Daflas on visits to their lowland friends. They were men of powerful physique and Betty viewed with some alarm their enormous calves and thighs, and expressed the hope that travel in these hills would not automatically result in such development of the leg muscles. Most of these stalwarts, who bristled with swords, knives and arrows, derided the suggestion that they should carry our loads ; their attitude demonstrated the limitations of Government's influence over the hillmen, who knew only too well that as long as they behaved themselves on this side of the Inner Line, they could come and go as they pleased and no one could compel them to do anything they did not want to do.

It would be tedious to describe all the details of our preparations. They included a visit to Charduar where I failed among other things to obtain from the Political Officer's store the blankets and waterproof sheets that I sought for the temporary porters. The Gallongs recruited in Sadiya had arrived fully equipped, and I was loath to take Plains Dafla porters into the high hills without adequate protection. Our own kit too was far from satisfactory, for no suitable Government tents were available in North Lakhimpur. Mills, in his first letter, had warned me that I could hope for little in the way of equipment in Assam, and had urged me to bring with me all that I owned. This I had done, but after four years of hard and continuous wear in the Deccan my light single fly-tent was in no condition to stand up to extensive touring in the Himalayas. There was also the question of Rajoni and the interpreters. No warm clothing could be procured for them and their tentage was even more dilapidated than ours.

There came a point, however, when it was clear that what we did not have we must do without ; it only remained to fix the date of departure and decide on our route. Range upon range of wooded mountains rising to heights of 7,000 and 8,000 feet separate the Apa Tani country from the plains, and there seemed to be no possibility of avoiding this tangle of forbidding-looking hills by following the course of a river. The only major river that breaks through is the Panior, known in the plains as the Ranganadi, and I was assured that even the most agile hillman, not to speak of heavily laden porters, would be unable to make his way along the precipitous banks of the Panior gorge.

The Miri Mission of 1912, returning from the Apa Tani country, which they had reached by a roundabout route, had crossed the Panior

5

above the main gorge and made their way to the plains through the Par valley and the hills to the west. But this route ran through Dafla territory, and everyone advised me against exposing an unarmed party to the possibility of attack by Dafla raiders. Our Apa Tani guides too showed little enthusiasm for any deviation from the paths with which they were familiar. They were accustomed to use tracks running to the east of the Panior, where there was little likelihood of encountering hostile Daflas.

Everyone from Political Officers past and present to Plains Daflas now weaned from feuds and raiding, painted the Hill Daflas in un-administered territory in the darkest colours. They were described as treacherous, cruel and unreliable, ever set on loot and murder, and quite unamenable to any approach other than one backed by armed force. They would, so I was told, ambush parties of unsuspecting travellers, carry off women and children into captivity and leave men with severed tendons to perish in the jungle.

I could not bring myself to believe in this picture of unmitigated frightfulness. But as I had only just arrived in the Subansiri area, I had to make allowance for the apprehensions and beliefs of the plains dwellers who were to accompany me, even if they should prove un-founded or exaggerated. I therefore decided on the route recommended by our Apa Tani guides, a route which was reported to involve a march of six days through uninhabited country.

With neither supplies nor shelter available *en route* every porter would have to carry rations not only for the six days' journey to the Apa Tani valley, but also for the return to the plains. It was when I began to work out the details of the porters' rations that I was struck with the full realization of what travel in these hills would entail. A porter's daily ration of rice, pulse, fat, salt, and tea weighs slightly more than one Indian *seer*—about the equal of two pounds—and twelve days' rations for one man thus amounted to half a man's carrying capacity, twenty-five *seer* being the maximum that the average hillman can carry over rough country. In other words, we needed on this six days' trek through uninhabited country two men for every load we wished to arrive in the Apa Tani country. The recruitment of sufficient porters to assure mobility was one of our most serious problems on that first journey as well as during the rest of the season, and it continued to be so throughout our travels in the Subansiri area.

In brilliant sunshine we left on the 6th of March from North Lak-

6

himpur, taking all the luggage, the Gallongs and the staff by lorry to the outskirts of the Joyhing Tea Estate. There, in a piece of bamboo jungle within two miles of the Inner Line we built a base camp for the Gallongs and made up the loads into porters' packs. The day passed in the cheerful bustle and chatter of a large camp, but I was worried because many of the Daflas who had allowed us to write their names on the porters' roll had not arrived, and messengers sent to nearby villages returned with a mere handful of men. By nightfall only forty Dafla porters had been added to our twenty-five Gallongs, and several of the less essential loads had to be dumped in a store-room lent to us by Mr. Farmer, the Manager of the Joyhing Tea Estate.

This first day in camp was in the nature of a dress rehearsal for our personal servants, neither of whom had ever been on tour before. I would have preferred to take hillmen with me into the Subansiri area, but in this as in every other matter I had had to take what I could get. In Shillong I had picked up a Muslim bearer, a tall cheerful boy called Jaffar, and in North Lakhimpur the caretaker of the Rest House had offered his nephew, Abdul, as cook. As long as we remained in the shadow of the uncle the meals Abdul put before us had been fairly satisfactory, but the food on that first day in camp was hardly eatable. And, as we journeyed further and further from civilization, Abdul's cooking grew worse. Far from becoming accustomed to camp conditions he seemed to lose heart, and after a few days he no longer tried to disguise the dreadful truth that it was the uncle, anxious to obtain a job for his thoroughly worthless nephew, who had done the cooking during our stay at the Government Rest House.

If our team was weak on the domestic side, it was strong on the political. Our interpreter Kop Temi (Kop being the clan-name and Temi the personal name), a Dafla of the plains village of Rangajan, was a man of outstanding qualities. He spoke Assamese as well as several Dafla dialects and though he had never been to the country of the Apa Tanis he had a good command of their language. Though faithful to tribal custom in other matters, Temi compromised in the matter of dress : he tied his long hair in Dafla manner above the forehead, transfixing the knot with a long brass pin, and he wore small wooden plugs in his extended ear-lobes as well as the plaited cane helmet without which no Dafla leaves his house. His usual clothes, however, were a khaki shirt and a pair of blue shorts which looked slightly incongruous when worn with a broad leather baldric and the inevitable Dafla weapon known as *dao*. This *dao* is a crudely fashioned broad-bladed sword, and though of different shape is used for much the same purposes as the Nago *dao*.

Temi's round full-moon face with its low nose, vivid dark brown eyes and rather small mouth usually wore a pleasant jovial expression, but the well-developed forehead spoke of determination and energy and in anger his eyes would flash, his brows contract and his lips emit a stream of the most violent invectives. Even the fiercest hillman quailed before Temi's wrath, when his soft and pleasant voice would assume the metallic strength of a deep bassoon. Outstanding honesty, reliability and strength of character were matched by keen intelligence and supreme tact. He had the rare gift of combining the skill of able and faithful interpreting with initiative and imagination in negotiations and on many occasions we were to leave the initial talks with suspicious tribesmen to Temi, trusting his diplomacy to smooth out difficulties. I have never met a hillman either on that frontier or in the Naga hills, in whose loyalty and ability I had greater confidence. Without Temi the whole expedition to the Apa Tanis would have been abortive, for at that time he was the only man who had a thorough knowledge of the Apa Tani language and was also fluent in Assamese.

Among the Plains Daflas Temi occupied a unique position. His house near North Lakhimpur was a centre for visiting Daflas, Apa Tanis and Hill Miris, who gathered there for shelter and advice when they came to buy salt, cloth and iron in the plains. In his youth he had received some instruction in a Baptist Mission School, and it was due to this contact that he knew how to read and write Assamese. But his faith in Dafla custom and Dafla religion did not allow adherence to any other way of life, and at the time I knew him he had severed all connection with the Mission. His domestic life was that of a prosperous and well established Dafla; in 1944 he had already three wives and several children and in a recent letter, written five years after he had last seen me, Temi mentioned that he had married two more wives, and he added : " They are very young ones and happy to live with me."

Another useful addition to our staff was Siraj-ud-Dhin, a young Muslim who had been working as a messenger of the local Sub-divisional Officer. Anxious to have a man whom I could put in charge of the Gallongs on their journeyings to and from the Apa Tani country, I had looked for a man of all works. Siraj had volunteered for the job, and we never ceased to congratulate ourselves on this fortunate accident. His skill and unfailing cheerfulness in dealing with tribal porters soon

8

made him an indispensable member of the expedition and his courage and humour carried us through many a difficult situation.

Two of the Apa Tani emissaries, Koj Karu and Nada Rika, were also given the status of members of the staff, and received the pay of interpreters ; although their Assamese consisted at that time of little more than a dozen phrases, they were willing and most helpful, and remained good and faithful friends up to the end of our time in the Subansiri area.

The enumeration of the members of the party would be incomplete if it omitted Chunki, a tiny, black, half-Persian kitten we had been given in Shillong. She accompanied us on all our travels and was soon a well-known and popular figure among the local tribesmen.

Nothing is more depressing than to set out on an expedition in rain, and on the evening before our departure the sky was so overcast that I feared a break in the weather. This would certainly have led to defections among the porters. But the night passed and next morning the sky was clear and blue. We breakfasted at five, hoping to make an early start. The reduction of luggage had, however, not been drastic enough and there were still more loads than porters. Again we checked over the packages and were eventually forced to shed yet more provisions and personal kit, a necessity which we were to regret at many a meagre meal.

The sun was high in the sky before we left camp. To watch the line of porters swinging along with their loads on their backs gave us a sense of achievement. After the fevered haste of the last few days it was strangely restful to walk through the luxuriant evergreen forest where giant trees rose from the dense undergrowth. The air was cool and fresh and we were excited by the prospects of our new venture.

An hour's walk brought us to the markings of the Inner Line, beyond which no plainsman may go without the Political Officer's sanction. The Line, however, is unguarded and the only deterrent to a plainsman's crossing it is fear of the hillmen against whose aggression he has no redress once he has left the provincially administered area. Soon we came to the Dafla village of Joyhing, a cluster of houses built on piles and surrounded by raised granaries. The inhabitants had gathered ostensibly to welcome us, but in reality to beg for the release of the men who had been recruited as porters and bridge builders. The porters left their loads on the ground and joined their voices to the women's clamour, pleading ill-health and old age ; one man tried to arouse our sympathy by opening his mouth and showing the toothless state of his gums, and

9

another claimed leave of absence for the sake of his young wife and fortnight-old child, dragging them forward for my inspection. I solved this problem by paying a small sum to a girl of another house to help the young mother, and turned a deaf ear to all other arguments.

A fair path led from Joyhing into the valley of the Jumni river. Our intention had been to bridge this river in two places. This I had been told would allow the route to be used during the rains. But even here, so near the Inner Line, our information proved faulty ; the path we followed crossed so continuously from side to side of the valley that not two bridges but twenty would have been required to keep the road open. There was, however, another route ; it was longer, but Temi thought that with three bridges it could be made passable at least until the middle of June.

We walked for two hours up the valley, picking our way in and out of the stream-bed, until we were forced up on to the left bank by a series of rapids. Here the path was so overgrown that our progress was slow and our Apa Tani guides, using their *dao* left and right, cleared the way as they went. I too wielded a broad sword which I had recently bought from Koj Karu, but my efforts were less effective and I contented myself with tidying up thorny branches and creepers so that they should not catch on the porters' carrying baskets.

After two hours of this wearisome going, we left the Jumni valley, and began to climb through the débris of a wild elephants' frolic, a tangle of broken bamboo and fern which completely obscured the path. Everywhere there were mounds of giant droppings and the peculiar acrid smell of drying elephant excrement. This climb was followed by a descent so steep that we had to cut steps in the clayey hillside to prevent the porters from slipping.

In our camp on the Gage river that night there were many complaints among the porters. A Gallong had sprained his ankle, others had cuts and bruises and everybody's legs were bleeding from leech bites. Betty, who had charge of the medicines, spent more than an hour attending to patients, a strenuous task after a hard march.

Early next morning I went with the Joyhing Daflas to view the sites on the new route where bridges would have to be built. They assured me that with these bridges I would secure our return during the rains. For building a bridge across the Gage river they demanded one hundred rupees, and this sum I gave them in advance, promising payment for the other two bridges when I returned from the hills.

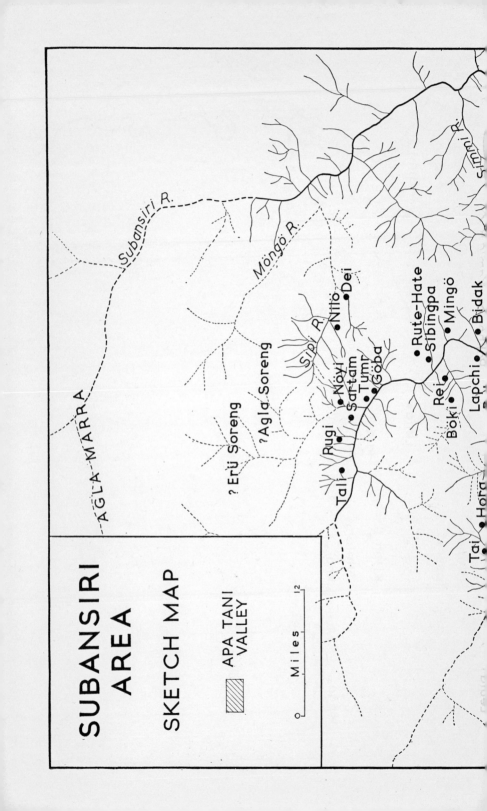

SUBANSIRI
AREA

SKETCH MAP

APA TANI
VALLEY

Miles

0   6   12

Subansiri R.

Möngö R.

AGLA-MARRA

? Erü Soreng

? Agla Soreng

Sipi R.

Niitö

Dei

Noyi

Sartam

Tumr

Goba

Rute-Hate

Sibingpa

Mingö

Bidak

Rei

Boki

Lapchi

Rugi

Tali

Tai

Hora

Simmi R.

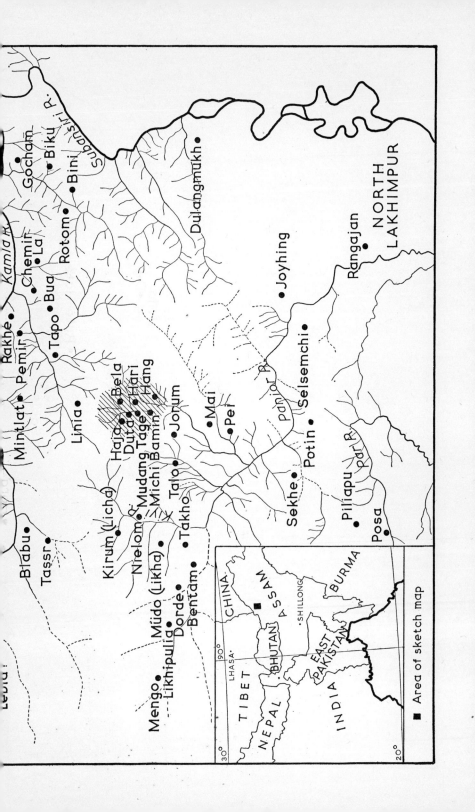

The porters had gone ahead and by the time we caught up with them they were toiling up the lower slopes of Mount Kemping, a ridge of some 6,000 feet. It was a long ascent and one which took us most of that day. At first the path was reasonably good, rising steadily through magnificent forests, but higher up we came into bamboo jungle through which the path zig-zagged at so steep a gradient that, looking back, we saw only the crowns of the porters' heads as they straggled behind us. In some places the Apa Tanis tied creepers to trees to give the porters handholds, but the latter found the way difficult and had to rest every few minutes. I too was not very happy and felt my right knee which once overstrained often troubles me at the beginning of a trek. Karu, the youngest of our Apa Tani guides, encouraged us in a rather charming manner, assuring us again and again in his few words of Assamese that the summit was near and that there was 'no more climb'. He did not seem to know the meaning of fatigue and though he carried quite an appreciable load, raced backwards and forwards, slashing through tangled bamboo and cane and helping porters who were in difficulties. With bare arms and legs and only a small, ragged cloth wrapped tightly round his body, his drawn sword, youthful strength and exuberant spirits he suggested the young Siegfried in his forest days.

We must have climbed some 4,000 feet when we reached the small spring beside which we were to camp. There was only a trickle oozing from the mossy ground, but as no other source of water was known to exist for a long way ahead, we made the best of this inconvenient site. A small ledge provided just enough level space to accommodate our tent, Rajoni's shelter and the servants' tarpaulin.

That evening Betty counted forty-two patients, more than half of our porters. To the aches and pains of the evening before were added coughs, headaches and feverish colds and we came to the conclusion that the Daflas of the plains and the foothills could not be very healthy. Indeed, this was so, Rajoni told me ; once settled at low altitudes, the Daflas easily succumb to malaria, and tuberculosis was spreading at an alarming rate.

The conditions under which the porters had to spend the night on Mount Kemping were not conducive to raising their morale. They found neither cane nor banana leaves suitable for thatching temporary shelters, and while the Gallongs, who served on a three months' contract, had been issued with blankets and waterproof sheets, the Daflas had received no such equipment and shivered in their flimsy cotton cloths. To make matters worse, a thunderstorm broke during the night, and no one got much sleep.

At dawn it was still raining and it became necessary to lighten the loads composed of tents and tarpaulins now wet and heavy. This repacking, and the Daflas' habit of splitting packages and rushing ahead carrying less than a full load, caused so much delay that it was nearly nine o'clock when we started to climb the last few hundred feet to the top of Mount Kemping. Once we had reached the crest, the path dropped steeply and despite the slippery ground we made good progress. The rain stopped, and we rejoiced at the thought that the Perre river, where we were to make our next camp, could not be very far.

Suddenly, however, we were stopped by excited shouts, and those who were ahead came back, saying that we were on the wrong path. The Daflas stood in an angry, *dao*-waving crowd, denouncing the Apa Tani guides, who, they claimed, had purposely misled us. But Karu and Rika took no notice of these accusations ; they plunged into the forest and disappeared downhill at right angles to the path we had taken. In twenty minutes they returned with the disheartening news that we were too far east : we must retrace our steps and take another path.

The Daflas, thoroughly disgruntled, blamed our guides and the Apa Tanis blamed the Daflas for running ahead. For over an hour, as we toiled uphill, they continued to upbraid each other with mutual and fruitless recriminations. Unable to understand a word I was not unduly perturbed, but Rajoni was worried when he overheard a Dafla say : " Why don't we drop our loads, and cut up these people who give us so much trouble. There are no sepoys ! We can finish them off here and now." I did not take this suggestion very seriously, but it showed a deplorable deterioration in the general atmosphere.

We climbed for nearly two hours up the slope we had so gaily and so swiftly descended, till we came to the turning we had missed. The new path led down into luxuriant forest. From rocky cliffs, which we negotiated with the help of cane-ropes, we looked down into large clusters of tree-ferns, their delicate leaves beaded with great pearly raindrops. Pale green moss enveloped the trees and hung tousled and dripping from every branch, and creepers hoary with lichen wound through space in grotesquely contorted forms.

The fairy-tale beauty of this rank and glistening vegetation temporarily banished our weariness, but as the way dragged on we knew that

12

we were both hungry and exhausted. We had eaten only a handful of dates since early morning and the slippery uneven ground called for continuous effort. Such glimpses as we gained of the landscape through gaps in the trees were not very encouraging, for there seemed no end to the misty space below and the slopes on the opposite side of the valley maintained their distance.

Late in the afternoon we heard at last the roar of water, and an hour later we came to the last steep descent, a cliff face as slippery as any we had met, with little hold for feet or hands on the dark grey rock.

As we stepped out of the forest, we found ourselves at a point of the river-bank that overlooks the confluence of the two rivers Panior and Perre. Fifty yards downstream a slender bridge of bamboo and cane spanned the Perre in an elegant arch and at its head a group of smiling Daflas stood to welcome us. They were men of Selsemchi and Potin whom I had commissioned to build the bridge, and they had just put the finishing touches to their handiwork. The bridge rested on two poles, firmly set between rocks on either bank and for added security it hung suspended by creeper ropes from great trees standing higher up the slopes. No cane of the kind usually used for the suspension bridges characteristic of the Himalayas was available in this gorge, but the Daflas assured us that the bridge they had built would stand the force of the Perre in flood.

On the opposite bank there was a broad shelf which seemed an ideal camping site for the porters, and a little lower down, close to the rushing waters, we found a sandy patch big enough to hold our tent.

It was nearly six o'clock when the last exhausted porter staggered across the bridge and flopped down on the sand. To continue next morning was only to invite protest, and before any complaint could be voiced I announced a day's halt. An issue of tea, sugar and country liquor and the prospect of a rest made everybody happy and our Daflas were soon busy cutting bamboo and banana leaves from which to build themselves shelters.

With our tent pitched and the porters settled round their cooking-pots we had time to survey the scene. Two valleys, both equally narrow, met at right angles, and as the Panior approached the confluence with its tributary, it thundered in a cloud of white foam and spray over a series of rocky steps. Then, joined by the Perre, it stormed against a wall of rock which, turning it, sent it roaring through a narrow gorge where it disappeared from view. It was this gorge which had

13

necessitated the lengthy and strenuous detour over Mount Kemping. As the crow flies the confluence of Perre and Panior is little more than four miles from Gage, but we had been forced to do two hard marches to make this small advance.

At dusk the mist that had lain over the valley cleared, and from behind a ridge which shut out one-third of the horizon the moon rose in un-clouded brilliance. Now we saw that the wooded hills flanking the river to the north was the first of three ranges, each one higher than the other. The walls of the gorge lay still in deep shadow, but the water caught the light reflected from the moonlit clouds. As the moon climbed the sky, the contrasts deepened : the waters of the river seemed to absorb all the silvery light while the black rocks grew darker and darker. It was a scene such as one sees only once in a lifetime, and we sat for a long time looking in silence at the turmoil of the foaming river and the play between light and darkness.

Next morning was fine and sunny. Some of the Daflas set conical fish traps in the rapids and Temi managed to shoot a fish otter. But the men of Selsemchi and Potin went to construct a small bridge over the Pei river, which we were to cross the next day. When they returned they told me of an easier route to the Apa Tani country, which for three marches runs due north and south through the foothills to the west, then crosses the river, and leads to the Apa Tani valley by way of the Dafla villages of Mai and Jorum. Next season, when I would have a better grasp of the situation, I thought we might try this way, but from their stories of conditions in the area, I considered I had been wise to choose the route advised by the Apa Tanis. Likha, a powerful clan inhabiting a tract of land near the upper course of the Panior, was terrorizing the country south of the river and in recent years Likha men had carried their raids into the lower Panior valley, wiping out whole villages, killing many people and carrying off others as slaves.

In the camp on the Perre river we all suffered from dim-dams, those yellowish flies which make life a misery in the low valleys of the Eastern Himalayas. They are about half the size of an ordinary house-fly and their bite, though painless, produces a small, highly irritating blister, which once scratched, easily grows septic. There seems to be no pro-tection against this pest except the wearing of long sleeves and long-legged trousers, for against dim-dams the most specialized insecticides are as ineffective as the country specifics of tobacco juice and salt. Even Daflas long resident in the area do not seem to have developed an

14

immunity and their naked limbs were peppered with pin-heads of dark congealed blood.

Next day Jaffar chose to wake us at three o'clock. And we, like he, were deceived into thinking the day had dawned until, emerging from our tent, we saw it was the moon that lit the white mist rising from the waters. We ate an untimely breakfast and should have got off early ; but one of the porters had developed a temperature during the night and we were kept hanging about arranging for his transport to the plains. Fortunately I could spare three men to carry him without abandoning any loads, for considerable amounts of rations had been consumed on the three days' journey.

We started the day's march by crossing the Pei river on the newly erected bridge. Then we began to climb the long shoulder of Mount Lai. The forest was so thick that we did not catch a single glimpse of the surrounding countryside. Now and then I saw a bird flitting from branch to branch in some distant tree, and once we came across two hornbills perched close overhead, but there was no trace of any of the larger animals which must surely inhabit such a lonely tract.

We climbed steadily through woods whose character changed as we gained height ; gradually the sub-tropical evergreen forest gave way to a semi-evergreen temperate type intermixed with some deciduous trees. At about 4,500 feet the trees grew smaller, the foliage sparser and instead of the ordinary type of bamboo, thick stemmed and heavy headed, there grew a small slender variety which is said to be poisonous. This is the bamboo which is used in game-traps, and the Daflas believe that even a man wounded by such a sharpened shaft will die in a very short time.

At an altitude of about 5,000 feet we found a good camp-site. The weather continued fair, but the night was unpleasantly cold so that in the morning we rejoiced in the warmth of the camp-fires around which we crowded as we waited for the loads to be packed. Karu, the only man who knew this route, urged us to hurry, saying that the day's stage was longer than any we had done so far.

A steady climb of two hours and a short steep ascent brought us to the top of Mount Lai, perhaps 7,000 feet high, and from there we had our first view over the outer ranges.

It was so fine a day that haze blotted out the distance and we saw nothing of the plains that we knew must lie beyond the ridges we over-looked. The shoulders and spurs around us swept up to summits as high and higher than the peak on which we stood. But not on a single slope was the mantle of thick forest broken and as far as the eye could see there was no sign of human habitation.

Northwards from Mount Lai the path followed the dented back of a ridge. Gradually we lost height and soon we returned to the region of high, damp forest where trees and stones were clothed in shaggy, dripping moss. Here at a height of perhaps 5,000 feet we saw the first flowering orchids, clusters of delicate white flowers, the inner calyx speckled with orangy yellow, growing from the crutch of an ancient gnarled tree.

We had been on the way seven hours when we sat down on a fallen trunk to eat our lunch. But on opening the boxes, we found that they contained nothing but a little pepper and salt, for our incomparable cook had forgotten to pack any lunch. He was not even there to be abused, but was lagging behind somewhere at the end of the long drawn-out porters' column. There was nothing to do but to continue on an empty stomach.

Soon afterwards we ran into a hailstorm, and Karu hurried us up a steep incline into a rock shelter. There we stood shivering as the wind tore the trees at the cave's mouth, but when the storm had spent itself the clouds parted and Karu, going to the edge of the cliff shouted : " Look, there is our country ! Look quickly, and you will see the fields of Hang ! "

Indeed far below we had for a moment a bird's-eye view of a wide open valley marked with the characteristic pattern of irrigated rice-fields ; then the clouds shifted, drew together, and the view was gone. Karu was delighted that we should have had this glimpse of the Apa Tani country and he explained how eagerly Apa Tanis returning from the plains looked forward to this first sight of their homeland.

Now the path dropped more steeply and passing quickly through the zone of tree-ferns and cane-palms we came to a river known as Pangen. Here on a level space we found a good camp-site and met the first and only travellers we had encountered on the five days' march. They were three Apa Tanis of Haja who were returning from a trading expedition to North Lakhimpur.

But of our guides Pila and Rika there was no sign ; they had gone ahead while we rested at the camp on the Perre river to purchase rice in the Apa Tani country for our improvident Dafla porters who, rationing themselves, were now running short of food. Karu was certain that Rika and Pila would arrive that night and just as we settled into camp

16

and Betty began her doctoring, there were loud shouts and Nada Pila burst out of the forest with thirty Apa Tanis behind him. Nothing could have dispelled our weariness more quickly. Their coming not only promised the end of our supply difficulties, but augured well for the attitude of the Apa Tanis as a whole.

The men crowding our camp were all dressed in more or less the same way, with cane-helmets, coarse grey cloths wrapped tightly round the body, red cane-belts with the characteristic tails and a flat cane-haversack carried on the back. Some had large cloaks of greyish cloth, and two wore a peculiar kind of rainshield made of black fibre. Many had feathers in their hats, and one man wore a little fluffy cap of black monkey skin perched on his hair knot. They were extremely friendly and seemed to bubble over with cheerfulness. The man with the fur cap made me try it on and this was thought a great joke. Most of the men were from Haja, and Karu was obviously proud that his arrangements had worked out so well. Not only had the Apa Tanis brought supplies of rice for our Dafla porters, but they had come prepared to carry our loads and this enabled me to pay off the worst grousers among the Plains Daflas.

The delight at the success of this first meeting was probably mutual. The only outsiders the Apa Tanis had ever seen in the vicinity of their country were officers surrounded by large escorts of sepoys with danger-ous-looking weapons, and the sight of a friendly traveller and his wife was an altogether novel experience. Any initial nervousness therefore turned to exuberant hilarity. Our position was much the same. We had been told so many stories of the hostility, treachery and unpredictable temper of the hillmen, and Government servants and tea planters alike had been so persistent in their warnings against entering tribal territory without adequate protection that we half believed in the difficult tempera-ment of the local tribesmen. The friendliness of these Apa Tanis reassured us and despite our weariness we did our best to charm and to amuse our visitors, who seemed as curious and as easily swayed by laughter as children. They crowded round our tent, touched and handled our belongings and were fascinated by the zip fastener which closed the tent door. When they saw the two camp-beds they wanted to know whether I slept on the one and Betty on the other, or whether we shared one. The information that each of us used a separate bed was received with astonishment. When I showed them my electric torch, a loquacious young man expressed the keenest appreciation of its usefulness. He thought it would greatly add to the interest of love-making in the dark and proceeded to demonstrate its usefulness with unmistakable gestures.

The cigarettes which we distributed were eagerly accepted, but what the men really wanted were matches. A few of them offered us eggs in exchange, while others hopefully expected to get them as presents, and at that first meeting were not disappointed in their optimism.

It was growing late when we sat down to eat our dinner, and the Apa Tanis, taking off their cane-rucksacks, rummaged in the dark interiors for the boiled rice and pork which they had brought from home. Then they squatted beside our fire piling the food on platters of hide and deer skin, and roasting small pieces of pork impaled on bamboo spikes.

Light rain fell during the night but next morning was fair and bright. We crossed the Pangen river, jumping from boulder to boulder, and decided that here too a bridge would be necessary if we wanted to secure our communications at the beginning of the rains.

Beyond the river there was a steep, slippery slope, and then we entered high forest lit by the blossoms of deep red, bright pink and pure white rhododendron. The Apa Tanis were pleased at our appreciation of these flowers and assured us that many more such trees grew in their homeland. When I picked a spray and put it in my buttonhole, Karu eyed it critically ; he came and picked off the green leaves, which apparently did not please his æsthetic sense, and then replaced the naked bloom in my coat.

We were still excited by the beauty of these enormous blossoming trees happily set against a deep blue sky, when we came on a small glade in the midst of the forest, a sunlit meadow studded with tall lilac-coloured primulæ. For us this was the first spring landscape, as we in Europe know it, that we had seen for five years and our delight must have been patent, for the Apa Tanis darted here and there gathering the bright heads into little bunches which they pressed upon us until our hands could hold no more.

As suddenly as we had come upon this flowery enclave as suddenly we found ourselves in forest of quite a different character : we trod on pine-needles and walked through colonnades of blue weeping pine. The Apa Tanis explained, like eager children showing off some cherished possession, that this pine was peculiar to the Apa Tani country, for, they said, their ancestors had brought the seeds with them when years and years ago they had come to the valley from lands in the far north-east.

18

1. Apa Tani men in the rolling meadow land at the southern end of the valley.

2. The Apa Tani valley after the rice harvest.

3. The Apa Tani village of Haja.

4. Apa Tani crowd assembled for the *ropi*-rite in Bela village ; in the centre the altar an
sacrificial sheep.

Once we had entered the pine forest, we dropped steadily along a well-trodden path and within half an hour came out into open country. On the edge of the forest we were halted by a scene of extraordinary beauty. An upland of flower-studded meadows and treeless hillocks extended into the dim, misty distance. The day had turned dull, but in the hazy atmosphere this particular landscape appeared all the more dreamlike and unreal. We sat on a grassy bank, and wondered at the violets, the white strawberry flowers, the delicate green of the curled fronds of young bracken, and the bushes tipped with the first pale buds of spring.

But this was not the moment to lose ourselves in the admiration of a landscape. Urged on by the Apa Tanis we followed the smooth path towards a broad, quietly flowing stream. It was unbridged, but before we could take off our boots we were lifted by strong arms and carried across the water. On the other side of the stream we came upon a small herd of mithan (*bos frontalis*) standing knee deep in a shallow pool. They were fine animals, some black with the usual white stockings, some piebald and others white with patches of black on back and neck. White mithan are unknown in the Naga hills, and I believe also in Burma, but I had seen such animals in the Abor hills. There were also some cows of the ordinary Assamese breed, but in this wondrous country they had greatly improved their appearance and had grown long and furry coats.

Soon we came to the first rice-fields, small fenced-in plots bearing the stubble of the last harvest. These, we were told, belonged to Hang and we had not gone very far when we met a band of men who had obviously been expecting us. Unlike the Apa Tanis carrying our loads they were beautifully dressed in long white cloaks with broad coloured borders, and some wore red rhododendron blossoms in their sleek black hair. Two of the new-comers, men of tall stature and ruddy complexion, were described as kinsmen of the chiefs of Haja, but despite our friendly gestures they maintained an air of studied indifference and went to follow us unobtrusively at the end of our column. With their arrival the mood of the Apa Tanis changed. The exuberance of the previous evening and the exhilaration of early morning gave way to a quiet purposefulness, and even Karu, who had kept so conscientiously to our side, encouraging us with help and advice, dropped behind and seemed anxious to avoid conversation.

We had arrived on a treeless wind-swept ridge lying close to a wooded range that separates the Apa Tani valley from the land of the Dafla village of Jorum, when the Apa Tanis put down their loads, declaring that this was where we must camp. We protested that the sun was still high in the sky and that there was ample time to reach the village of Haja before dark. No, they said, this was a much better camp-site than any we could find near Haja village ; they pointed to the wooded hills and the stream meandering through flowery meadows. Here, they said, there was ample wood and water, and near an Apa Tani village neither would be available. Betty and I surveyed this exposed ridge surrounded by treeless hillocks with growing apprehension. The Apa Tanis had themselves advised a difficult route through un-inhabited country so that we might avoid encounters with potentially hostile Daflas. It seemed altogether unreasonable to lead us, now that we had gained their own country, to a camp-site within striking distance of Jorum, a large and notoriously warlike village, which some twenty years before had been burnt as a punishment for raiding into the plains of Assam.

Yet, there was nothing we could do. To force the issue and go, if necessary without luggage, to Haja would have been unwise. Chobin —to whom our guides referred as chief—had not come to meet us and the men present seemed to be acting under orders. To rush things might have prejudiced future relations and would certainly have appeared undignified. If we were doubtful as to the security of the proposed camp-site, we could not admit our nervousness to the Apa Tanis.

So we made *bonne mine à mauvais jeu* and found a shallow ledge just behind the ridge that offered a little shelter from the driving wind. The Apa Tani carriers immediately set to work organizing our camp. Some went to fetch wood from the forest, others brought water, and the rest helped in erecting shelters. They were most efficient and when the tents were up we paid each man two rupees, a box of matches and a leaf of tobacco. Money, as we were soon to discover, is not much good in the Apa Tani valley, but these were men who went occasionally to the plains and understood the value of silver coins. We gave cigarettes and match-boxes to the disdainful gentlemen in the gorgeous cloaks and these they graciously accepted, thereafter withdrawing to a nearby hillock from which they could watch our camp.

After a little, Karu, Pila and Rika came to say good-bye. They would go to their houses, they said, and return to us in the morning. We tried to persuade them to change their minds, but they were determined, and this again seemed a somewhat disturbing sign. Rajoni, who was used to touring with escorted parties, grew alarmed, fearing not so much that the Apa Tanis had led us into a trap of their own devising, but that having heard of the hostile intentions of neighbouring Daflas, they were anxious to dissociate themselves from our party.

To clear the atmosphere I walked over to where the prominent-looking men were sitting and drew them into conversation. Through Temi I explained that we had come as friends, without an armed escort, and that we hoped to stay with them in their villages and learn something of their customs and their way of life. This speech evoked many signs of assent, a nodding of heads, and a few polite words in reply. I explained that as visitors to their country we expected the hospitality and protection due to guests and that we would like the three men, Karu, Rika and Pila, to stay with us that night so that they could explain our presence to any one who might come upon us unawares. The men consulted together, and after a little delay I was promised three men. Karu and Pila were to return to Haja, but Rika with two other Apa Tanis would remain with us in camp.

Meanwhile, more and more men came walking over the downs to see us, and I was pleased to see that some of them were accompanied by children—always a good sign in a doubtful situation. Gradually the tension eased, and by the time we sat down to a cup of badly needed tea, we were surrounded by interested and laughing spectators. One man's eye fell on our table and without a word he picked up Betty's knife and, putting it into the sheath at his waist, offered her his own formidable instrument in exchange. How was such a gesture to be taken ? We had hardly time to make up our minds, for another spectator repeated the procedure with the knife beside my plate. I am afraid our exchange partners must have had a poor impression of European products, for our camp cutlery was ill-suited to such arduous tasks as carving up pigs or fashioning bow staves. But the mock ivory handles looked smart at a warrior's waist, and for many months we were to see these ornamental weapons carried side by side with those that fulfilled more useful functions. Having lost our table knives we hoped that the Apa Tanis would not extend their barter operations to the crockery and offer us deer-skins for platters and bamboo vessels for teacups. I had, however, no time to contemplate such emergencies, for a long side of smoked pork was pushed under my nose. I used my newly acquired knife to slash a small piece off the joint, and later we had the meat cut into scrambled eggs ; it was so good that I was sorry that I had taken so modest a portion.

Many men offered us eggs, one egg for one box of matches, but one man wanted two strings of red beads for four eggs, and preferred to take back the eggs rather than accept a lower price. At this early stage in our trading relations with the Apa Tanis I felt it would be unwise to establish unreasonable rates that we could not later maintain. It was much better to make outright gifts than to purchase at exorbitant cost.

As dusk fell, the Apa Tanis began to depart ; in small groups they straggled off home leaving us to the cold and the night. A biting wind blew over the downs, and the temperature dropped to 50° F. ; I was anxious about the porters who were not only cold but nervous. The Plains Daflas, raised on stories of raids from which their elders had escaped to the plains, were not happy in this lonely camp within range of several war-like villages, and their uneasiness was communicated to the Gallongs and even to our staff. I cannot claim that I was entirely free from anxiety, but to take any precautions seemed futile, and we were both so tired that once in bed we slept dreamlessly through an uneventful night.

2

RIOTOUS RECEPTION

WE WOKE to find blue smoke drifting into the tent. The porters were cooking their morning meal, and looking down on their shelters we were relieved to see them laughing and joking over the steaming pots. The strained atmosphere of the previous evening had vanished and in the crisp morning air even the Daflas had regained their good spirits. We dressed hurriedly and were still at breakfast when Apa Tanis began streaming into camp; they came, it seemed. partly to trade and partly to look.

Karu had promised to return at sunrise, but when at nine there was still no sign of him nor of any of the more important men who had been in camp the previous day, I decided to set out for Haja without them. If there was any misunderstanding our presence could perhaps prevent the crystallization of a hostile attitude, and if all was well no harm would be done by proceeding to the village. We left the camp in charge of Siraj and set off up the valley with Temi, Rajoni and Rika and a Gallong porter to carry a basket of 'political' presents.

The path over the rolling hills was well trodden and the surrounding meadowland was bright with primulæ and other spring flowers. Every few yards we came on bands of men on their way to our camp, but meeting us on the way, they turned in their tracks and quietly followed us on the way to Haja. We had not gone far when we saw Karu coming towards us at the head of a large party. He greeted us with a broad smile and an arm raised shoulder high. The barbarian Siegfried, dressed in coarse rags hacking a way through the jungle, was transformed overnight into a handsome, well-groomed Greek youth. His body-cloth of hand-woven silk was tightly wound round loins and chest and from his shoulders fell a wide cloak of white quilted cotton, bordered with bands of light blue and red. His long-handled sword hung from a fur-trimmed baldric and instead of a cane-helmet, he wore an elegant snood of metal rosettes on his newly oiled hair. Proudly he announced that Haja awaited us. We should send for our luggage—Apa Tanis would carry whatever loads we could not move with our own porters. With these words he waved forward the whole contingent of his followers and I sent them off with a hastily written note to Siraj telling him to pack up the camp and follow us to Haja.

From now on our progress resembled a triumphal procession. At every cross-road and on every hillock groups of men, women and children had gathered to gaze, and as we passed they came from their vantage-points and fell in at the end of the column, until the file on the narrow path drew out to such a length that the end could no longer be seen. We must have done two or three miles when Karu pointed to a small group standing straight and tall on a grassy knoll. Here were Chobin and Roza—described to us as ' chiefs ' of Haja—who, with the Apa Tanis' sure sense of the dramatic, had chosen a place where they could receive us in a position that dominated the crowd.

But there was no need for a special setting to impress us with the importance of these men. Roza was a tall, slim, old man with a wrinkled face, a narrow hooked nose and eyes deep set under prominently arched brows. The cast of his features reminded me of certain Red Indian types and the dignity with which he greeted us was that of a man great and respected among his own people. Chobin, also tall and slim, and equally self-possessed, was, though a good many years younger, well advanced in middle age. From Karu's conversation, we had judged Chobin to be the ruling chief, and Roza the old chief retired from active affairs, whose consent must yet be added to Chobin's if we were to enter Haja. And at this first meeting, and indeed for some time to come, we dealt with Haja as if Chobin wielded authority over the whole village.

It seemed an excellent sign that both these men had come to the borders of their village land to meet and escort us to Haja. They offered us rice-beer in large mugs and we drank a few gulps of a rather thick, white brew. Roza smiled at once, and Chobin's glance grew friendly as we drank, and he began to finger and examine our clothes. His attention was caught by the field-glasses hanging from my shoulder, and he was delighted when I showed him how they brought the distant hills closer.

After this brief interlude we continued on our way ; Roza and Chobin led the procession, their white cloaks billowing in the breeze, and behind came the Apa Tanis in their hundreds, moving one after the other in single file along the narrow dykes of the rice-fields ; to either side the young boys and girls raced abreast of us on the yellow-coloured stubble. Looking back on the anxieties of the day before they seemed to have as little substance as a bad dream.

Soon we left the area of hillocks and meadows, and came to the wide expanse of rice-fields which occupies the whole of the central bowl. The first settlement we passed was Michi Bamin, the smallest of the seven Apa Tani villages. The houses were built on raised ground, and the browns and greys of thatched roofs were broken by the pale pink and deep rose of flowering fruit trees.

The elders of the village stood to welcome us beside the path and after drinking a little more rice-beer we resumed our zig-zag course through the rice-fields. All this land, said Karu, belonged to his own village of Duta and a few minutes later we came in sight of the houses. Beyond lay Haja, and there on a grassy meadow, dominated by a huge pine tree, was the place which the Apa Tanis had chosen for our camp. It seemed a truly delightful site. But we had hardly time to appreciate its beauty for the multitudes following in our wake spilt over the smooth turf and we were soon the centre of a dense crowd all of whom shouted and pushed in their eagerness to catch a glimpse of their unusual visitors. Women had secured the best places under the pine-tree, and grouped round its enormous trunk they stood watching us with open-mouthed interest. I was anxious to talk to Roza and Chobin and, as there seemed no chance of intelligible conversation as long as we were packed in a swaying crowd, I edged towards the old pine-tree and made them sit down beside me on its great sprawling roots. There, below a gallery of giggling girls, I tried to explain the purpose of our visit. I do not know how much they understood, but they smiled pleasantly and promised their help during our stay in their village.

There was no doubt of the friendliness of the Apa Tanis. Hour by hour the crowd grew, and looking over the sea of heads, we estimated that at least two thousand people must have gathered on that grassy patch. About midday our luggage arrived, carried partly by Gallongs and partly by Apa Tanis, and Karu and Rika persuaded some young men to bring bamboos and wooden stakes with which to rig up shelters for the porters and the cook sheds.

It was quite a task to move the crowd from the small areas of ground required for our tents and shelters, and when at last the camp was up, it was equally difficult to preserve it from the pressure of the onlookers.

25

Karu and Rika made several attempts to ward off the curious but eventually they decided that the only sure protection was a fence and they surrounded our tent with a double railing of bamboo poles. It was now well past two o'clock and we were hungry. So we called for Abdul and he came pushing his way through the throng that separated us from the cook tent, with the dishes carried well above his head. He seemed very jittery and his hands trembled as he put the plates of dal cakes and wheat bread on the table.

Our manner of eating created new excitement; the crowd surged forward the better to see what we were doing until the railing began to crack; Karu, ever quick to deal with a new situation, immediately organized a guard. He hailed some stalwart youths out of the crowd and stationed them on the inside of the palisade, thus preserving our precious little vacuum, some two feet from the jostling mob. Our every movement drew comment and we ate our frugal fare to the incessant clamour of hundreds of voices. The first European landing on a South Sea island can hardly have been the object of greater curiosity. Comparatively few Apa Tanis had ever been to the plains of Assam, and Haja had never been visited by an official party. For the majority of the Apa Tanis of Haja we were thus the first outsiders on whom they had set eyes.

After lunch we would have liked to visit the village, but Temi explained that the headmen did not want us to enter Haja until the first excitement had died down. They feared that the excited crowds would swarm over the village and cause damage by overloading the bamboo verandahs. That this was a very real fear I understood some days later when on our first visit to Hang a high verandah collapsed under the weight of spectators.

To escape the crowds I suggested to Chobin and Roza that they should walk with us across the fields to the pine-woods at the edge of the valley. Only a modest number of people followed, for even without us, our camp with the strange figures of the Gallongs, the Plains Daflas and our Assamese servants was sufficient to engage the attention of the Apa Tanis. Once out of sight behind a bamboo grove, however, the two headmen changed their minds and, quickly turning down a narrow gulley, led us into the back streets of Haja where granaries built on piles stood in closely packed rows.

A short climb brought us to a cluster of houses and from an open platform on the top of a hillock we looked down on the roofs of Haja.

26

It was a surprising and beautiful sight. Hundreds and hundreds of houses —I later found there were six hundred and forty—their high gabled roofs thatched with yellow and grey rice-straw, were crowded together within a circle of well-tended groves of bamboo and pine. Here and there the pink blossoms of fruit trees broke through the regularity, and high above the gables rose tall poles bearing tasselled cross-beams that swayed in the wind. These, I was told, were used for the *bobo* game played on festive occasions in the spring.

A narrow street flanked by houses raised on high piles led us into the village, and as we passed, the verandahs filled with women wrapped in loose jackets of grey quilted cotton. The street opened on to a small piazza and in the centre stood a rectangular platform some five feet high on which we were invited to sit. Such platforms, made of enormous wooden planks often twenty to thirty feet long and perhaps a foot thick, are used for public gatherings, for no Apa Tani house is spacious enough to hold a large assembly. Beer, made partly of rice and partly of millet, was handed round and, before drinking, we followed our hosts' example and poured aside a libation for the departed.

We returned to camp refreshed, to find our servants exasperated by the importunities of the sightseers, and we sat down to dinner watched as before by hundreds of eyes. Even when we retired into the tent and zipped up the door, the crowds remained, and their curiosity and ceaseless chatter endured until far into the night.

The next day brought no change in the attitude of the Apa Tanis. We remained the great attraction to be gazed at and commented on from early morning till late at night. Long before dawn we were awakened by laughter and voices outside, defying the cold and the discomforts of early morning sightseeing. At breakfast and ever after we were surrounded by several thousand men, women and children but now, added to the desire to see, there was the wish to trade. Men wanted matches in exchange for eggs and women tobacco leaves for puffed maize ; others hoped to barter chickens for cloth, but we had to husband our trade goods, for most of the cloth we had been able to carry with us was required for the purchase of such basic supplies as rice for staff and porters, and could not be expended on luxuries for our own table. That rice was available locally, and that the Apa Tanis were prepared to barter it for salt and Indian mill-cloth was soon apparent, and this not only facilitated our transport arrangements but offered great possibilities for the development of the Apa Tani country as a base in the following season.

27

Our most immediate problem was to get settled in a permanent camp. The present site was not satisfactory for, though commanding a beautiful view, it was out of sight of the village, and had the added disadvantage of being one of Haja's burial grounds. When we went to talk the question over with Chobin and Roza we took with us presents of blankets for the two headmen as well as mirrors and other trinkets for their wives. The gifts appeared to give much pleasure, especially to the wives who giggled at themselves in the looking-glasses and proudly added the strings of blue beads I had given them to the innumerable necklaces that already hung round their necks. Having paved the way for a business talk, we explained to Roza and Chobin that as we wished to stay in Haja for several months, we would like to live in something more solid than a tent. Would the Apa Tanis, we enquired, lend us a house in Haja or build us one in the immediate vicinity?

Chobin replied that there was no vacant house in the village but he would gladly arrange for a new one to be built. There might be difficulty over the site, for no Haja land could be sold to outsiders, but if we chose a suitable place he would buy the land himself and then lend it to us for as long as we required it. Of course this could only be done with the owner's consent, for no Apa Tani could compel another to part with his land.

We set out at once to make a tour of the village. Chobin sent two eager-faced youths to show us the way, but it soon became evident that to find building land in Haja would be no easy matter. We walked round the outskirts of the village, and then we crossed it back and forth in several places. With the houses standing as close as in any mediæval walled town, and every plot fenced in as garden or grove, there seemed little chance of finding any vacant plot large enough for our purpose. The only likely spot was on a small hillock overlooking the village ; but here bamboos had recently been planted out, and the owner refused to sacrifice even the smallest part of his newly created grove.

We had despaired of finding a suitable site when Karu, emerging from a whispering group of elders, suggested a piece of land which belonged not to Haja but to Duta village. He led us across a short stretch of rice-fields that lay below the Haja granaries, and up on to a small grass-covered island shaded by a group of magnificent pine-trees and backed by groves and gardens.

We saw at once that this was an ideal place for a permanent camp ; it was in a fairly central position, and as the ground was village property

28

the question of compensating an individual did not arise. I told Karu to tell the elders of Duta that I was delighted with the island. That afternoon an oldish man with a broad face and small wistful eyes appeared in camp to take the omens for our stay. He carried a small chicken and holding it cupped in two hands he began chanting in a peculiar sing-song voice. Temi, coming up at that moment, whispered to me that this was an illustrious priest and one of the most important men of Duta. He stood before us invoking the gods and spirits of the land, praying that they should favour our plan of settling on Duta soil. Then he cut the chicken's throat, tore off one wing and slitting open the belly, gazed long and searchingly at the liver ; turning it over and over he scrutinized it carefully from all sides and then he licked it. To our relief he pronounced the omens favourable.

The priest's name was Chigi Nime, a great character with an irrepressible sense of humour whom we soon learnt to value as a good informant and a sincere friend. At this first encounter he astonished us by announcing that misfortune would strike us if we paid for either the site or the building of the houses. Whether Chigi Nime and his co-villagers believed in the prophecy or whether it was a wise stratagem to prevent us gaining permanent rights on tribal property I never learnt, but we were well content to accept the generous offer of free land and labour.

In the afternoon we returned to the prospective camp-site, which, we were told, was called Pape, and pegged out the ground plan for our houses. Koj Roza, a man with a full-moon face and prominent incisors which, when he smiled, gave him a tigerish look, threw himself enthusiastically into the task. He knelt and, bending forward till his chest touched the ground, used the measure of finger-tip to finger-tip to mark off the width and the length. When I suggested that the houses he had outlined seemed rather narrow, he declared that all Apa Tanis houses were narrow. No one knew how to build any other kind of house than the ones they built in their own villages. Narrow they must be, but as to length we could please ourselves. The men of Duta and Haja promised to begin collecting the building materials at once, but they did not commit themselves as to when the two houses would be ready.

For two more days we remained on the burial ground at Haja. The Gallong porters, accompanied by a few Apa Tanis, left for the plains to bring up provisions while we familiarized ourselves with the highways and by-ways of the two villages and grew acquainted with the leading

29

personalities of Haja and Duta. Unfortunately the weather changed for the worse, and hour after hour of heavy rain transformed the smooth green turf round the camp into a brown clayey bog. Our old alpine tent, though leaking in two places, was yet the driest place in camp and gradually everything of value we had with us was transferred there. Sacks of rice, salt and flour as well as the bales of cloth, tobacco, cigarettes and matches which were our principal barter goods, were piled on the floor until there was hardly room in which to turn round, and the interior looked more like a junk shop than a dwelling-place. But the others were even worse off. The shed used by Siraj and Temi was an inch deep in water and rain streamed through the ancient tent which served as a kitchen.

The curiosity of the Apa Tanis, on the other hand, had hardly lessened. There were twenty thousand of them living in this one valley, all within easy walking distance of our camp, and though the crowds who stood round our tents must have changed from hour to hour, the number of spectators at any given time did not appreciably diminish. This constant attention was trying enough for Betty and me, but Jaffar and Abdul, cooped up between saucepans and kitchen paraphernalia, began to wilt under the strain of being stared at morning, noon and night. They were irritated by the filching of small articles whenever they turned their backs and were terrified when at night some playful Apa Tani twitched the blankets from their sleeping forms or tweaked a protruding toe. It was interesting to see the different way in which the two boys reacted. Jaffar, even in the most wretched conditions, could be persuaded to laugh, but no amount of joking would induce Abdul to treat anything in a light-hearted manner. The truth was that he was scared, and the Apa Tanis, gauging his malady to a nicety, singled him out as a most rewarding subject for their endless pranks.

As the days passed and there was no sign of the rain stopping, I decided that something must be done. So when next Chobin and Roza with several other elders strolled into camp, cheerful and dry under their rain-shields, I took them round the bedraggled shelters, now ankle deep in mud, so that they could see for themselves our miserable plight. I asked once more if there was not perhaps some house or granary in which we could temporarily reside until the buildings at Pape were ready. But they hedged and voiced all manner of misgivings. At first they tried to put us off by saying we would not like the smell of their houses, an idea they must have picked up from someone in our camp, but when

30

I pressed them, they came out with the real reason for refusing to allow us to live in the village. Their houses, they explained, where on feast days powerful rites were conducted, were the abode of gods, and the entry of strangers would surely arouse their wrath. Someone suggested that once more omens should be taken to see how the matter could be resolved, but Chobin side-tracked the issue by proposing that we should all go to Pape, and see how the house-building was progressing. " As long as you are here," he added, " all the young men come only to stare at you, and no work is done on your house."

How well Chobin knew his Apa Tanis. We arrived at Pape to find a mere handful of men at work on the buildings. The poles and bamboo flooring were already standing, but everywhere great heaps of bamboos and thatching grass lay on the ground untouched, tied up in the bundles in which they had been delivered. After some argument and much persuasion the crowd that had followed us from the village set to work, and even old Roza squatted down and helped to split bamboos from which to weave the wattle walls. Neither he nor Chobin seemed to have much control over the other villagers and it began to dawn on us that the word 'raja' which Temi used to describe these notables was altogether misleading. With the translation of a tribal language into the simple Assamese used as lingua franca such an error can easily occur, and it was only fortunate that we discovered our mistake so early in our relations with the Apa Tanis.

After two hours of consecutive work, a storm swept up the centre of the valley and everyone sought shelter under the pine-trees, two of which, being completely hollow, offered excellent protection. No Apa Tani can remain silent for any appreciable length of time and before long some of them began discussing the necessity of felling these hollow trees lest in just such a storm as this they fall and squash our newly built houses. Karu, however, had quite definite views on this subject; the pines had been as hollow and as tall as they now were ever since he was a small boy, so why should they fall now ? I agreed with him. They were wonderful trees, some hundred and seventy feet high, and much too beautiful to be felled for the sake of a temporary camp.

The driving rain continued to slow up proceedings, and as there seemed no chance of it stopping we decided that no more work could be done that day and returned to Haja, slithering in all directions over the sodden rice-bunds. Karu lent Betty a rain-shield made of two layers of plaited cane and interlined with leaf wadding. It gave perfect

31

protection to head and back and forthwith we adopted this easy method of keeping dry.

When the men of Duta, who had followed us to the Haja camp, saw the sorry state of our tents, they began discussing among themselves, and after a little, they came to us saying that Koj Tini, a poor man living on the outskirts of Duta, had declared himself willing to act as our host. If we liked we could move to his house in Duta that evening.

Rajoni, however, was not enthusiastic ; the smell and the dirt would surely be intolerable in an Apa Tani house. Temi too declared that a Dafla of his status could not sleep in an Apa Tani village and Siraj decided that he would rather continue to wallow in the rain and the mud of the burial ground than share the home of an Apa Tani family.

But smell or no smell, I was not prepared to forgo the opportunity of breaking down tribal prejudice. Here was a chance to prove that nothing untoward would happen if we entered an Apa Tani house. Besides, the mud of the burial ground had become for me more intolerable than any smell could ever be. We decided to move at once, and lending our tent to Rajoni and Siraj, we departed for Duta before the villagers could change their minds about admitting strangers to their midst.

With us we took Jaffar, who had sufficient pluck and sense of humour to cope with Apa Tanis, Tade, a young Dafla boy who had worked in the tea-gardens and spoke some Assamese and a little Apa Tani, and Chunki our cat.

It was getting dark when we moved with a few necessities over the rice-fields to Duta. Koj Roza, our amusing friend with the fang-like teeth, who still wore our ivory-handled table-knife as a symbol of our first encounter, shouldered my dispatch-box and capered ahead like a faun. Perhaps he was a little drunk after the day's round of drinks which, in our honour, had probably been rather more liberal than usual. He was certainly more affectionate than he had been on the evening of our first lonely camp. He encouraged us with smiles and the exclamation *dza!* and now and then he would turn and vigorously pat my cheeks.

There were smiles on the faces of the people who watched us pass through the village streets and when we arrived at the house in which we were to stay we found Tini the householder and Chigi Nime, the priest who two days previously had taken the omens, waiting for us on the verandah. As we climbed the ladder Nime began a long incantation and we paused before entering the house to allow him to complete what was obviously a protective rite. Tade was incapable of providing a

32

running and coherent translation, but he gave us an idea of the general meaning of the prayers ; they called on the local deities and spirits to bless our entrance. We had come from a far land at the request of the Apa Tanis, and no evil should come of our living in their houses. Nime then took a chicken in his hand, tore off a breast feather which he blew into the air and cut off the head and one of the wings ; these he tied to his wand, and proclaiming that he was master of all evil spirits, none of whom would now harm either us or the people of the house, he set up the bamboo wand at the sacrificial place in front of the house.

Having safeguarded our entrance against supernatural dangers, Chigi Nime led us through the small entrance hall into the dark interior of the house. A fire burnt in the middle of a longish room, and round it were gathered a small group of ten or twelve men and women. They moved aside to allow us to sit down by the hearth and warm our hands at the comfortable glow. Those that had come with us from Haja followed us in and soon the room was crowded to full capacity. Tini, anxious lest the bamboo floor, not built to hold such gatherings, gave way under the weight of so many visitors, tried to prevent others from entering by bolting the door with a stick. But he was not very successful. Again and again some man or woman lifted the latch and after much argument Tini was persuaded to let in just one more visitor.

Chigi Nime produced a bamboo vessel of rice-beer and invited us to drink. The beer was clear and good and the mug went round several times but I noticed that only the more important men were offered refreshment. Meanwhile our host cleaned the sacrificial chicken, removing the intestines and singeing off the feathers. He slashed off the limbs with quick strokes of his knife and, impaled on bamboo sticks, they were set over the fire to roast. We were given the choice pieces and we ate them gladly ; not only were we hungry, but in this overcrowded house we saw no chance of preparing a meal that night.

After the cold and damp of our rain-sodden camp we appreciated the cosy atmosphere round the fire. We took off our heavy boots and the Apa Tanis scrutinized the thick leather soles and iron nails with immense interest. Chigi Nime tried mine on and was very disappointed when they proved too narrow for his widely splayed feet.

Our hosts may already have eaten, or they may have decided to do without dinner that day, for there was no sign of an evening meal. Some of the guests, however, gradually left, lighting splinters of pinewood to serve as torches on the way home. When the circle had thinned,

33

I produced a bottle of country liquor and gave it to Nime as a present. He poured out a little in a brass bowl, and, without tasting it, handed it to Koj Roza. With an expectant but slightly suspicious expression Roza sipped, and then with one gulp finished the contents. As he swallowed the fiery liquid he sucked in his cheeks, pursed his lips together and then, opening them suddenly, let out a noise that sounded like the pop of a cork being drawn ; with a broad grin and sparkling eyes he returned the bowl to the priest. A similar sequence of expressions appeared on the faces of the guests as each in turn was served. There was one youth who refused even to taste this new beverage, while the wife of our host, the only woman remaining in the gathering, took a cautious sip, but not liking the taste spat it out in disgust.

On the whole the men drank moderately, and Nime asked me if he might take the remainder of the liquor home. He emptied the bottle into a bamboo vessel slung round his neck and smiled happily at the prospect of a further round in his own house.

In the comfortable atmosphere that settled over the assembly, Nime broached the subject which was foremost in the minds of the Duta and Haja people ; the danger from Licha, the warlike Dafla village to the east. For years, he complained, Licha had robbed the Apa Tanis of cattle and captured their men, releasing them only on payment of enormous ransoms. The Apa Tanis never had a chance of fighting the Licha Daflas, for they always shunned open battle and treacherously ambushed small parties from hide-outs in the jungle. Now we had come they hoped that the Government that ruled the people of the plains would put an end to the depredations of Licha and give protection to the Apa Tanis.

It appeared that the Apa Tanis were under the impression that I had come solely in response to the messages conveyed by Karu and his companions, and at this time it did not seem necessary to disabuse their minds and tell them that it was only by the merest chance that my tour coincided with the appearance of their envoys in the plains. But the subject of help against the Daflas was a very ticklish one ; I replied that for the moment I had come to see and to hear and to report on the position to Government, but that it was too late to arrange anything more before the onset of the monsoon.

The Apa Tanis were not very satisfied with this pronouncement. They had heard vague and garbled accounts of the recent Japanese bombing of Assam and they often saw American planes flying overhead on their way to China. Could we not do a comparable magic and

34

5. Padi Layang, an Apa Tani notable of Bela village.

6. Apa Tani woodcutters tripping along the rice-bunds on their way to Duta village.

7. Apa Tanis planting out the rice seedlings.

hit Licha from above? It would not be necessary even to cross the mountains that surrounded the Apa Tani valley, for the whole village of Licha, suggested Nime, could be destroyed from the air without one of us leaving the Apa Tani valley.

I was in a difficult position. I could not of course commit Government to any course of action and though I knew that Government might find it necessary to curb the warlike spirit of the Dafla villages that lay on the routes to the McMahon line, I was not empowered to make any specific promises. So I hedged, and the sharp-witted Apa Tanis were not slow to notice my hesitation.

If we were unable to deal with Licha now, persisted Chigi Nime, would we not at least bring soldiers to guard the Apa Tani country? Licha would certainly laugh and swell with pride if we left without doing anything in the matter. There was no end to this kind of talk, and man after man added his persuasions to Nime's with so rapid a flow of speech that Tade had little opportunity of translating even one-tenth of what they said.

It was getting late and I did my best to break up the gathering. We were thoroughly tired and weary, and had eaten nothing but part of a tiny chicken and some puffed maize since midday. When Nime and the other guests withdrew, I hoped that at last we should be left to ourselves and that Tini and his family would retire to a neighbour's house for the night. But nothing of the kind happened. While Betty and I spread our bedding at one end of the room, and Jaffar and Tade settled down at the other, our hosts stretched themselves out on either side of the fire. But first they opened a small door in the side wall and politely showed us the sanitary arrangements. Under the eaves a narrow shelf ran the whole length of the house, and sitting or standing on this one looked down on to a fenced-in enclosure under the house, where three small pigs eagerly awaited the droppings from above. This seemed an admirable arrangement, fulfilling in the simplest manner the triple function of kitchen sink, rubbish bucket and lavatory.

Betty went to sleep at once and Tini, wrapped in his cloth, was soon snoring peacefully, but his wife was troubled, and troubled me, as I sat by the fire writing my diary till two o'clock, by continuous coughing. Nevertheless we spent quite a comfortable night. The atmosphere was perhaps a bit stuffy, but it was warm and dry and the smell was not half as bad as Rajoni had predicted. In the early hours of the morning, while still half asleep, we heard the doors of the house being pushed open.

H.B.—D

35

Tini had already raked the ashes together and was putting on some new logs, and when we opened our eyes we found ourselves the centre of a semi-circle of women all with their eyes fixed on us. Tini's wife soon left to fetch water in a large gourd vessel of the type the Apa Tanis use for carrying liquids, and then she began cooking gruel in a coarsely made pot.

We managed to wash and to have some breakfast but the crowds began to gather and Tini made frantic efforts to prevent the house from being overrun. He removed the ladder leading up to the verandah, and threatened to pelt the assembled village youth with stones which he had stacked in a basket for this purpose. But being a man of little importance, he could do nothing against the elders of the community, and many an assertive woman succeeded in pushing her way up in spite of Tini's remonstrances. The floor began to creak and the house posts groaned as more and more people crowded in. Indeed it seemed that the only thing that could save the house was for us to leave it and take the crowd with us.

During the day the construction of the houses at Pape made rapid progress, and by five o'clock it was evident that at least ours would be ready before evening.

As the leading men of Duta and Haja continued in their refusal to accept payment, partly perhaps from pride and partly on account of Nime's prophecy that we would die if we paid either for the site or for the houses, we decided to reward the workers with small gifts of tobacco and matches. They were told to collect in groups according to village and clan, and Karu and Tini went about distributing two match-boxes and two leaves of tobacco to each man. At first all went well, and we were quite impressed by the efficiency with which they handled the crowd. But when Karu and Tini declared that all had now received their reward, there arose a chorus of loud cries from those who asserted they too had worked but had been omitted from the distribution of gifts. Karu and Tini, jealously guarding our interests, made it their business to deny these claims. They abused those claimants whom they suspected of having idled away the day as spectators and there was complete pandemonium as fists were raised and sticks brandished. In the excitement Karu brushed clusters of small boys from the railing of our newly finished house, and hurled an unfortunate dog through the air, while Tini, making his way to the house through the crowd, was almost mobbed.

The noise was terrific and I, unable to make anyone understand or to translate what I said, found myself leaning helplessly in a corner of the verandah, while the Apa Tanis struggled below in what seemed to be the beginning of a free fight.

Rajoni, who had for many years been accustomed to the arguments of excited tribesmen, said afterwards that he had never watched such a scene. Had the men been Daflas, he added, they would certainly have drawn their swords and bloodshed would have been inevitable.

Not until late in the evening did the noise subside and we enjoy the comfort of our own house. It was just what we wanted. Built on piles, it was above the dampness of the ground, and the new bamboo floor looked fresh and clean. In front a short ladder with six rungs led up to a verandah which was partly protected by side-walls and the protruding roof. The main room, long and narrow in shape, was big enough to accommodate two camp-beds and our personal baggage, and there remained sufficient space for a small gathering round the fire, which was built on an earthen hearth in the centre of the room. The back of the house was partitioned off to make a small bathroom. But as we did not intend to keep pigs, our sanitary arrangements were not in Apa Tani style ; we had a little hut built over a deep hole in the ground at some distance from the back door.

With a solid roof over our heads and a cosy fire at which to warm ourselves, most of our material troubles were over. Food too was no great difficulty. We were able to barter rice, eggs and some vegetables, and occasionally a piece of smoked pork. The rice, it is true, was mostly of a coarse red variety, and the leafy vegetables rather tasteless, but with communications as precarious as they were, we had no other choice but to content ourselves with local produce. What we missed most was milk for our tea, for Apa Tanis do not milk their cattle, and powdered milk was then unobtainable in the bazaars of Assam. In the Naga hills I had lived largely on chickens, but the Apa Tanis fixed the exchange rate of their fowls so high that we could not afford them. Once or twice we purchased some venison from a successful hunter, but as a rule we fed on rice, *chapatti* made of wheat flour brought from the plains, *dal*, eggs, some Apa Tani greens, and strictly rationed quantities of butter, sugar and tea. It was a dull but adequate diet and life among the Apa Tanis provided sufficient novelty, distraction and variety to make us careless of such material things as food and drink.

3

RAIDS AND RANSOMS

WE COULD not have chosen a more beautiful spot for our house nor one that was more favourably placed for the observation of Apa Tani life. From our verandah we looked down the whole length of the valley, which, stretching southwards for nearly six miles, lay tranquil and lovely within a ring of sheltering hills. To the west, a few minutes' walk across a narrow tongue of rice-fields, lay the twin villages of Haja and Duta and beyond, a little to the south but still close at hand, were Michi Bamin and Mudang Tage. Hari stood on the valley's eastern rim, a compact group of houses framed in dark pines, and backed by mountains rising to close on 10,000 feet. While to the north, beyond a low ridge and just out of sight, was Bela, the largest of all Apa Tani villages.

During those first days of our stay the fruit trees were in bloom. The edge of the island was fringed with flowering pear, and patches of pink peach and deep red prunus brightened the groves of pines and bamboos. The contrasts of colours and shapes in this heavenly valley never ceased to delight us and often we would sit and wonder at the curve of mound and hillock that so perfectly broke the flatness of the central bowl, lending it enchantment where only monotony might have been. Often at sunset we would pause in the day's work to watch the forested hills turn purple above the stubble-covered fields spread like a golden carpet over the valley bottom. Then we would wait for that magic moment when the thinly etched line of Tibetan cranes (*grus nigricollis*), flying in a giant V across a yellowing sky, returned to roost in the gardens beside our house.

We had hoped that once we lived in a house, the Apa Tanis' curiosity would die a natural death, but this was not to be. Our verandah remained the focus of attention, and the central position of Pape on the paths linking four of the seven Apa Tani villages facilitated the visits of sightseers. Many a passer-by who had an hour to spare would clamber up and make himself comfortable on our verandah, and during the first months we lived largely in the public gaze. Even in our so-called 'bathroom' we had little privacy, for the Apa Tanis amused themselves by making peep-holes in the bamboo walls, skewering their knife-points into the bamboo lattice so that they might spy on our ablutions. As the days passed we grew quite hardened to this perpetual prying and expert at gauging, from the height of the eye-holes, whether men, women or children were the uninvited spectators.

Among our first formal visitors was Talyang Bokr, one of the clan-heads of Bela. His narrow, well-cut face wore a gay, whimsical expression. Wiry, slender and swift of movement he suggested a woodland sprite, rather than an elder of a large village community. When I thanked him for coming to see me and proposed that I should pay him a return visit next day, he hesitated. At any other time we would be welcome, he said, but to-morrow the villagers would be engaged in certain ceremonies. Further questioning drew from him the information that next day the villagers were to celebrate the final rites connected with the disposal of a hand captured by his kinsman from a Dafla of Pemir.

I had heard that Daflas performed rites with the hands of slain enemies, but I did not know that the Apa Tanis too valued this type of trophy. Careful to betray neither surprise nor disapproval, I told Bokr that I would very much like to see the ceremonies. In that case, he replied, he would welcome us to the triumphal rites.

Bokr had hardly departed, and we had just sat down to our midday meal of red rice and *dal* curry, when a band of young men from Hari scrambled up on to the verandah flourishing a large side of bacon. Would we like to buy it?—Yes, we would be pleased to do so. What did they want in exchange?—The price, they said, was ten strings of red beads and if we had no red beads, then they wanted white beads. I shook my head sadly. We had no beads left, but we would like the meat and were ready to pay for it with money or with salt.—No! they were not interested in salt or money. They wanted beads.

The argument continued in this sterile fashion until Karu and Tini, infuriated at the boys' obstinacy, bounded up the ladder and showered them with abuse. The next moment a sword flashed, and I saw Karu draw his knife, and lunge. As I caught Karu's arm, Betty flung herself at the Hari swordsman so that both nearly tumbled off the verandah.

Other bystanders helped to separate the combatants and the Hari youths were hurried away; they retired to the edge of the turf where, surrounded by their own people, they stood cursing Karu and Tini.

After a little I went down to try and re-establish friendly relations. The Hari youths were very aggrieved. They had come peacefully, they declared, to trade their pork for my beads. Why should the Duta and Haja men abuse them as though they were common thieves? After some argument I succeeded in calming their wrath and bought the pork for five rupees. With this, I assured them, they could buy red beads from us when the porters brought fresh supplies from the plains, and to smooth over any unpleasantness I gave them each a few boxes of matches and a small quantity of tobacco.

Later I explained to Karu and Tini that although I fully appreciated their solicitude, they should not loose their tempers in our service. If they must shed blood, they should not do it on my verandah during lunch. I did not mind barter at breakfast, but objected to murder at meals. Nevertheless, it had all looked very fine! A Shakespearean scene in Apa Tani dress.

The 21st of March, the first day of spring, was cold and rainy. At midday the thermometer scarcely reached 52 degrees and as none of us had coats which could be called warm, we all suffered in the unexpected cold. Once inside the house, however, we were tolerably comfortable. The blaze of an open fire radiates at least good cheer and from our camp-beds, which stood at right angles to each other, we were both able to throw on new logs without getting out of our blankets. It was only when the wind blew that we were badly off, for our dwelling stood on piles and the floors and walls woven from plaited bamboo shook in every puff of air and in stormy weather offered about as much protection as a suspended bird-cage.

For days the Haja men had talked of giving me a full account of their grievances against Licha, and at last it was arranged that there should be a meeting under the pine-trees below our house. At the appointed time the elders of Haja and Duta arrived in force, bringing with them bundles of short sticks; a long bamboo rod was dragged into the centre of a large circle and several hundred Apa Tanis gathered round to watch old Roza set the scene for his opening speech. Squatting down he arranged the sticks from his bundle in systematic order, leaning them in a row against the bamboo rod. He grouped the sticks by connecting them in threes, fours or fives with horizontal cross-bars, and began his tale, checking the points against the bamboo tallies. Each group of tally sticks represented an incident, and the individual sticks stood for the losses in mithan, valuables, and persons killed or captured which the Nada clan had suffered.

Most of the incidents which Nada Roza recounted at great length seemed to be straightforward cases of kidnapping for the sake of the high ransoms the Licha Daflas could extract from the Apa Tanis. On the face of it, it appeared that the robbers beyond the western hills had done remarkably well out of this particular type of banditry. But did old Roza tell the whole story? Were all these attacks on Apa Tanis unprovoked, or was there perhaps another side to the tale? If there was, we would certainly not learn it from Roza. He was out to prove that the peaceful and unoffending Apa Tanis were harassed by the wicked men of Licha and every incident he recounted bore out this contention.

Quite recently, he complained, ten men of Licha had ambushed and captured his nephew, Nada Neha, while he was out hunting on the borders of Haja territory. For four months he had been held captive in Licha, and the ransom which had ultimately to be paid consisted of one mithan, two brass plates, two Tibetan bells, two Assamese silk cloths, two swords and one axe.

Such captures for the sake of the ransoms the Apa Tanis were prepared to pay seem to have been the order of the day, and later Chige Nime related a number of cases in which he had acted as go-between and negotiator. As a priest and a practised public speaker, he was a great believer in detail, and he prepared his account even more elaborately than Nada Roza had done. After invoking the gods, swearing by sun and earth that he would tell the truth, he laid out some hundred and twenty tally sticks. Certainly his memory was remarkable for he remembered every sword, cloth and piece of pork or beef that had ever figured in a transaction between the Apa Tanis and the Daflas of Licha.

Nime began his account by citing the case of Pura Pejang and Pura Tade, who had been captured in the previous year while working in the forest close to Haja.

"Tell us what happened to you," said Nime, turning to Pura Tade, who was sitting next to him.

Tade seemed reluctant to relate his adventures, but eventually was coaxed into telling the story.

"While we were cutting cane in the forest," he said, "four men of Licha and four of Blabu fell upon us. There was no chance of escaping for they were eight and we were only two. They bound our hands, and fastening ropes to our hair-knots led us away like dogs to be sacrificed. We walked through the forest for a whole day and a night and on the next morning we reached Blabu village.

"There our legs were encased in logs and our left arms hammered numb with the blunt edge of swords. We could crawl about inside the house but the pain in our left arms and the logs on our legs prevented us from trying to escape. The house in which we were held captive belonged to Bebi Tem, a great warrior and an ally of Licha. He assured us that he bore us no ill-will, but that he held us to ransom to oblige his friends in Licha."

At this stage, Nime took over the narrative, and told how the victims' families had waited in vain for their return from the forest. When the men had been missing for three days, the Haja people began to suspect foul play and they sent two men, Kago Takar and Haj Plagang, to Licha to find out what had happened. Both these messengers were poor men and therefore in no danger of being captured, for like other Daflas the Licha men do not kidnap men whom none will ransom. In Licha the two Haja men stayed the night in the house of a Dafla acquaintance, and there they heard that the missing men were being held captive in Blabu. They returned the next day and reported what they had heard to the elders of Haja.

"Then I was asked to act as negotiator," continued Chigi Nime. "With three Apa Tani companions I went to Licha and I engaged five Daflas with whom I am on friendly terms to act as go-betweens and help me with the negotiations. I had taken with me four Tibetan bells, but the Licha men were not content with these and in the end I had to return to Haja to fetch three mithan and various valuables which the Daflas demanded as ransom for the two captives.

"For Pura Tade we paid two mithan, four Tibetan bells, three silk cloths, one white cloth, four Apa Tani cloths bordered in colour, three brass plates, three Tibetan swords, three Apa Tani swords, four axes and four hoes. The ransom for Pegang was a little less and amounted to one mithan, two Tibetan bells, three brass plates, three Apa Tani cloths, two Tibetan swords, two country swords, two axes and eight pounds of salt."

Nime added that, besides these ransoms, appreciable fees were paid to the go-betweens at Lichá. He remembered and enumerated these fees down to the last pound of salt. For his services as chief negotiator Chigi Nime received one Tibetan sword, one Apa Tani sword and four pounds of salt, which seemed to me a rather modest reward compared to the fees paid to the Dafla mediators.

But it was not only to effect the rescue of captive kinsmen that the Apa Tanis sent their shrewd priest on diplomatic missions. He was more frequently employed to secure the release of cattle stolen by Dafla marauders from woodland grazing grounds. Apa Tani mithan do not live in the intensively cultivated valley, where they would do incalculable harm to the fences and fields, but are left to graze in a semi-wild state in the wooded country that lies between the Apa Tani valley and the surrounding Dafla villages.

Nime told us how a few months previously he had been asked to negotiate the return of a mithan cow of Haja which Licha Sera had stolen from its grazing grounds. In this affair Nime had sought the assistance of two Daflas, one of Talo village and the other of Licha, and finally effected the return of the mithan cow against the payment of one mithan calf, one large pig, one brass plate, two cloths and one sword ; the Dafla mediators received the combined fees of four cloths, eight pounds of salt and one brass cup, while Nime was paid one axe and twelve pounds of salt. When I remarked that the ransom paid for the mithan cow appeared to me more than the value of the mithan itself, Nime admitted that this was so.

"But we Apa Tanis must ransom our animals," he explained, " if we left them in Dafla hands the spirits would be offended."

It seems to be a point of honour to effect the return of a stolen animal just as it is a point of honour to ransom a captured kinsman, and this attitude may be connected with the prestige-value of mithan. Being neither milked nor used as draught or pack animals, these domestic bison are only kept for the sake of their meat, as sacrificial animals, as symbols of wealth and as currency for all ceremonial payments and land transactions.

The relations between the Apa Tanis and the Daflas were of a peculiar nature and it was a long time before I began to understand the true import of the feud with Licha which loomed so large in all discussions with our Apa Tani friends. From the evidence produced by the Apa Tanis it appeared that a gang of bold and unscrupulous Daflas, concentrated in the group of settlements loosely known as Licha, had taken to the capturing of men and mithan for purely mercenary purposes. They relied on the Apa Tanis' reluctance to take concerted and decisive action and grew fat on the ransoms individual Apa Tanis paid for the return of their captured kin and cattle. In this the men of Licha were extraordinarily successful for, without exposing themselves in open fight, they crept close to the forest paths frequented by Apa Tanis and captured many an unsuspecting woodcutter or hunter. At home in the forest and expert in handling the bow, they outmanœuvred the Apa Tanis, who lived in fear of the Daflas' poisoned arrows. Nevertheless the inaction and policy of appeasement of the large Apa Tani tribe was difficult to understand. Man for man the Daflas might have been better fighters, but why, I wondered, did not the Apa Tanis exploit their vast superiority in numbers and crush Licha with a force of overwhelming strength?

The key to this problem lies in the fact that the relationship between Haja and Licha is not one of unremittent hostility. The economies of the Apa Tanis and the Daflas are complementary and each of the seven Apa Tani villages has hereditary trade ties with those Dafla and Miri villages whose lands adjoin its hunting grounds. Thus Haja and Licha are traditional trade-partners, even though their relations have often been marred by savage feuds.

The Apa Tanis are primarily agriculturalists, who despite the concentration of a large population in a very limited space, produce a surplus of rice. For the raising of domestic animals, however, there is little scope in their intensively cultivated valley, and their requirements of animals for slaughter and sacrifice are largely met by imports. The Daflas, on the other hand, are indifferent cultivators, but have at their disposal vast grazing grounds and a considerable aptitude for breeding cattle, pigs and goats. Trade relations based on the exchange of surplus Apa Tani rice for surplus Dafla or Miri cattle is therefore to the advantage of both tribes.

A Dafla or Miri in need of grain usually comes himself to the village of an Apa Tani friend and if he succeeds in concluding a deal, he and the members of his family carry the rice back to their own village. Usually the price is paid at once, and I have seen prospective buyers crossing the hills between the two territories driving their cattle before them. But to needy Daflas the Apa Tanis sometimes give rice on credit and quarrels arising from a failure to pay such debts have been the cause of many a blood-feud.

44

Trading with the Enemy

The Apa Tanis seem inclined to use these advances of grain as a means of manœuvring their debtors into a relationship of dependence. According to Apa Tani custom it is perfectly regular for a man unable to repay a loan to work for his debtor until it has been cleared. But although an impecunious Dafla, who has perhaps quarrelled with his own village, may temporarily accept a position of economic dependence hardly distinguishable from the status of a slave, he will often grasp the first opportunity of going back on his bargain and making good his escape. Such one-time bond-servants have often used their familiarity with the Apa Tani country and Apa Tani personalities to the detriment of their former masters and have acted as guides or even as the leaders of raiding parties.

Cattle robbery and kidnapping were normally not sufficient cause for the severance of all trade relations between two villages, and even in times of tension a measure of trade was maintained by slaves and poor men who could go backwards and forwards without fear of capture.

Such was the position until shortly before our arrival. Apa Tani slaves went to Licha and bartered pigs, tobacco and cotton for salt, swords and cloth; and even in the previous year some Haja and Duta men had sold large quantities of rice to Daflas of Licha, who, unable to pay the whole price, were still indebted to individual Apa Tanis. I asked the elders why, if the situation was so desperate, did they not forbid trade with Licha and thereby cut off all her supplies of Apa Tani rice. They answered that the enforcement of such a general boycott was beyond their power; there would always be people who would put considerations of personal gain before the interests of their village.

But now things had come to a head. Since our arrival in the Apa Tani valley all trade with Licha had ceased. The Licha men had announced that anyone coming from Haja or Duta would be killed and they would wipe out any Government party that dared to approach Licha.

It was rather unfortunate that we had been drawn into this feud, and were being labelled as the ally of one and the enemy of the other party. We would have preferred a more neutral position, but the Haja and Duta men had spread it far and wide that we had come to support them, and the Licha men had drawn the obvious conclusion when we built a house in the Apa Tani country. In these circumstances, there was little possibility of making any direct contact with Licha, but

45

whenever Daflas from other villages came to visit me I tried to impress on them that Government kept an open mind in the quarrel and would like to see a peaceful settlement of the whole conflict.

The next day brought a vivid—and not altogether pleasant—demonstration of the Apa Tanis' nervousness and fear of Licha. Early in the morning we went to Bela to watch, as we had been invited to do, the rites accompanying the disposal of the hand of the Pemir woman killed by Talyang Bokr's cousin. The weather was dull and chilly, and the paths running along the dams of the rice-fields were covered in mud. We entered the village by a narrow lane, and made our way to a piazza in the centre of one of the quarters. It was thronged with men and we were greeted by Talyang Bokr, who wore a magnificent black cloth embroidered in white, red and yellow. Bokr ushered us on to a large wooden platform where we were raised above the jostling crowds. But the rites seemed forgotten in the excitement of our arrival and it was quite impossible to understand a single word in the great clamour that arose as soon as we climbed on to the platform. I did not know then how much or how little influence Bokr had : it was only evident that he was unable to command even a modest measure of silence.

The commotion lasted about ten minutes, and then we were shown a miniature hut, less than five feet high, of the type which is called *nago* and serves as the ritual centre of a group of clans inhabiting the surrounding part of the village. In front of the *nago* a temporary structure of bamboo and leaves had been erected as an altar and before this a small fire smouldered.

We had missed the major part of the rite, for this was all that was left of the fire that had consumed the hand trophy ; there seemed to be a lull in the ceremonies and I took the opportunity of asking about the events that had led up to the capture of the hand.

Some months previously Bokr's cousin, Talyang Nipa, had gone north to hunt in the borderlands between Pemir and Bela. There he had been ambushed and overpowered by Pemir people, who took him to the village and kept him in stocks for three months. The negotiations for his release were delayed by unfavourable omens, but eventually he managed to escape. Unlike most Apa Tanis in a similar position Nipa was not content with his freedom ; bent on revenge he returned to Pemir, hid near the granary of his captor, and when a woman of the household came to fetch rice, he followed her into the building, slew her and cut off her hand.

46

With his trophy he returned to Bela. For three days the hand was kept in the *nago* shrine, and the rites for its disposal had begun on the previous evening : the priest of the Talyang clan, assisted by the other priests of the village, had called upon the spirits of the dead woman's deceased and living kinsmen to come and partake of the offerings of food and rice-beer placed for them on the altar ; the men and boys of the Talyang quarter had danced most of the night ; and early in the morning the hand had been taken out of the *nago*, covered with pigs' fat and then burnt to ashes in the fire which we still saw smouldering.

This rite, known as *ropi*, has much in common with the head-hunting ceremonies which some years previously I had watched among the Konyak Nagas. Talyang Nipa had brought home only the hand of his victim, but it is more usual, the Apa Tanis told me, to secure also the eyes and tongue of slain enemies and at the time of the *ropi* ceremony to bury these in a bamboo receptacle. The Konyak Nagas dispose of the tongues of slain enemies in the same way and the stones set up near some of the Apa Tani *nago* to mark the place of burial reminded me of similar collections of stones at the ritual centres of Konyak villages. In burying the eyes the Apa Tanis seek to prevent the spirits of their victims from revenging themselves on the slayer and his kinsmen.

The priest ministering at the rite was in full ceremonial dress. On his head he wore a cap made of panther skin with the panther's tail hanging down his back. His cloak was of a black cotton fabric, almost completely covered by an elaborate embroidery in yellow and red wool. A thick, embroidered muffler round his neck was perhaps a symbolic protection against sword thrusts or perhaps just part of a warrior's normal outfit. Just then he was busy tying offerings in small leaf parcels to the bamboo altar in front of the *nago*.

A little later the crowds parted to let in the dancers : a line of young men and boys, the oldest being perhaps fifteen or sixteen and the youngest not more than ten years old. They all wore cane-helmets and carried drawn swords and rectangular shields made of mithan hide. The priest took his place at the head of the dancers, and at the end of the line came Talyang Nipo, the hero of the day. He was a stoutish, middle-aged man and his determined and rather set expression were in marked contrast to the aristocratic nonchalance of his cousin Bokr. With small tripping steps the dancers filed past the *nago*, uttering long-drawn-out shouts. Then the line broke up, and two by two the dancers faced each other, and enacted a kind of sham fight. They exchanged no

47

blows but were content with advancing and retreating on each other to the accompaniment of threatening gestures.

Compared to Naga head-hunting dances this was a very tame affair : the spectators remained aloof and were apparently more interested in us than in their hero and his dance of triumph.

But suddenly there was a stir ; the complacent atmosphere of a minor victory celebration changed to one of anxiety. Someone whispered to Bokr, and a moment later the air was buzzing with alarming news :

" Daflas are advancing."

" A force of Daflas, many hundred strong, has been seen in the forest."

" Fighting has broken out in Haja and Duta."

" Men of Licha are storming Haja."

Temi translated these rumours as he picked them up, and it was clear that for the moment they were given general credence. Everywhere was confusion and consternation, and the brave warriors who had leapt about so gaily in the sham fight, showed singularly little inclination to rush to the defence of the valley.

I did not like the situation. To be caught by a raid in a village where we had practically no friends and did not know the topography, was not a pleasant prospect. The raiders might well be Daflas from Pemir intent on avenging the murder of their kinswoman.

Yet, the rumours insisted that the attackers were Licha men about to raid Haja and Duta. In that case our camp lying so close to both villages was endangered and I wondered whether it would be possible to rally the Bela men and go with them to the help of the threatened villages.

However, the rumour died as suddenly as it had sprung up. How it ever arose I never discovered. The general nervousness of the Apa Tanis regarding Licha or the expectation of some retaliation for the killing of the Pemir woman may have produced a psychological tension which found expression in this sudden mass-delusion. Or perhaps some Apa Tanis, meeting a group of Daflas on the edge of the valley, mistook peaceful traders for the advance guard of an attacking force and spread the news that Daflas were approaching.

A few weeks later we would hardly have been taken in by such fantastic rumours ; a daylight attack by Daflas in the very heart of the Apa Tani country was against all precedent besides being wellnigh

48

impossible. No village or combination of Dafla villages could ever marshal the force required for such an expedition. But at this early stage of our acquaintance with the Subansiri tribesmen we could not gauge the credibility of the rumours.

When we had seen enough of the *ropi* ceremony we went for a walk round the village. With over a thousand houses, Bela is the largest of the seven Apa Tani villages ; it is divided into three quarters, Reru, Kalung and Tajang, each of which functions, in a way which at that time was still obscure to me, as a separate social and political entity.

From the Kalung quarter, which was the scene of the hand-taking rite, we went to Reru, the largest of the three quarters of Bela. Our guides led us through a labyrinth of fenced-in lanes, till we came into another broad and long main street, lined with houses built eave to eave on bamboo poles of varying height.

One of these houses aroused our interest. It was surrounded by a high bamboo fence, and we wondered why this one house, standing safely in the main street of the village, was protected by so elaborate a palisade ?

The explanation was surprising, for it appeared that the owner of the house, Nani Jile, was living behind the palisade in a kind of self-imposed, protective imprisonment. There had been a family quarrel over the inheritance of some rice-fields, and in the course of a long and bitter dispute Jile had kidnapped the wife of his cousin Nani Tane and held her captive for more than a month. Even when her husband had negotiated her release and paid a ransom of five mithan, Jile would not set her free, and eventually her husband and some of his friends had broken into Jile's house and carried her off.

Thirsting to revenge the insult Tane swore that he would capture Jile or a member of his household, and Jile, fearing that this threat was likely to be carried out, shut himself up in his house, which he surrounded with a high palisade of bamboo. When I first saw this improvised fortress in the main street of Reru, Jile's voluntary house-arrest had endured five months, and neither he nor his wife and his children ever went out. He had two male slaves who fetched water and brought in foodstuffs without risk of capture and his wife's relatives helped to cultivate his land. But his own kinsmen, who were also the kinsmen of his opponent, were too deeply involved in the dispute to be of much assistance.

Sitting on the front verandah Jile could chat to the passers-by through the bars of his bamboo ' cage ', and friends could climb the palisade and come to his house. But subsequent events justified his anxiety. In the following autumn, when I visited the village again, the palisade round Jile's house had gone, but there was an even higher fence round his cousin's house a little way down the street. I was told that soon after my first visit to Reru, Jile had grown careless, and venturing out one day into the public street, had been carried off by his cousin. Tane refused to set Jile free until he received full compensation for the loss of property and prestige he had suffered at Jile's hands. When I finally left the Apa Tani country the dispute, which had dragged on for close on two years, was still unresolved, but I had little doubt that ultimately Jile would be ransomed or forcibly freed, and that the cousins would reach a compromise which would obviate the necessity of fortifying their houses.

On that first visit to Bela we called at the house of Padi Layang, who, we were told, was a most important man. It seems that he had already visited our camp, but finding us surrounded by slaves and men of little account he had maintained a dignified reserve. Now that we had come to call on him, he received us most courteously. In the months to come Padi Layang became one of our staunchest friends and one of our most valuable contacts, but he was always a little unpredictable, and often, for no apparent reason, would suddenly withdraw and hold himself aloof from our council.

I have known few Apa Tanis as attractive as Padi Layang. He was rather small but beautifully built, with a slim athletic body and delicately shaped hands. A fine, curved nose, and eyes set deeply under well-arched brow-ridges were matched by broad and prominent cheek-bones. The skin showed a rosy flush on a light-brown base, and the black hair was slightly wavy. Padi Layang could look serious and dignified but usually a humorous smile twisted his well-shaped mouth, a smile so wistful and good humoured that it gave him almost a gamin expression. Though fully conscious of his status he was never pompous or stiff. When the villagers showed off their skill in high jumping, he would compete with boyish enthusiasm ; and when a discussion of political affairs on my verandah had gone on too long and our heads were buzzing with mithan, Tibetan bells and swords, paid, claimed or robbed, he would quietly leave the verandah and, stretching himself on the grass below, rest his head on his arms and peacefully smoke his silver pipe (Pl. 5).

8. Acrobatics in Hang village : a girl propelled into the air as the *bobo*-mast swings back.

9. Ponyo Tamar's fourth wife : a young patrician woman of Hang.

Padi Layang invited us to sit down on his own private platform and offered us rice-beer. Our conversation was inconsequential. I knew too little of Apa Tani life to ask the right questions, and to badly formulated questions one usually receives loose answers. My question, for instance, of what part of Bela village Padi Layang was the headman, presumed—as I later realized wrongly—that there are single headmen for whole villages or at least for such sub-villages as have individual names. Padi Layang promptly told me that he controlled the whole of Reru. The truth was that owing to his wealth and personality he happened at that time to be the most prominent of Reru's clan headmen, but a ' headman ' of Reru exists as little as a ' chief ' or ' raja ' of Haja.

A few days later Padi Layang paid us a return visit. He too had grievances against neighbouring Daflas, and he told us how many of his mithan had been stolen by people of villages lying to the north of the Apa Tani country. Like many Apa Tanis he did not tend his own mithan, but gave them into the care of Dafla friends and trade partners. He had ten mithan in Tapo and seven in Linia, and as a reward for their care the Dafla herdsmen received one calf out of every three born to his cows. He now claimed that within the past three years Daflas of other villages had stolen four of his mithan farmed out to Linia and Tapo. When I suggested that he would save himself a lot of trouble if he were to keep his mithan in the Apa Tani valley, Padi Layang explained that they would do far too much damage to crops and gardens. " If we all kept our mithan near our villages, we might as well give up raising crops of rice and millet."

After this conversation I wrote in my diary :

In their cattle economy the Apa Tanis remind me of capitalists who are not energetic enough to run their business themselves and not strong enough to protect their investments against encroachments ; therefore their continuous trouble with mithan which are robbed or withheld by the men into whose care they have been entrusted.

Though not entirely without foundation this diagnosis was an over-simplification of a very complex situation and was due to an insufficient knowledge of the intricate relations between the agricultural Apa Tanis and the cattle-breeding Daflas. In so far as my judgement reflected on Padi Layang's lack of courage and energy it was particularly wide of the mark. When I got to know him better I discovered that he was not only one of the most successful war-leaders of Bela, but that on

H.B.—E

occasion he could evince a ruthlessness not at all in keeping with his smooth, amiable manners.

The story which he told me of his raids on the Dafla village of Dodum, when his party had killed thirteen people and captured and sold as slaves ten women and children, revealed some of the fiercer aspects of the feuds between Apa Tanis and Daflas ; it also showed that Haja's present weakness *vis-à-vis* Licha was by no means typical.

Though by temperament much less warlike than the Daflas and far more interested in the growing of rice than in the planning of raids, the Apa Tanis seem to be capable of a cold-blooded and deliberate ruthlessness. For years they will tolerate the pin-pricks of their militant neighbours and attempt every measure of appeasement if only they can keep their avenues of trade open. But once they have decided to take up arms they will pursue their revenge with a single-minded purpose, more anxious to injure and humiliate their enemy than to profit from fat ransoms. Daflas have a more professional attitude to war, regarding it as a mercenary affair which must yield rich dividends. I have heard Dafla war-leaders wrangle about the damages due for the killing of their nearest of kin as if there was no injury and no insult which could not be wiped out by the appropriate payment.

Apa Tanis too are calculating, but once their feelings are roused, they tend to lose all sense of proportion. It is only in the relations between the inhabitants of their own valley that the desire for revenge is subordinated to the necessity for maintaining the social harmony vital for the smooth functioning of its elaborate and delicately balanced economic system.

4

BEGINNINGS OF CIVILIZATION

IT WAS a one-sided picture of Apa Tani life which emerged from our early talks with the leading men of Haja, Duta and Bela, the three villages most directly involved in the feud with Licha. War and foreign trade loomed large in all these discussions, and we seldom succeeded in turning the conversation to other subjects. I did not fully realize at the time that it was only a limited number of prominent men, owners of mithan and creditors of defaulting Daflas, who were vitally interested in political relations with Licha and other neighbouring Dafla villages ; the great mass of the Apa Tanis were engrossed in the all-important task of growing rice and millet, and gave little thought to the quarrels between a set of wealthy families and a troublesome Dafla clique beyond the mountain barrier which surrounded their homeland.

What I did sense, however, was the quickening pulse of Apa Tani life, as with the coming of spring the rice-fields increased their demands on the time and energy of every able-bodied man, woman and child. Each morning, long before the sun dispelled the thick white mist that usually filled the valley at dawn, strings of women with hoes on their shoulders and small work-baskets on their backs would trip along the paths that led past our house on their way to distant fields and gardens. The digging over and the manuring of dry fields and the weeding of vegetable and tobacco plots were early morning work, and soon after sunrise most women would return to cook a meal and do the house-work. Then, together with the men, they left for the irrigated rice-fields, where young and old spent the major part of the day.

These rice-fields, extending in an unbroken series over the whole length of the valley, and watered by an ingenious system of channels and ducts, were the source of the Apa Tanis' wealth. There was produced the rice which bought slaves, mithan and pigs from truculent neighbours, and which enabled the Apa Tanis to maintain a standard

53

of living far superior to that of any other tribe in that part of the Himalayas. Tradition relates that when their ancestors first arrived from distant lands in the east, they found the valley filled with swamps and stagnant pools, in which lived lizard-like monsters of enormous size. They drained the swamps and pools, killed the huge inoffensive reptiles and set to work on the land.

No Apa Tani legend, however, tells of the damming of streams, the planting of bamboo and pine-groves, and the construction of terrace after terrace of irrigable land. The story of this complete transformation of a useless swamp into land whose every square yard now serves the needs of man would be an epic of absorbing interest, but tribal memory retains no recollection of the immense civilizing labours of the early Apa Tanis. We do not know how they set about draining the valley, but the results of their handiwork are there for all to see. In a valley with a total area of less than twenty square miles there live to-day about twenty thousand people, who produce in this small area sufficient food not only for their own needs, but even for sale to neighbouring tribes.

Yet their agricultural methods are based entirely on human labour. Such inventions as the plough and the wheel as well as the principle of animal traction, are unknown, and if we are to believe the old men, it is only during the last two generations that the Apa Tanis acquired iron hoes. Before the establishment of the Assamese tea-gardens, which are now their main source of supplies of iron, they tilled the soil with a wooden hoe fashioned from a forked branch. In other words, despite the importation of metals, which to-day have many uses in Apa Tani life, their economy retains the basic features of a system characteristic of the later Stone Age.

Such a persistence into modern times of an economy of neolithic type is nothing very extraordinary, for there are many backward peoples who have never progressed beyond the stage of subsistence agriculture based solely on human labour. What is remarkable, and perhaps without exact parallel, is the concentration of so large a primitive population on so narrow a space. Remarkable also is the isolation and uniqueness of a culture confined to a single valley of twenty square miles. There is a fundamental and striking difference between the Apa Tanis and all their neighbours. None of the peoples of the Himalayas east of Bhutan resemble the Apa Tanis to any great extent, nor can any other tribe boast of a similar mastery of nature.

It is this mastery of nature effected not through mechanical devices,

but through ceaseless effort and loving care, which has made possible
the phenomenal growth of the Apa Tani population within a strictly
circumscribed area. In the Apa Tani valley nothing is left to chance.
Every foot of land is put to some purpose ; it may be a house site,
a village street, a path, a rice-field, a garden plot, a bamboo or pine-
grove, or a burial ground, but not one square yard remains waste land.
Plants grow because they are planted or at any rate encouraged to grow,
or they are not allowed to grow at all. There are no clusters of un-
productive shrubs or useless trees, and weeds have a very short life.
In fact the whole valley has the character of a garden, tended by thousands
of eager gardeners who know for which crop each plot is most suited
and spare no labour to give it the best chance of yielding the maximum
produce.

When we arrived in the Apa Tani valley, the agricultural season
had only just begun. The preceding two months—January and February
—had been spent in repairing dams and ducts damaged by the winter's
rain and snow, and this work was still continuing. Everywhere we
watched groups of men and women, or youths and girls, building
dams and dykes, re-shaping fields and re-arranging the flights of terraces.
Splashed with mud and wielding large iron hoes, they moulded the
sodden soil to their purpose and levelled the contours of the cultivable
area by shifting soil on oval wooden trays drawn sledge-like over the
slimy surface. At an average temperature of 50° F. they seemed un-
mindful of the cold and wet and particularly the younger people always
appeared to be in high spirits.

The pleasure of working in good company no doubt lightens the
burden of monotonous toil, and many agricultural tasks are performed
in gangs rather than by the members of individual households. From
the age of seven or eight every Apa Tani belongs to a *patang* or labour
gang, which consists of the boys and girls living in a particular quarter
of a village.

Until they marry the young people spend most of their working
days with their own *patang*, and those boys and girls who are not of
the same clan may become lovers or even marriage partners when they
are older. As a rule the members of a *patang* work in turn on the
fields belonging to the members' parents, and receive from the field-
owner no other reward than a midday meal and some rice-beer. But
rich men can hire a *patang* out of turn for wages and then the day's
hire is divided equally among the boys and girls of the gang. To

some extent the association of *patang*-members continues in later life. A man who has to rebuild a rice-terrace will invite his *patang* friends to help him, and he in turn will work on their fields whenever his assistance is required. Similarly women often co-operate in the tedious work of transplanting rice-seedlings, a group of four or five working in turn on each other's fields.

One day, while I was watching a new channel being dug on the fields below our house, I noticed an unusual number of people going southwards from Duta and Haja. All wore long white cloaks and seemed to be particularly well turned out. Karu said they were going to attend the Mloko celebrations which were being held in Hang. The beginning of these celebrations had coincided with our arrival in the valley and we now heard that it was because of the Mloko festival that we had been led to a camp in the south-western corner of the valley, so that we should not see the houses of Hang and insist on going through the village. The excitement of our arrival had in any case kept the Haja and Duta men from attending the festivities, but now that life in their villages had returned to normal, they were going to take part in the last rites. This feast is celebrated by each of the three groups of Apa Tani villages in turn, one year by Haja, Duta, Mudang Tage and Michi Bamin, one year by Bela and Hari, and one year by Hang. At the time of the festival men and women from all the other villages in the valley pay ceremonial visits to their friends in the village that holds the Mloko and there they are lavishly entertained with rice-beer and meat. It is a time of gaiety and merriment which comes each year with the spring.

As the day was fine we also went to Hang to watch the Mloko celebrations and arrived to find the streets full of visitors. On every *lapang* squatted men in ceremonial dress gazing upwards at a bouncing rope on which a small figure was doing aerial acrobatics. Now I understood the purpose of the high poles which are so characteristic a feature of the sky-line of every Apa Tani village. At the time of the Mloko new poles, sometimes fifty to sixty feet high, are set up at each sitting platform, and a cane running from the head of such a mast to a stake in the ground some sixty to a hundred feet away, produces a long slanting tight-rope. Groups of young men and girls work the rope by pulling the lower end up and down so that the pole bends backwards and forwards. When by this rhythmical action sufficient momentum has been gained, all but one youth let go, and the rope, soaring up, carries the acrobat into the air, where high above the house-tops he performs all sorts of gymnastic feats.

Although I was invited to take my turn, I lacked the courage to entrust myself to the flying rope and was content to record the antics of the game with my camera.

In Hang lived Ponyo Tamar, the Apa Tani best known outside his own country. Not that he had ever ventured to the plains of Assam or even travelled to any distant Dafla village. Among the Apa Tanis, experience of foreign lands and high social status stand in inverse proportion. But for two generations Tamar had been one of the leaders of Hang. His extensive economic interests had involved him in many business deals, as well as in a number of feuds with Daflas of the foot-hills, and they and his numerous slaves and dependants had for many decades spread the fame of Tamar far and wide. Indeed one of these slaves, a Dafla naturalized in Hang, continuously referred in broken Assamese to Ponyo Tamar as the ' Anka Raja ', Anka being the Assamese term for Apa Tani.

Shortly after our arrival in Hang, I sent word to Ponyo Tamar that I would like to visit him, and having learnt that one does not please a prominent Apa Tani by arriving unannounced on his doorstep, I waited for him on the public platform of the Ponyo clan. After a short while Tamar appeared accompanied by slaves carrying bamboo vessels of rice-beer. He was a white-haired old man bent by years, but apparently still quite active. A fleshy hooked nose dominated an expressive face which, furrowed by deep lines, often broke into a charming smile. He was very friendly and explained that he was too old to walk long distances and only for this reason had not come to visit us at Pape. He offered to vacate a slave's house for our use if we wanted to come and stay in Hang, and when it began to rain he invited us into his own home. Either he was free of the prejudice against the entry of strangers into a dwelling house, or thought that good manners demanded taking a risk. To match his spontaneous hospitality I made him a present of a woollen blanket from my stock of ' political presents ' and he seemed immensely pleased with the gift, immediately wrapping it round his shoulders.

Settled by his fire we could talk more freely than on the platform surrounded by spectators, and I found the opportunity of gaining some idea of the Apa Tani system of ownership and land tenure.

Tamar told us that he had five sons and fifteen daughters ; the children of three wives. As each of Tamar's sons married, he had given him a site on which to build a house, several fields, one mithan, one cow and a quantity of beads and cloths. Only the youngest son still lived in Tamar's house, and cultivated jointly with his father.

"When I die," said Tamar, "all the property which I now hold, several rice-fields, bamboo and pine-groves, this house and some hundred mithan and hundreds of cows, six male slaves and four female slaves will go to my youngest son."

Before the division of his property Tamar possessed fifty slaves, five of whom were Daflas. Ten slaves he had 'freed' in recent years, giving them house-sites and land of their own. The gift of rice-fields to a freed slave is a sign of great favour, for land is expensive, and a slave thus provided with irrigable land is economically better off than many a son of poor patrician parents.

Land can as a rule only be bought for cattle. Pigs, cloth or swords may go with the price, but the basic payment must be made in mithan and cows. Only very small patches of dry land, such as are used for vegetable plots, sometimes change hands for a large pig or some other valuable, but the proper currency for transactions in real estate is and remains cattle.

Irrigated rice-fields are the most important part of a man's property. On these he grows the bulk of his food supply, and the price of such wet land is so high that unless an Apa Tani inherits at least two or three terraces, he has little chance of ever building up a holding sufficient for his own needs. Near the villages, where land is most expensive, ten mithan or more may be paid for a single terrace about half an acre in size. It is only in the outlying side-valleys, where irrigation is difficult and fields dry out during the winter, that a terrace of half an acre can be obtained for as little as two or three mithan.

We left Ponyo Tamar with the assurance that soon we would return to his village and camp there for several days. In the weeks that followed I found Hang a valuable testing ground for information on Apa Tani custom which I obtained in the villages nearer our camp. Ponyo Tamar was a good informant and seemed always willing to spend his time with me. Despite his wealth he had remained fundamentally simple and unostentatious. Once he surprised me by pointing out that he had himself woven the ceremonial, heavily embroidered cloak he wore, and not only the cloak but also the waistcoat and scarf. The wool used for the manufacture of such ceremonial clothes used to reach the Apa

Tanis in the form of white Bhutia blankets that were traded in the plains of Assam. These they unravelled and, dyeing the yarn in different colours, wove it into cloth of traditional design. But, for some years, Ponyo Tamar complained, no more blankets of this kind had been available in the bazaars of Assam, and there was consequently a great shortage of wool in the Apa Tani country.

How the Apa Tanis obtained the wool for their embroidered textiles before they began to trade with the plains of Assam is an intriguing problem. The techniques employed in the manufacture of part or wholly woollen ceremonial cloaks and scarfs, show every sign of an old-established craft, and I wondered whether in the old times the Apa Tanis had perhaps been able to buy wool from their northern neighbours. To-day small quantities of woollen cloth of Tibetan origin reach Miri villages very close to those occasionally visited by adventurous Apa Tani traders, and it is quite possible that long before they began to descend to the bazaars of Assam the Apa Tanis obtained Tibetan wool through the same channels through which they still obtain Tibetan swords and beads.

Though apparently a man of simple tastes, Ponyo Tamar seemed to know how to employ his wealth to secure the good things of life. His fourth wife, a girl some forty years his junior, for whom he had paid a bride price of four mithan, was one of the prettiest and most charming Apa Tani women. A few days after our first visit to Hang, she came to our camp at Pape to repay the visit to her husband's house ; she brought us a gift of eggs, and stayed on our verandah for most of the morning, obviously enjoying herself in the rôle of a great man's wife. The black nose plugs which lend most Apa Tani women so strange an air did not seem to disfigure her beautifully cast features, and indeed against her rosy skin, the blue-black nose plugs produced a harmonious link with the blue chin-tattoo. These nose plugs are as peculiar to Apa Tani women as the red cane-tails are peculiar to Apa Tani men. Holes are pierced in a girl's nose in infancy and the small wooden pins which are first inserted are changed from time to time into progressively larger studs until the nostrils are sufficiently extended to take the plugs of blackened wood. The ambition of every woman is to be able to wear the largest possible nose plugs and those that are most admired are as big as a two-shilling piece. But the attainment of such an ambition is a risky business, for if vanity triumphs over caution and the plugs are too quickly enlarged, the dilated nostril will tear—a catastrophe for an Apa Tani belle.

It was in the sphere of beauty operations that our doctor, newly arrived after an appalling journey in almost incessant rain, had his first great success. Ajitkumar Bhattachariya, a young Bengali, fresh from college and hospital training, joined us at Duta on March 28th and threw himself into the novel task of ministering to the tribesmen with admirable enthusiasm. During the following year he accompanied us on many tours, proving always as cheerful and as stout of heart as on that first day when in clothes utterly inadequate for the climate of the Apa Tani valley he arrived caked in mud and shivering with cold. He was a great success with the hillmen, and though it was some time before the sick summoned him to their houses they eagerly sought his aid in the matter of torn nostrils and ear-lobes, and day after day his bamboo house was besieged by long queues of battered belles patiently waiting for the doctor to restore their beauty with needle and thread.

Towards the end of March the Duta priests performed the Korlangni rite in honour of the deities of lightning, forest, water and fields ; slaughtering a chicken they prayed that lightning should have no power to strike men or houses and that the crops in the fields might prosper. This rite precedes the transplanting of the rice and is followed by two days of ritual abstention from work. The taboo extends to wood-cutting and the Apa Tanis insisted that even our Gallongs should not cut wood during this period ; rather than risk a violation of the taboo they brought us sufficient fuel from their own stores to last the camp for two days.

A few days later Mokum, a female deity dwelling in the earth, was propitiated with offerings of fowls and eggs, and this too entailed one day of ritual leisure. After that everyone was free to begin transplanting the young rice.

On those fields in the centre of the valley which were already flooded and fit to receive the seedlings, women now worked in small assemblies. But many fields still needed levelling, and those that were situated high in side valleys had yet to be dug over. There are two types of rice-fields cultivated by the Apa Tanis ; those permanently kept under water and those that are drained soon after harvest and replanted in the follow-ing year. On the former the stubble of the previous year's crop sprouts in the spring, and the same plants bear fruit in two or three successive seasons. In March, women go over the field, planting seedlings in barren patches, but the earth is not dug over for many years and manure is only scattered on the surface. Nowhere else in India have I seen

60

such perennial rice, and I believe that the practice of allowing the same rice plants to grow and bear fruit year after year must be unique.

Close to many of these permanently flooded terraces lie fields which are allowed to dry out and harden as soon as the crop has been reaped. At the beginning of the agricultural year they are dug over with hoes and kept flooded until the soil is thoroughly soaked. The mud is then puddled by men and boys who, supporting themselves on two poles, churn the mud to a smooth consistency with their feet. This is not considered a pleasant task, and one in which, I was told, well-to-do men over middle-age never choose to engage. During this phase they usually confine themselves to supervising the activities of women, young boys, and slaves, whereas at the time of planting or reaping, they may work alongside hired labourers. Yet even the very rich differ in their attitude to agricultural work. The Haja men laughed at the idea of Chobin, an elder of the Nada clan and the richest man of the village, labouring on his fields. But they pointed out that Roza, Chobin's much older and almost equally wealthy cousin, often worked on his lands with his own hands.

The transplanting of the rice-seedlings from the nurseries—patches of thick, luscious green in small well-watered squares on the outskirts of the village—began at the end of April. It was a time of great activity. Everywhere we saw men and women standing ankle-deep in the flooded fields ; bent-backed, they moved forwards, not backwards as they do in Assam, pressing the seedlings into the soft soil. Soon the wide expanse of the central valley was a mosaic of different shades of green, ranging from the pale yellowish hue of rice newly transplanted to the vivid, emerald tone of the vigorously growing crop.

Looking out over this sea of luminous green, we regretted that we would not be there to see the harvest when, as Karu told us, the whole valley is covered with golden rice, and all Apa Tanis work together at great speed to gather the crop as it ripens.

Besides rice, the Apa Tanis grow millet, maize, a number of vegetables, and a coarse variety of tobacco. Millet (*eleusine coracana*), which is sown in nurseries and then transplanted, is mainly used for the brewing of beer, but it is sometimes crushed and made into a rough kind of bread. Tobacco is both smoked and chewed, and even small boys are seldom seen without a pipe in their mouth. During our first weeks in the country, when the local crop had not yet ripened, tobacco was the most sought-after commodity and Apa Tani women pestered us day and night for tobacco leaves which they wanted to barter for eggs and puffed maize.

The growing of food crops and tobacco, however, is not the only preoccupation of Apa Tani husbandmen. The natural resources of the forests surrounding their valley fall far short of the tribe's requirements of firewood, bamboo and building material. Were it not for the systematic preservation of tree growth, some five thousand hearths burning from morning till evening would divest the valley of every trace of forest in a very short time. Further and further would the Apa Tanis have to go for firewood, until the bringing in of timber and bamboo from the higher hills would become so difficult and so un-economic that only dispersal could save the whole population from a famine of fuel and building material.

Daflas will ruin a whole tract of country by the unregulated felling and burning of forest and then move on, leaving a treeless, desolate wilderness with the fertility of the soil exhausted and the hill-slopes covered in useless grass too coarse even for fodder. But not the Apa Tanis. They have taken care to preserve all the resources of their country, and have even added to them by the introduction of new trees and plants.

Extensive parts of the valley have been turned into carefully managed groves and gardens, and every householder, except the very poorest, owns at least one fenced-in grove in which he cultivates a few pines, several types of fruit trees as well as a special type of male bamboo. This variety of bamboo does not occur anywhere in the surrounding country ; being male it neither flowers nor seeds, and the only way of propagation is by separating and replanting the roots. In good soil these bamboos grow to a size usable for house-building in four years, but only bamboos of seven to ten years' growth are strong enough for ridge-poles or rafters.

While a man laying out a bamboo grove secures his own supply of bamboo for buildings, fences and implements, an Apa Tani planting pine-trees acts entirely from a sense of responsibility towards future generations. Neither he nor his sons are likely to profit from his action, but grandchildren or even more distant descendants may require the tree for house-posts or firewood. Nevertheless, pines are regularly planted and one sword or a valuable cloth may be paid for four or five saplings by those who have no young trees in their own groves.

The Apa Tanis believe that both the pine and the male bamboo were introduced by their ancestors when they first settled in the valley, and it is claimed that the small clusters of pines found on their traditional route of migration in the area of the Kamla river were also planted by their forefathers. Whether this is true I cannot say, but it is a fact that neither *pinus excelsa* nor the Apa Tani bamboo occur anywhere else in the immediate vicinity of the valley.

The preservation and development of a country's resources are signs of civilization and in the Apa Tani valley we were able to observe the working of an incipient civilization in miniature, a civilization perhaps not unlike those centres of neolithic culture from which—under conditions more favourable than those prevailing in an isolated Himalayan valley—sprang the great prehistoric and protohistoric civilizations of Southern Asia.

In all the ordered activity, which was quietly resumed as soon as the excitement caused by our arrival had subsided, there seemed to be a sense of urgency, an urgency which found its most obvious expression in the peculiar short-stepped trot of people hurrying along the rice-bunds and village-paths, as if they were struggling to overcome a perpetual shortage of time. Indeed time must be short if one wants to achieve the results of civilization without having developed its full mechanical equipment. These men and women did individually very simple and ordinary jobs, but collectively they performed a civilizing act such as no other people had performed in those wild and lonely hills ever since the beginning of time. With their industriousness, their passionate sense of order and tidiness and their budding feeling for beauty, they had created and maintained an oasis of stability within a world of semi-nomadic, improvident tribesmen. While their Dafla neighbours despoiled the land wherever they settled, in this one valley the fertility of the soil was preserved indefinitely for the benefit of future generations and every gift of nature was bent to the service of man.

5

PATRICIANS AND SLAVES

THE LONGER we watched from our vantage-point in the centre of the valley the smooth rhythm of Apa Tani life, the more puzzling became the question how this large community with so little elbow room and so argumentative a temperament prevented internal friction from disrupting their highly specialized economy. It was obvious that blood-feuds and raiding in the Dafla manner would have spelt the doom of Apa Tani civilization. With their complicated irrigation system, the proximity of the seven villages, the dovetailing of their land and the vulnerability of closely packed and highly inflammable settlements, the Apa Tanis had to live in peace with each other or perish. But what social controls maintained the balance between conflicting economic interests? What common ground was there between the rich landowners and the poor men compelled to hire out their labour, between the cattle-owners mourning the loss of mithan at the hands of Dafla raiders and the adventurous traders who journeyed to the villages of those very Daflas to sell the products of Apa Tani craftsmen and purchase raw materials and livestock?

Where was the authority to assure security of life and property, to settle the quarrels of rivals, and to punish or restrain those criminals who exist in every society, be it primitive or advanced, barbarian or civilized? Who had the final word when it came to determining the course of an irrigation channel that would affect the fields of many owners, who decided boundary disputes, and who formulated popular opinion when an emergency demanded an extraordinary appeal to the gods or the community's ritual abstention from work?

To all these questions we found at first no answer. The Apa Tanis, talkative to the point of garrulousness when discussing their land and their business-deals, readily prepared to relate the details of a scandal or to enumerate the items of a ransom paid or a compensation received,

64

were unable to explain the social order which was to them as natural and as obvious as the growth of the rice and the change of the seasons.

It did not take us long to discover that in an Apa Tani village there was no man capable of giving an order which was binding on anyone except his immediate dependents and slaves. Men such as Nada Chobin of Haja or Padi Layang of Bela undoubtedly wielded considerable influence and could order about a number of people who lived in their houses and worked on their land. But other members of their clan, men of good status though of no great wealth, did not exert themselves to do their bidding, and reluctantly we came to the conclusion that a ' headman's ' promise, because not binding on his clansmen, was something to be taken with a grain of salt.

We soon realized that those of ostentatious behaviour, men who gave themselves airs, shouted commands and boasted of their achievements, were of little social consequence in Apa Tani society. These were largely men who went year after year to the plains of Assam there to trade and earn perhaps a little cash by casual work in the tea-gardens or Government forests. The real power in the valley was concentrated in the hereditary upper class, who, quiet in manner and calm in an emergency, were reticent in their dealings with outsiders. It was only after I had learnt their names and could seek them out in their own villages that we became acquainted with the more important men.

Gat Tadu, one of the clan-heads of Hari, for instance, held aloof and did not visit our camp until I had paid him a personal call. He was courteous but reserved when he greeted us, and though he dispensed a liberal hospitality on the verandah of his house, I felt at once that at this level contacts must be expanded slowly if they were to result in lasting relationships. As one of the most aristocratic Apa Tanis, Gat Tadu represented a physical type found mainly in a few families of high status. His face was long and narrow, the nose straight and finely shaped, and the comparatively light eyes were set under strongly marked brow ridges (Pl. 13). He was tall and slim and of a most dignified bearing ; his voice was low and he spoke softly and deliberately. Indeed he was a striking contrast to the blustering, loud-spoken lower class Apa Tani.

From Gat Tadu I understood that there was an upper class, whose members, known as *mite*, never intermarried with those of the lower class called *mura*.

65

" There is nothing," said Tadu, " that can turn a *mura* into a *mite*. He may become rich and acquire much land, he may be a great warrior, he may be so clever that his voice will be heard in the council of the village, but a *mura* he remains ; even in the Land of the Dead he will be a *mura*."

Similarly a man of patrician birth can never sink to the level of a plebeian. " If a *mite* is very troublesome we may decide to kill him. But he cannot be made a slave. He is free by being born a *mite*. Of course he may be unfortunate and fall into the hands of Dafla raiders, and then who can say what will happen ? Recently my own sister was captured by Daflas. She went to Jorum Temi's house to buy cotton, and her host seized her and kept her in stocks for three months. At last I was able to ransom her ; she is a widow and so it was I who had to buy her freedom ; if I had not done so she would surely have become a Dafla's slave. But in our own valley a *mite* cannot become a slave. If he is poor and has debts, his kinsmen will pay them rather than see him serve his creditor."

The social superiority of the patricians is undisputed, but most of their privileges are undefined. There are some very poor patricians who have lost their land through misfortune or bad management ; they make a living by working on the land of others and going far and wide on trading expeditions. But their status in the rank system is not affected by such poverty, though obviously they have little influence in village affairs.

Gat Tadu told me that originally all *mura* were the slaves of patricians, and that although there are to-day many free *mura* families, they are all the descendants of slaves. This traditional status is perpetuated by the ceremonial association which links every *mura* clan in a client-relationship with a patrician clan, and by the institution that is the tangible expression of this dependence : every member of a *mura* clan, however rich or well situated he may be, stands under the ritual obligation to give his ' patron ' the heads of all the animals he kills in the chase or sacrifices to the gods. If a free *mura* dies without heirs all his property goes to his patrician patron.

The modern world looks upon the very principle of slavery with horror, and the trade in African slaves and their exploitation in countries far from their homeland, partly under conditions of appalling inhumanity, is certainly one of the least creditable chapters in the history of Western nations. But it would be a mistake to condemn out of hand the domestic

66

10. Kago Bida, a leading patrician of Haja.

11. A Dafla conference : Likha Teji arguing his case in the *mel* with Nabum Epo.

12. Apa Tani justice : a girl with one leg encased in a log tied up at a public sitting-platform in

slavery of a self-contained tribe such as the Apa Tanis. There are no great barriers between patricians and slaves and a young slave-boy living in a patrician's house works alongside his master's sons and daughters. Like all young Apa Tanis he joins a work-gang consisting of both *mite* and *mura* and as he grows up he flirts with the girls of his own gang as well as with other unmarried girls of the village. As long as he observes the rules of clan-exogamy he is free to associate with patrician as well as with slave girls.

The Apa Tanis do not disapprove of sexual intercourse between unmarried boys and girls or even of the sexual play of children too young for intercourse. Indeed most boys and girls take their first steps in the courts of love long before they reach maturity. The young couples meet in the granaries, in bamboo groves and sometimes even in their parents' houses, and at this age an attractive slave-boy has nearly the same opportunities as the son of patrician parents, and no one objects if he enjoys the favours of patrician girls. All Apa Tani youth delights in secret and often short-lived love-affairs and adult society looks with tolerance and amusement on the romantic adventures of the young people.

Premarital pregnancies are not frequent—the relatively infertile period immediately after maturity probably saving most girls from such predicaments—but even should a patrician girl bear the child of a slave-boy there is no scandal and little recrimination. The child remains with the mother's family and grows up as a member of the mother's clan. Such children are known as *hipa*, and some clans do not allow them full participation in certain ceremonies and ritual meals.

" Why should any one blame a girl for becoming pregnant ? " said Karu, our gay interpreter, " is it her fault ? No. It is the will of the gods. But such pregnancies are rare. Girls play about with boys for years and nothing happens, but once married they soon have children."

The suggestion that a girl might become pregnant after one or two night's dalliance with a man was greeted with hilarity. My Apa Tani friends thought it impossible ; they denied all knowledge of contraceptive practices but explained that a continuous relationship was necessary before a child could be conceived.

We may assume therefore that despite the strict ban on marriages between patricians and people of slave descent, a certain amount of miscegenation does occur. But it is certainly not enough to blur the very distinctive physical type found in the leading patrician families.

H.B.—F

The assertion that most girls do not conceive before marriage is probably true whatever may be the cause.

The free relationship between all the young people of both classes has, however, very important social consequences. In the days of childhood and youth ties of friendship and comradeship are formed which no subsequent hardening of class distinctions can completely obliterate. The patrician's wife retains a friendly feeling towards the lovers of her young days even if they are the dependants and slaves of her neighbours, and the ease with which slaves join in the conversation round a fireside is undoubtedly the result of the early intimacy between boys and girls of the same work gangs.

Though usually treated with consideration and even affection, a slave has hardly any legal rights. As long as he lives in his master's house and has not been given land of his own, he may be sold at any time. A slave-owner faced with the necessity of paying a fine, ransoming a captured relative or providing a mithan for the appeasement of spirits, may find the sale of a slave the quickest and sometimes the only way of obtaining the necessary funds. But young children are normally not separated from their parents and married couples are always sold together. Moreover, it is an unwritten law that an Apa Tani slave should not be sold outside his own country. Public opinion is very much opposed to such sales, because even a slave has a certain dignity as a member of the Apa Tani tribe. This practice prevents a good deal of hardship, for Apa Tanis of all classes love their beautiful valley and feel unhappy in the very different environment of a Dafla village. Sales within the Apa Tani community, on the other hand, mean hardly more than a change of residence to the modern town-dweller. Even if sold to another village, an Apa Tani lives within sight of his old home and has innumerable opportunities of meeting his old friends.

Though Apa Tanis will not sell their own tribesmen to outsiders, they themselves purchase a good many slaves from Daflas, usually children captured in raids, who can be easily assimilated. Such Dafla children are brought up as Apa Tanis, speak only Apa Tani, marry Apa Tanis, and bearing their master's clan-name, do not appear as strangers even to the other villagers. Thus a continuous stream of Dafla blood flows into the slave population of the Apa Tani valley and this no doubt contributes to the physical distinctiveness between the Apa Tanis of *mura* class and the members of the more prominent *mite* families. Some of the Dafla slaves owned by Apa Tanis come

68

from distant places in the valley of the Upper Khru and have been traded down by such intermediate villages as Licha. And all Apa Tanis will tell you that they prefer to buy slaves from far-off regions who, if they escaped, would have little chance of reaching their home village, and are therefore resigned to remain with their masters.

Some Dafla slaves, however, enjoy their lives in Apa Tani villages and often Nielom Tacho, a young Dafla whom later on I met in Talo, joked about his captivity among the Apa Tanis. He was a striking young man with handsome features, and startling eyes which, bulging from their sockets, gave him a fierce expression.

"I was quite a small boy, living with my parents in Nielom, when one day I accompanied my elder brother on a friendly visit to Haja. While we were there Kemli Koi captured me on the pretext that my brother had failed to repay an old debt. My father was too poor to ransom me and so Kemli Koi sold me to Hage Polü of Hari. But Polü did not want to keep me, and he took me to several Miri villages, hoping to find someone to buy me. He had no luck. All the Miris said, 'How can we buy a boy with a face like that? He would certainly seduce our wives, and in the end he might even murder us.' So Polü took me back to Hari and I remained in his house for many years. It was not a bad life and I had lots of fun with the girls. Apa Tani girls are very forthcoming," Tacho grinned, "I cannot even remember how many I slept with.—Whether I prefer Apa Tani or Dafla girls? Oh! I think they are much the same. Outside they look a bit different, but they all feel alike. In the end I got tired of life in Hari, and so I ran away to Talo. Hage Polü was very angry with the Talo people for sheltering me, and he stole two of their mithan in order to recoup his loss."

Years in the service of an Apa Tani master had not embittered Tacho in the least and it may well be that in peaceful, prosperous Hari, with lots of girls to respond to his masculine charms, handsome Tacho had a better time than he would have had in his home village. But for a full-grown Dafla of initiative and spirit, the position of an Apa Tani *mura* offered too little scope, and one day he walked off to Talo.

Although such a course is open to any enterprising Dafla slave sure of a welcome in another village, there are a good many Daflas who voluntarily remain in the service of wealthy Apa Tanis.

I will always remember the pride with which Taj Tako, an old Dafla of Hang, assured me again and again that he was a man of the great 'Anka Raja' Ponyo Tamar. No henchman of a mediæval baron can have basked with greater glee in the glory of his lord and master.

Taj Tako's parents were Daflas of Licha, who after a family quarrel found refuge in Haja. There his father supported himself by hunting deer and wild pig and selling the meat, while his mother worked in the fields of wealthy Apa Tanis. Tako was born in Haja, but after some time his parents moved to Mai, his mother's home village, and subsequently his father was killed in a clash with some Apa Tanis of Michi Bamin. When Tako was about ten years old his mother married again and his step-father sold him to Tani Doni, a Dafla of Talo. There Tako stayed for seven or eight years and then he ran away to the plains of Assam. For nearly a year he lived in Rangajan, a Dafla settlement near North Lakhimpur.

At the time of his separation from his mother he had been too small to ask about his father, but when he grew up he decided to go to the Apa Tani country in order to discover the circumstances of his father's death. There he met Ponyo Tamar, who, like other wealthy men, must have had a good eye for potential dependants. He suggested that Tako should come and live with him in Hang, and Tako, who did not relish the prospect of spending his whole life in the plains, readily agreed. Ponyo Tamar paid three mithan to Tako's former owner in order, as he said, to avoid the odium of harbouring a runaway slave, but presumably also with the idea of acquiring some legal title to Tako's services.

At first Tako lived in Ponyo Tamar's house. He cut wood and worked on the fields, and often went hunting. Among the Daflas of Talo he had learnt woodcraft far superior to that of the Apa Tanis, and so he made himself popular by supplying Tamar's household with game. Tamar had a Dafla slave with an Apa Tani wife, and Tako found favour with their daughter. She dressed as an Apa Tani and spoke only Apa Tani, but Tako had no prejudices in this respect and married the girl. When their first child was born, Tamar gave them a separate house close to his own, and a garden plot in which to grow vegetables.

"Ponyo Tamar would also have given me some rice-fields, but I did not care to own land," explained Tako. "Why should I not be content to work for Tamar? He gives us all the rice we require, and we are never short of food. Both my sons have been given land, even though they are not yet married ; one of them lives in Tamar's house and the other has joined the household of his sister. I taught them to be good hunters, but otherwise they are just like Apa Tanis.

"I myself have become half an Apa Tani," he said laughingly, "and at home I speak only Apa Tani. Life here is very pleasant, far better than in a Dafla village. As a man of the Anka Raja Tamar I am in want of nothing."

It is unlikely that many Dafla slaves share Tako's unqualified enthusiasm for the life in the Apa Tani valley ; and there are numerous instances of Dafla slaves escaping from Apa Tani masters.

Apa Tani slaves, on the other hand, rarely run away. Every year, scores of slaves go to the plains of Assam to trade both for their masters and for themselves, and they know very well that if they remained there, and found work in a tea-garden, their masters could do nothing to recover them. Yet the only Apa Tanis who in recent years had availed themselves of the asylum that is granted to all slaves choosing to settle in the plains of Assam were two young men who lived near Rangajan. But even though it was known that they were free and made a reasonable living, no other Apa Tanis had been encouraged to follow their example.

Indeed the average Apa Tani slave would seem to be content with a fate which is not without prospects. Slaves established in separate houses with a little land of their own are known to have become wealthy, and their descendants can rise to positions of influence and a certain importance in village affairs.

In the material standards of living there is little to choose between slaves and the poorer people of patrician class ; both live in similar houses, eat similar food and do the same kind of work. It may be, however, that on an average slaves have to work harder ; even when middle-aged they must engage in such arduous tasks as wood-cutting, work which among free patricians is left to boys and young men. The main disabilities of the slaves, however, lie in the social sphere. They are excluded from the competition for social prestige which is an engrossing and extremely important part of Apa Tani life, and one of the incentives for the accumulation of wealth. And to be caught in a criminal act may have more serious consequences for a slave than for any free man or woman. A master embarrassed by a slave's tendency to petty crime will first try to sell him ; but if the slave is of notoriously bad character, no buyer may be forthcoming. Cutting his losses, the

71

owner may then withdraw his protection and even initiate proceedings which may result in his slave being put to death.

Such a case had occurred in Hang some time before my arrival, when a slave-girl of irresponsible character kept straying from her master's house. Her promiscuity would have been a matter of indifference to the villagers, but her thieving habits caused general annoyance. One day, she was caught red-handed, and her owner declared that he would no longer be responsible for her. He had her seized and tied up at the sitting platform of his clan, and then called the leading men of the village to decide her fate. They resolved unanimously that she must pay the penalty for habitual theft. Her master's other slaves dragged her to the execution place at the Kale river, and there she was hacked to pieces and thrown into the river. Subsequently a nominal *ropi* ceremony was performed at the *nago* shrine, because before she died she had been tied up like an enemy at the clan platform.

The Apa Tanis, who live in crowded villages in a strictly limited area, must have a fairly severe code of justice, and criminals must be drastically dealt with if serious friction is to be avoided. As there are no prisons or other means of segregating bad characters, the death sentence is the only effective means of eliminating anti-social elements. Banishment from the tribal territory might be an alternative, but one that would not be free from danger ; for an Apa Tani with a tendency to crime might involve his home-village in a dispute with the Dafla community in which he found asylum.

It is only in extreme cases, however, that an Apa Tani thief will pay with his life for his crimes. More usually a show of force and public condemnation will be followed by an arrangement whereby the thief is compelled to make amends in a less drastic manner. So it was when Sano Rali, a *mura* woman of Hari, was accused of the theft of a brass plate and tied up at one of the Haja *lapang* (Pl. 12).

One morning when I was walking through the village I came upon a large crowd gathered at the assembly platform of the Taru clan. At the foot of the platform, protected from the rain by a projecting plank, sat a young woman, her foot stuck through a hole in a large wooden log which was secured by an iron peg. Cane-ropes bound her to the posts of the platform, her hair-knot had been cut off, but she was still wearing her large brass ear-rings and a few other ornaments. Nada Pila, one of the men who had come to North Lakhimpur as Haja's envoys, was talking to her in serious and persuasive way, and considering

72

her precarious situation she seemed extraordinarily composed. The cane-ropes that bound her arms were so tightly drawn that the flesh was red and swollen, but Nada Tomu, one of Chobin's cousins, humoured me by loosening these when I pointed out that they must cause the girl considerable pain. Beside her was a small fire and some cooked rice in a broken gourd and Karu whispered to me that she was only a scape goat, the real culprit being Dani Pila, a respectable patrician who had engineered her capture in order to direct attention from himself.

If this was his intention he had certainly succeeded. Chobin, the leading clan-head of Haja, had elastic views on questions of justice, and was only too willing to sacrifice the interests and good name of a poor widow in the interests of patrician solidarity within Haja village. Slaughtering a pig and a goat he gave a feast to reconcile the aggrieved owner of the brass plate and Dani Pila, the suspected thief, but recouped his expenses by attaching Sano Rali to his household and making her work for him. The elders found no flaw in this situation. They could not establish who had stolen the plate, and Chobin's proposal meant the end of the troublesome dispute. Sano Rali, at whose expense harmony had been restored, entered Chobin's house as a bond servant. She was allowed to go about freely and spent most of her time weaving, a craft in which she was expert. I doubt whether this arrangement meant any great hardship for her. As a poor widow without the support of close kinsmen, she had in any case to live on casual labour, and as a member of a rich man's household her position was rather more secure than it had previously been.

To the Apa Tanis there is a subtle difference between common crime and certain acts of violence which are not considered disreputable. The preservation of social harmony is the supreme aim of Apa Tani justice. The man or woman of low social status, who, through habitual petty theft, becomes a nuisance and a source of irritation and disunity, is eliminated by public action, whereas the rich man who picks a quarrel with an equal and in its course captures men and mithan, is allowed to carry such a dispute to considerable lengths if at the same time the general peace of the village is not disturbed and no one suffers except the two quarrelling parties. Indeed, the capture of one's opponent is a favourite and usually fairly effective means of pressing a claim and is employed mainly in what we may call a 'civil' dispute. But if an Apa Tani of wealth and high social status considers his honour at stake, he resorts to a very specialized procedure in order to restore his prestige

73

and humiliate his enemy. He challenges his opponent to a competition which involves the ritual destruction of wealth and recalls in this respect the *potlatch* rites of the Indians of North-west America. The challenger starts by killing one or several of his mithan in front of his opponent's house, leaving the meat for the other villagers to eat. For good measure he sometimes adds to the holocaust by breaking such valuables as Tibetan bells, bronze plates and swords. If his opponent accepts the challenge he must slaughter at least the same number of mithan and destroy property of equal value in front of the challenger's house.

Ponyo Tamar of Hang told me with pride of such a competition. It had occurred a good many years ago, but hearing Tamar describe it one would have thought it had happened yesterday.

" You know my Dafla *mura* Taj Tako," began the old man. " Some years ago another Dafla, Licha Seke, came to live in his house. People said that this Seke had had a hand in robbing a mithan belonging to Belo Lampung, my sister's kinsman by marriage, but the matter seemed forgotten and for a whole year Licha Seke lived unmolested in Hang. Then one day when he was going to cut firewood, Belo Lampung and his clansmen fell upon him and dragged him off.

" What could I do but offer to ransom the man ? Had he not been living with my slave ? It was just as if he had been living in my own house ! I was responsible for his safety, and Belo Lampung had no right to kidnap a man who was as good as my guest. I offered Lampung five mithan as ransom for Licha Seke. But Lampung refused to accept them, declaring that nothing but Seke's death would satisfy him. Next morning he and his clansmen took Seke to the Kale river, beheaded him, cut the body into pieces and threw them into the water. I was very angry. I seized two of Lampung's cows and killed them within sight of his house. But he did not dare to retaliate and like a coward ignored the killing of his cattle. However, I was determined to show that people could not dishonour me and kill my slave's guests with impunity. So I challenged him to a *lisudu*.

" The first day I slaughtered three of my mithan cows in front of Lampung's house and smashed one bell, one bronze plate and one sword. Lampung replied by slaughtering four mithan in front of my house, but he did not destroy any valuables. Next day I killed ten mithan and Lampung killed twenty. I more than matched these by killing thirty on the following day, but Lampung, far from admitting defeat, collected sixty mithan and killed them on the fifth day. Then I called upon all my kinsmen to lend me mithan and when I had gathered eighty I was ready to slaughter them. Lampung could not have matched this number, and his defeat was certain. But then the elders of all the other clans in Hang intervened ; they persuaded me to kill only sixty mithan, to end the *lisudu* by equalling but not outstripping Lampung. I agreed, provided Lampung admitted his fault, and compensated me for the killing of my slave's guest. This he did ; he paid me a fine of one mithan cow."

The squandering of so much wealth for the vindication of personal honour may appear senseless, but it is arguable that the *lisudu* nevertheless plays a useful rôle in maintaining the equilibrium of Apa Tani society. Excessive wealth easily leads to exaggerated self-confidence and high handedness in the Apa Tani valley as anywhere else in the world, and the accumulation of too much cattle in the hands of a few rich families is not in the interest of village harmony. From the point of view of the average villager it is therefore a good thing if two men competing for prominence and leadership relieve each other of some of their surplus wealth. The flesh of the slaughtered mithan is not wasted, for in a village like Hang, with well over four thousand mouths to feed, even dozens of mithan are easily consumed, and visitors from other villages are not lacking when a *lisudu* is in progress. Indeed the whole valley enjoys a feast at the expense of two rich men who emerge from the contest with their wings considerably clipped. After all, mithan are meant to be eaten, and the *lisudu* helps in the equitable distribution of the available meat.

While personal rivalries within the village can be settled by a *lisudu* competition, disputes between members of different villages cannot be solved so easily. If a quarrel arouses strong feelings on both sides, the two communities consider their collective honour at stake, and all attempts at mediation fail, the only way of easing the tension may be a pre-arranged fight or mass duel.

Such a conflict, called *gambu*, usually starts with an armed demonstration of strength of the villagers, who consider themselves aggrieved, and sometimes such a demonstration suffices to end a deadlock or to induce the other party to meet demands for compensation. But often the challenge is accepted and both sides line up for battle. The actual combat is governed by various rules and conventions, and as soon as there are one or two casualties on either side the fight is called off.

Some years before our arrival in the valley, Hang and Hari had been involved in such a *gambu*. Men of Hang who had a quarrel with the Dafla village of Bua, ambushed and captured two Bua women when they were on their way to visit friends in Hari at the time of the Mloko celebrations. Both women were put in stocks and Hari's demands for the release of their guests were refused.

Hari considered this a slight on their own honour, for they were responsible for the safety of their guests, all the more as the captive women had been accompanied by a Hari man when they were ambushed. After some rapid consultations with Bela, Mudang Tage and Michi Bamin, all villages friendly with Bua, Hari challenged Hang to a *gambu* and the challenge was accepted. The Hang men replied that they were ready to fight ; ' they would shoot arrow for arrow, hurl spear for spear and draw sword for sword.'

On the day fixed for the contest, the men of Hari and their allies, all carrying enormous pikes some fifteen feet long, and large rectangular shields of mithan hide, lined up on the fields below Hang.

The Hang men, enraged by the challenge, killed one of the captive women and burnt her body in front of a *nago* shrine. Then they came out to fight. There was a great deal of shouting, but the combatants kept at a respectful distance. Flights of arrows were exchanged, and the Hari men and their allies dashed forward with their pikes, but there was no general mêlée. Vastly outnumbered, the Hang men gradually gave way, and the attackers entering the garden area began to damage the fences and bamboo groves. Men of Haja and Duta, the only villages who had remained neutral in the quarrel, had come to watch the fight and suddenly the rumour spread among them that Ponyo Tamar's son lay dying from an arrow wound in the chest.

This sobered the men of Hari. To kill the son of Hang's leading man was more than they had intended, and they feared that if the boy died, relations with Hang would be embittered for a long time to come. Though on the threshold of the village, they withdrew and broke off the contest.

Subsequently it was discovered that the rumour was exaggerated. It was true that the boy had been wounded, but the injury was not serious. Hari's casualties were two wounded.

Two months later the surviving Bua woman was ransomed by her husband, but there were never any formal peace negotiations between Hari and Hang. The fight had been the final word in the dispute and normal relations were gradually re-established.

As the weeks passed and we got to know most of the prominent Apa Tanis, I collected more and more accounts of incidents that reflected the interaction of social forces. But it was not until much later that I discovered the organization which underlies the whole system of village government.

When you walk through an Apa Tani village, you find that here and there the streets broaden and a raised platform of enormous planks stands in a little piazza. Such a platform is the meeting place of a clan, and it appears that the clans are more or less localized, the houses of each occupying a separate quarter. In most villages there are patrician as well as plebeian clans, and many of the latter share an assembly platform with their patrons of *mite* class.

Each of these exogamous and localized clans is represented by one or two *buliang*, men of character and ability, who are appointed either from among the members of a family of high status and wealth or on account of their personal popularity. There are three types of *buliang* : the *akha buliang*, men of mature experience, but too old to take a very active part in village affairs, the *yapa buliang*, middle-aged men who carry on negotiations and sit on the village councils, and the *ajang buliang*, young men who are employed as messengers, go-betweens and assistants of the *yapa buliang*.

Collectively the *buliang* are the arbiters of tribal law and the up-holders of tribal justice, but the individual *buliang* are primarily the spokesmen of their own clan or group of clans, and not village headmen wielding absolute authority. The duties of the *buliang* are not those of a police, and they do not take action unless a dispute has become a public issue and concerns the community as a whole.

For all his social sense and capacity for co-operation in economic matters, the Apa Tani is a great individualist. His first reaction to any wrong is to hit back and retrieve his loss or vindicate his honour, rather than to appeal to the *buliang*. As a rule, it is only when a quarrel has dragged on for a considerable time, or when it threatens to spread to persons outside the immediate family circle of the opposing parties and thus to endanger the peace of the whole community that the *buliang* enter the field and restore the peace either by initiating negotiations or by coercive action.

If the most unobtrusive government is the best, the Apa Tanis score heavily over many primitive races and even a good many civilized nations. They certainly do not like to be told what to do and in most enterprises they fall almost instinctively into so smooth a co-operation that any strong leadership would seem superfluous. I learnt to appreciate this discipline and automatic co-operation when travelling with Apa Tani porters, but I also experienced how difficult it was to impose on Apa Tanis any outside authority. Even their own *buliang* will be ignored if, under the pressure of such an authority, they overstep their normal functions as mediators and representatives of the public will, and try to give effect to unpopular measures.

Just as the Apa Tanis' economic system is admirably adjusted to the potentialities of their environment, so the social order, stabilized as it seems during centuries of peaceful development, ensures the security of property necessary for the free play of economic forces with a minimum of interference in private affairs. Compared to the hazards of life in a Dafla village, there is also a great sense of personal security; the number of Apa Tanis who meet with a violent death at the hands of fellow tribesmen is small and a man must have a long criminal record before such extreme retribution overtakes him.

Patrician Apa Tanis, however, are extremely sensitive to any slight on their family honour, and husbands of well-born girls are careful never to touch the pride of their parents-in-law. More than one young man confessed to me that he would like to marry a second wife, but that he was afraid his first wife's parents would consider such a marriage as an insult to their daughter and themselves and take drastic action.

Relations between a man and his parents-in-law can be the subject of great stress and this was exemplified by the curious case of Ponyo Tamo of Kach, a small hamlet just outside Hang, who captured his own son-in-law, Tapi Pusang, and kept him tied up for many months. Ponyo Tamo was a rather gruff, elderly man, with a worried look on his face and a ridiculously small hair-knot. Tapi Pusang was young, handsome and obviously a favourite with the ladies.

Many years previously Tapi Pusang had married Ponyo Tamo's sister's daughter, but the match ended in a divorce, and Ponyo Tamo, giving him a second chance, consented to Pusang's marriage with his own daughter Sante. The couple had no children, but for ten years they lived together without major dissensions.

Suddenly, however, Pusang took a dislike to Sante. "What would you think of a husband," asked Ponyo Tamo, "who drove his wife from his house? Again and again Sante tried to return to him, but every time her husband turned her away. Time after time, I tried to make him see reason, but he was as stubborn as a mithan bull. At last he had the impudence to come to my house and ask me to take my daughter back. This gave me my chance. My two sons happened to be at home, and we got hold of Pusang and put him in stocks. This was half a year ago, and all this time we have had to keep him tied up. It is a lot of trouble, but Pusang won't give in. Would you like to see what my house looks like?"

I said I would, and we climbed through bamboo groves to the top of a small hill above the houses, which we used as a *pied-à-terre* whenever we stayed at Hang. The four houses of Kach stood on the crown of this hill, and one of them had been transformed into a miniature fortress. It was surrounded by a palisade that towered above the roof; there was no front entrance but at the back a high ladder led up to a gate in the fence twenty feet above the ground, and another led down into the courtyard of the house. What a job the women must have had bringing home the water twice a day! High above the ladder a small platform had been built on stout bamboo poles and seated on this one member of Tamo's family kept a nightly watch.

I admired Tamo's ingenuity in making his house proof against escape and he told me that unless his son-in-law agreed to take back his wife or to pay a ransom of one hundred mithan-values,[1] he would continue to keep him prisoner, however inconvenient it might be for the other inmates. Negotiations with Pusang's kinsmen had started, but no definite offer had been made.

Sante, the cause of all the trouble, was too shy to give her version of the story. She was a thin and inoffensive-looking woman of about thirty, lacking the jolliness and rosy cheeks which makes so many young Apa Tani women attractive. Unhappiness was written on her face, and I doubted whether her father's policy of securing her husband's person was much help in brightening her domestic life. The atmosphere at family meals, when she had to serve her captive husband, must have been a little strained.

When I revisited Kach a year later the fence had been removed from Tamo's house. Pusang's clansmen had ransomed him by paying forty mithan-values as compensation for the loss of face his wife had suffered. The parties were reconciled, but Pusang and Sante had

---

[1] The measure translated as 'mithan-value' is used for assessing the value of cattle and corresponds roughly to the value of a small calf; a full-grown mithan is worth four 'mithan-values'.

separated. In the negotiations leading to Pusang's release the *buliang* of Hang village played an important part, but it is significant that for many months they took no action to prevent the imprisonment of one fellow villager by another. Their attitude was that the quarrel concerned only two families, and since it did not disturb the general peace their intervention was not called for until the parties approached them with the request for mediation.

Disputes arising from dissension between husband and wife are not frequent, however, and there are few divorces. The great freedom in matters of sex which both men and women enjoy before marriage seems to make for stable unions in later life and in contra-distinction to many Middle Indian tribes the Apa Tanis are not greatly addicted to the pastime of abducting each other's wives. The general stability of marriages does not preclude casual love-affairs between young married men and unattached girls, but only if the first wife agrees can a husband add a second wife to the household.

Such agreement seems to be rarely forthcoming and in Haja, a village of some six hundred and forty houses, there were only three men with more than one wife. Kago Bida, however, one of the richest and most influential of the younger men, told me laughingly that he hoped to build up a polygamous household in the fashion of rich Daflas. I did not doubt his ability to content several women. Rosy-cheeked, powerfully built and always well and rather expensively dressed, he was the picture of a man fond of good living ; the aplomb with which he would enter an assembly must have won him the heart of any woman admiring virility matched with elegance, and his person radiated the good cheer of a man in harmony with the world and himself (Pl. 10).

His irrepressible good humour, however, endeared him to both of us, and Betty encouraged his confidences with the assurance that no woman could hope for anything better than to find a place in his home even as a second, third or fourth wife. The number four was indeed in his mind, and he told us that three girls—whose names he did not withhold—had agreed to be his additional wives. One was from Duta, one from Hari, and one from Bela. His first wife, who had born him two daughters, but as yet no son, had already given her permission and her kinsmen too had been sounded. He had spoken—and probably more than spoken—to the girls of his choice, and when he was sure of their willingness, he had obtained the consent of their fathers. All was arranged and next year he would begin the series of weddings by marrying Chigi Papu of Duta. He would kill a mithan and feast all their friends and kinsmen, but there would be neither ritual nor a priest to consult the omens.

The other marriages would follow and we thought it considerate of Bida to space his weddings so that each bride should have a honeymoon of her own. It is customary in polygamous households for every wife to have a separate hearth and her own granary and Bida was already speaking of extending his house.

But only a man very sure of his position can marry more than one wife. Karu, who looked so dashing and adventurous, was very much under the thumb of his pretty young wife. He once confessed that although he could easily get any number of girls to marry him, his wife and her family would never allow him to take a second wife. Whether he was averse to casual adventures, I cannot say, but he always seemed anxious to return to his own house. Once when I was camping in Hang, and we were sitting round the fire in the evening, Karu deliberated whether he should walk back to Haja in the moonlight or spend the night in Hang. He was not frightened of being captured by Daflas, he said, but a spirit might seize him on the way and make him ill. The Hang men teased him for his eagerness to return to his wife : " Have you no girl friends in Hang ? " they questioned. But Karu was not to be drawn and retorted that the Hang people had all dark complexions —he did not even want to look at the women of Hang. None of them were as light-coloured or as pretty as the girls of Duta and Hari.

I was surprised to find this preference for a light complexion—so widespread through the length and breadth of India—current also among the Apa Tanis, and I wondered whether the comparatively lighter pigmentation of the more prominent patrician families might have led to the expression of such a preference.

Apa Tani women have great freedom in managing their household affairs. They can sell grain and cattle without consulting their husbands, while a man will rarely dispose of any part of his crop until he has discussed the deal with his wife. Indeed Ponyo Tamar told me that if a household was short of food, a wife might even sell a piece of her husband's land. Should husband and wife enter independently into conflicting commitments regarding the sale of, say, the same mithan, the wife's arrangement would be upheld, even at the expense of the husband's plans.

The marriage bond does not end with death. In Neli, the Land of the Dead, husbands and wives live together again and a woman who on this earth had more than one husband will rejoin the man with whom she was first united.

Though an Apa Tani marriage is believed to outlast life itself, its conclusion is a casual affair unaccompanied by ceremonies or religious rites. There is no function which could be described as a wedding. If a young couple have agreed to get married, either the girl comes to live in the young man's house, or he joins her parents' household, both being temporary and informal arrangements until such a time as the young couple can build a house of their own. It is a father's duty to provide his sons with house-sites, but the establishment of a separate household may be deferred for many months.

When a young couple move into their own house they invite the clansmen of both parties to a kind of house-warming party and entertain them with the meat of mithan or pig, rice and large quantities of beer. Patricians and well-to-do *mura* usually pay a bride-price, which varies from one to five mithan, and the girl's parents give their daughter a dowry of ornaments, household vessels and clothes. Both bride-price and dowry are paid only after husband and wife have lived with each other for some time, and the bride-price does not constitute an enforceable obligation as among Daflas, but is rather in the nature of a gift of good-will.

By allowing their children full freedom to choose their marriage partners, the Apa Tanis dispense with marriage alliances as an operative in the competition for social status. While to the Dafla marriage is one of the principal devices for securing a favourable place in the network of friendships and alliances on which wealth, power and life itself depends, the Apa Tanis lay little emphasis on this aspect of marital relations. To them marriage is predominantly a private affair, and though both patricians and *mura* must seek their permanent partners within their own class, they do not usually marry for the sake of status and wealth. Whether the infectious cheerfulness of most Apa Tanis is the result of happy and satisfying relations between men and women, I would not dare to say. But the paucity of marital disputes, elopements and divorces that are brought before the village councils certainly speaks for a matrimonial system which on the whole leads to harmony and contentment.

We have only to look across the borders of the Apa Tani country to find cases of abduction as one of the more frequent causes of blood-feuds.   Among the Apa Tanis such cases are rare.   Women are neither objects of politics nor articles of wealth.   They do at least half of the work and control a large part of the tribe's economic resources ; they rule and sometimes intimidate their husbands about as much as the women of more civilized societies do, but it seems that both men and women thrive on this arrangement and the laughter that you hear wherever Apa Tanis are gathered is the best proof of the friendliness and warmth of human relations that despite all factions and feuds normally pervade the tribe's social life.

6

ROUTES TO THE NORTH

ONE COLD and stormy evening at the end of May I was sitting up in bed writing my diary when Chigi Nime burst through the door, he paused on the threshold and then rushed in, blown from behind by a squall of rain. Seeing nothing untoward in our night attire he hung up his dripping rain cloak and sat down beside the fire. He had, he said, just performed a rite to bring about an improvement in the weather and, returning from the sacrificial place under the Pape pines, he had judged it more pleasant to spend an hour at our fireside than walk back to Duta in the mud and rain. He produced a green bamboo culm that contained the twenty-four eggs he had offered to the gods : the shells had been left to deck the altar, but the whites and the yolks were the perquisite of the priest, and he proposed to share them with us. He threw a few logs on the fire, prodded the embers to a blaze and then he put the eggs to bake inside the bamboo receptacle, which ultimately he split open with his sword.

We spent a pleasant evening sitting round the fire, and the eggs baked in green bamboo sap were an excellent snack to eat with rice-beer. After a little I began to coax Nime into telling me of his experiences in the villages to the north of the Apa Tani country. I had known for some time of his occasional excursions into this area, but as any information on the villages of the Upper Khru and Kamla valleys was of the utmost importance to us if next season we were to explore the borderlands adjoining Tibet, I had curbed my curiosity until I found the right moment in which to broach the subject.

Here was the opportunity : on this dreary evening it seemed improbable that any other Apa Tani would brave the rigours of the night and break in on our conversation.

Nime never needed much encouragement to talk, and after a few rounds of rice-beer, he plunged into the tale of his adventures with great zest.

84

Five years ago, he told us, was the first time he had ventured on a trading excursion to the far north. He had been visiting friends in Licha, and it was they who had persuaded him to accompany them. Since then he had twice repeated the exploit, and on both occasions he had travelled with his Dafla friends. But now, he remarked sadly, the quarrel with Licha had put an end to all such lucrative trading expeditions.

Considering Nime's rôle at the meeting of elders when he had acted as spokesman for those who demanded the extermination of Licha, I was not a little surprised to learn of so recent a relationship of trust between himself and the current enemies of the Apa Tanis.

On all these trips Nime had set out from Licha, and with his Dafla companions journeyed through the Palin valley. The first night they had reached Blabu, a village from which he could see the Khru river in the valley far below. There the people were friendly and he had paid for the hospitality he had received with salt. From Blabu he had travelled westwards along the hills flanking the Khru, and on the second day came to the Lebla area. It was open, grass-and-bracken country ; the mountains were steep, covered even in March with deep snow, and the settlements were large with long lines of houses built against the hills. The people cultivated like the Licha Daflas, growing rice, millet and maize on hill-slopes, but they seemed to have more plentiful supplies of grain than the Daflas he knew in the Kiyi and Panior valleys.

In the country round Lebla, a great deal of a rubber-like substance used for waterproofing baskets is found, and on two trips Nime brought back as much 'rubber' as he could conveniently carry. He paid for his purchases with salt, Tibetan swords and an Assamese silk cloth, and made a considerable profit from reselling the rubber in the Apa Tani country. On his third trip Nime bought not rubber, but three white beads as large as hen's eggs : these he wore with his priest's regalia and for them he paid twelve pounds of salt.

In Lebla he had met people from many neighbouring villages and some of them told him of their trade with Tibetans who came over a pass several days' march to the west to barter valuables for skins, furs and dyes. Nime particularly remembered the men from the villages of Yando and Yambu. Who could forget people who wore such scanty clothes, declared Nime, and he roared with laughter as, pulling up his own cloth above his stomach, he demonstrated how the Yando-Yambu men used little bamboo shields to cover their private parts. When

85

guarding the crops, he added, they beat on their penis covers with wooden sticks and the noise was sufficient to scare the birds from the ripening crops.

Returning from his last trip to Lebla, Nime had brought with him one of his Yando friends. This man had been eager to see for himself the valley about which Nime had doubtless related many tales and he had spent several months in Duta. I enquired whether he was still in the Apa Tani valley, but learnt that he had died less than a month before our arrival. This was disappointing, for he must have been a most remarkable character—the only man, I judged, in the Subansiri region who had crossed the whole breadth of the Himalayas : he had been a frequent visitor to Tibet and from the Apa Tani country he journeyed to the plains of Assam, where he stayed many months. When I asked Nime how his Yando friend had enjoyed his sojourn in the Apa Tani valley, he replied that of course he had enjoyed it very much, and no doubt as the honoured guest of the influential Chigi Nime of Duta he had received the best the Apa Tanis could provide. But this much-travelled man had held no high opinion of Assam, and had compared it unfavourably with Tibet. In Assam he, as a traveller, had been offered nothing, neither food, lodging nor alms, but the Tibetans had entertained him hospitably wherever he went, and in some houses his host had even slaughtered a sheep to provide meat for his journey.

Nime's account of the Lebla area which lay outside the area surveyed by the Miri Mission tallied on the whole with the information I had gathered from the Daflas who had visited our camp. But it was more detailed and in one important point his information was of particular interest. Nime was sure that the Khru valley did not extend much beyond Lebla—he had had the source of the river pointed out to him from a hill-top. On the Survey of India maps the course of the Upper Khru is tentatively marked as flowing from the Great Himalayan range, and now there seemed two possibilities. Either the Khru is much shorter than it had hitherto been assumed, or having left the valley of the Khru before ever reaching Lebla, Nime had mistaken a tributary for the main stream.

The Miri Mission had been told that the only route to Tibet leading through the Khru valley, left the right bank of the river, and, striking nearly due west, crossed the Himalayan main range by a high pass. Nime's story encouraged us to believe that this might be the one used by the people of Yando and Yambu and that after the monsoon we might with his help be able to reach the area in direct touch with Tibet.

But all such plans depended on two factors : the co-operation of the Apa Tanis as porters and the settlement of the Apa Tanis' feud with Licha, the village which straddled this route to the Upper Khru and dominated the political scene.

The attitude of the Daflas was still anybody's guess. Those of Licha undoubtedly regarded us as the friends and allies of the Apa Tanis, and therefore with suspicion if not with hostility, but many Daflas from other villages had been to visit me at Pape and I had found them pleasant men, more virile and perhaps more ' savage ' than the Apa Tanis but certainly amenable to friendly overtures. I was convinced that an understanding with the Daflas was not only possible but necessary for the success of next winter's expedition towards the Himalayan main range and I took a great deal of trouble to impress all those who came to see me of the advantages of friendly relations with Government.

The largest Dafla villages that lay on the fringe of the Apa Tani valley were Jorum and Talo. The leading men of Jorum had been among my first visitors, but Toko Bat, the most prominent man of Talo, and a figure of almost legendary wealth and influence, had maintained his distance during the three months of my stay. When in a friendly message I invited him to Duta, he excused himself on the plea of pressing business, but sent his wife as a personal envoy. She was a very self-possessed lady of dignified bearing, whose beauty was greatly disfigured by an enormous goitre. With her came a grown-up son and two slaves to carry a present of fowls and a very good brew of millet beer.

Toko Yoyum, for so she was called, spoke very pleasantly of this and that, but she succeeded in misleading me on one most vital point. Loud in her protestations of friendship, she pretended that Talo too suffered from the aggressions of Licha and that every year the villagers of Talo lost many mithan and cows as a result of raids by Licha and their ally Nielom. At the time it seemed a likely story, but later I learnt that Toko Bat had the closest family ties with both these villages, and through him our intentions and our movements were relayed to the Daflas of Licha.

As the time of our departure drew near the Apa Tanis of Haja and Duta began pressing me for an assurance that after the rains Government would send ' sepoys ' into the hills and so end their troubles with the Daflas of Licha. One day they underlined the urgency of their pleadings by bringing one of their publicly owned mithan to Pape ; the mithan they declared was to be sacrificed in the interests of our friendship. At a nearby altar the animal was tied to a tree and there ceremonially fed with bamboo leaves. Chigi Nime drew his sword from its sheath, and lunging at the animal began one of his long incantations. He called on the mithan not to grieve over its death—it would die in a good and worthy cause—the strengthening of the friendship between the Apa Tanis and Government. As Licha was the enemy of the Apa Tanis, so should the mithan's soul become Licha's enemy, go to Licha and trouble the inhabitants. It should not complain at being sacrificed, for the gods had given the Apa Tanis mithan for slaughter. In such a vein Nime continued for a long time, but at last the mithan was killed, and the meat was divided into equal shares and distributed among all the households of Duta and Haja. We too received a share and rejoiced in the succulent flesh, which was the first mithan meat we had tasted since our arrival in the Apa Tani country.

The Apa Tanis' frequent bids for a definite promise of help against Licha caused me some embarrassment, for I could not commit Government on a specific course of action in the political field. I knew that the extension of political control over a large part of the tribal area was part of Government's policy and that the establishment of some outposts manned by Assam Rifles would be the inevitable concomitant of such control, but no decisions had yet been taken on the details of this policy, nor on the programme for next season's touring.

So I discussed with Nada Chobin, Chigi Nime, Padi Layang and other Apa Tani notables the part that they were prepared to play if a more substantial expedition came into the hills in the following winter. Such an expedition would certainly require a great many porters, I explained ; no number short of two hundred would be able to keep up the communications of an adequate escort of sepoys. The Apa Tani elders assured me in their grandest manner that two hundred, nay four hundred porters, would be readily forthcoming in the cold weather when the harvest had been brought in.

But when I mentioned that I would soon be returning to the plains and would need some thirty porters to take me as far as Perre, they were not so confident. They pointed out that the time of the year in which the Apa Tanis were used to leave their own country had long passed. The men were fearful of making the journey to the plains, or indeed undertaking any long trek once the rains had come, for in the damp low valleys of the foothills they were certain to fall ill.

This fear was unfortunately a well-founded one, and several of the Apa Tanis who had lately enlisted as porters and accompanied parties of Gallongs to the plains, had gone down with malaria soon after their return and one of them had died. The Apa Tanis, whose own country lies above the danger zone, seem to have very little resistance to this disease, and it was only the untiring exertions of our doctor which kept the casualties so low. At first he had been hampered by the inflexibility of Apa Tani belief and custom which decreed that, for three days after the propitiation of disease spirits, no stranger should enter the house of sickness and that the patient should not swallow any medicines which came from outside the house. Gradually, however, he overcame these prejudices, and by the end of the season it was quite an established routine for people to fetch him as soon as a man who had been to the plains went down with fever.

The Apa Tani women were always nervous when their menfolk left the valley on some errand for us, and would come and worry us over their welfare if their return was overdue. I well remember the night when Nada Bida's wife harried us so persistently that we hardly had an hour's consecutive sleep. Nada Bida was a young man of patrician family whom we often employed as a messenger, and one evening, having returned from North Lakhimpur with our post, he sat a while by our fireside and warmed himself with a mug of liquor before going to the village. At about eleven that night we were lying peacefully in bed, when the door of our room was pushed aside and in came Bida's wife : she wept and poured out such a long tale of woe that I got up and woke Temi so that he could tell me what was the matter. Bida it seemed had not reached home. What had happened to him ? Temi patted her paternally on the arm and assured her that her husband had returned from his journey early in the evening, and after delivering our post had left Pape in good health several hours ago. Somewhat reassured she went away, and I went back to bed. But it was not long before once more we heard her cries of " Bida, Bida ", and there she was standing in our doorway again, demanding to know where Bida was. Throughout the night she woke us at intervals with her call of " Bida, Bida ", a call so insistent and so plaintive that in the early hours we grew anxious in spite of ourselves, fearing that some misfortune had overtaken him on his way from the camp.

We need not have worried, for next morning Karu, hearing of the night's disturbance, came to tell me that Bida had spent the night in a granary with his girl-friend. At cock's crow he had gone to Karu's house to establish an alibi and the two friends pretended that Bida had joined Karu for dinner and, being tired, stayed on for the night.

I asked Karu whether Nada Bida, whose marriage of ten years' standing was childless, could take his girl-friend as second wife. "He would not dare," was the answer. "His wife's relations are important people of Bela. They would feel insulted if he took a second wife: they would certainly kidnap him and cut off his hair, if they heard that such was his intention."

Though of good family and a distant relative of the powerful Chobin, Bida was not well off. His improvident father had been too fond of rice-beer and had sold most of the family land while Bida was quite young, and Bida himself, easy-going and unaggressive, had few prospects in a fiercely competitive economy. Though unsuccessful in material matters he had attained the status of the Nada clan's principal priest and spirit caller.

Apa Tani priests must have good memories so that they can recite the long chants which are a part of every sacrificial rite, and in their dreams they must be able to visit the world beyond and bargain with the spirits for the soul of the sick who have been carried off prematurely to Neli. But they need not be models of respectability. No Apa Tani considered Bida's amorous adventures incompatible with his position as mediator between men and the spirit world, and while he was doubtless afraid of his wife and her influential kinsmen, his dalliance with pretty girls did not offend the moral laws underwritten by supernatural powers. The gods and the spirits are particular in matters of respect and the exact nature of the offerings they are tendered, but they are indifferent to the sexual behaviour of the priest who conducts the rites. And so were the worshippers, who liked Bida for his good humour and smiled at his wife's exhibitions of jealousy.

At the beginning of May we began to wonder how much longer we could safely remain in the hills. In the south of India it is generally assumed that the monsoon breaks about the 7th of June and further north popular belief has fixed the 15th as the day on which the rains break. So we had thought it safe to plan our departure for the first week in June. But on the 5th of May a party of Gallongs returning from North Lakhimpur brought the news that the waters of the Perre had nearly reached the bridge. The Gallongs spoke of the terrific scene at the confluence of the two streams ; if the waters rose a few feet more the bridge would be swept away. This was their opinion, and I thought sadly of the Daflas' self-assurance when they declared that the river would never reach the level of their lofty structure.

If the bridge were washed away our return to the plains would be difficult and there was uneasiness in the camp as the more imaginative members of our staff already saw themselves marooned in the hills for the duration of the monsoon. How would they live without salt, sugar, tea or without any fat but the rather doubtful Apa Tani pork ? Karu, overhearing our deliberations, stated categorically that after the lunar month ending late in May, none of the Apa Tanis would undertake the journey to the plains.

Reluctantly we decided to advance the date of our departure to May 21st. The Gallongs were to begin at once moving the camp equipment to Joyhing and then they were to return to meet us half-way on our downward journey, while the Apa Tani clan elders promised to raise the porters to take us as far as the Perre river.

On the appointed day many notables came dressed in their white cloaks to see us leave Pape, and before the assembled crowds Chigi Nime and Koj Talo presented me in the name of Haja and Duta with a Tibetan sword in a bamboo sheath. Solemnly Nime hung the halter round my neck saying I should always wear it as a symbol of our friend-ship ; then, making the gesture of taking his heart from his own breast he laid it on mine, declaring that the Apa Tanis and I should for ever be as brothers.

I was touched ; it had been a simple act but a sincere one and I felt churlish when I could no longer delay my enquiries for the porters who were to carry our luggage. They were, we were told, making ready for the journey and would soon arrive in camp. Another hour elapsed, in very pleasant conversation it is true, and once more I ventured to make some enquiries, only to be assured that the porters were eating their morning meal. How could they start on empty stomachs ?

It was ten o'clock before the first men came straggling over the fields ; they were the most miserable of slaves, men who were obviously so dependent on their masters that they could only obey when they had been bidden to carry our luggage to the plains. The slave-owners had perhaps hesitated to send their more robust workers on a journey which everybody considered dangerous and had deliberately limited their losses by sending only those who were old, infirm and of little value.   Or perhaps they had not commanded men of whose compliance they were not certain.   Many young men, as strong and as fit as anyone could wish, stood idly by as we upbraided the elders for not making better arrangements ; they scorned the idea of enlisting as porters, work they considered demeaning for those of noble birth ; and they saw no reason to exert themselves in order to earn a few rupees.

After several hours' haggling we were still five men short.   The elders declared they could do no more, and it was Chigi Nime who saved the situation : he announced that he would give rice and meat for the journey to any shouldering the loads lying about on the grass, and when this failed he made a grand gesture, announcing that he, greatest of spirit callers, would himself accompany us as far as the Perre river.   He rushed off to Duta and within the hour he returned magnificently dressed in a large black fibre rain hat and cloak with bottles of rice-beer and cooked food dangling from both shoulders.

Thanks to Nime's gallant example we soon had a porter for every load, and as we left the sun broke through the clouds.   Had it rained at this crucial moment, I do not think we should have got off.

It took us all of the day that remained after our late start to reach the camp on the Pangen.   The Gallong porters who had frequently spent the night here on their way to and from the plains had built a number of small huts on the raised ground beside the stream and in these the porters quickly made themselves at home.   They divided into groups of three and four and began cooking the food they had brought with them.   Only Chigi Nime ate his food alone.   He felt it did not become him to sleep with ' all the slaves ' and insisted on sharing our tent.   Saying that ' we should sleep as brothers '—a sentiment which fortunately included Betty—he stretched himself out between our two camp-beds.

The night was disturbed by one distraction after the other and when at last I had succeeded in going to sleep I was woken by a terrific noise. It sounded like wild elephants charging through the undergrowth, but it turned out to be a tree which on this stormless night crashed, without cause as it would seem, a few yards from the camp.   At 1.15 a.m. I was woken again, this time by the blast of Temi's whistle.   He had mistaken the hour, and thinking that the dawn was near wanted to rouse the porters in good time.   As it was three hours too early I went out into the chilly night and sent everyone back to bed.   During all these disturbances Chigi Nime slept peacefully between us, but in the grey and cheerless morning he decided that he had had enough of this type of picnic, and having brought us to the edge of the Apa Tani valley, he bade us a ceremonious farewell and returned to Duta.

The Apa Tani porters proved good camp fellows, far better indeed than the Daflas who had brought us up. Each man took up the load he had carried the day before, none haggled over the weight of his burden and no one complained of the path. The way was long, steep and difficult, and though we climbed the shoulder of Mount Lai with halts only just long enough to allow the stragglers to catch up, the passage took us a little over ten hours.

Next day we came down to the Perre river. Neither it nor the Panior carried appreciably more water than they had done in March, but drift-wood strewn high up on either bank bore witness to the higher level the water must have reached not so very long before. Siraj waited for us on the further bank and with him were the Gallongs and a party of Plains Daflas.

During the night the fair weather ended. It began to rain and by morning the waters of both Perre and Panior had risen several feet. This frightened the Apa Tanis, who were anxious lest another day of rain would see the swamping of the bridge, which they were reluctant even to cross. A few volunteered to complete the journey to Joyhing in order to bring up another load of salt, but the majority returned to the Apa Tani country, and with them went Karu. We were sorry to say good-bye, and it was not long before we regretted the loss of such good carriers. For hardly had the Daflas taken over when we had our first casualty. Our covered basin, perched on top of the kitchen load, became entangled in the suspension ropes of the bridge, and the Dafla carrying it disengaged himself with such a jerk that he sent it spinning into the river where it soon disappeared in the foamy waters. Unhappily it contained most of the medicines which for years we had hoarded against an emergency and which were at that time irreplaceable in India.

We had expected the return journey to be unpleasant and the climb from the Perre valley to the top of Mount Kemping came up to our grimmest expectations. The path was sodden and the slimy clay so slippery that every step was difficult to hold. Progress was slow, and we found the heat oppressive and the continual complaining of the Plains Daflas irritating. Walking in nothing but our cotton shirts we

93

were soon drenched to the skin and like the porters covered with dim-dam blisters and the blood that oozes from the bite of a half-satisfied leech.

It rained all night, and on into the morning and the camp on Kemping was a slough of mud soon churned by porters' feet to a fine paste. We set out early, largely because it was so uncomfortable in camp, and accomplished the descent from 6,000 to 2,000 feet in little more than five hours.

It was midday when, smeared from head to foot with the yellow mud into which we had all fallen innumerable times, we arrived at the confluence of the Panior and Gage rivers. A day's stage was behind us but the Daflas urged us to continue. If we hurried, they assured us, we could reach Joyhing by nightfall.

We picked a way along the water's edge over slippery stone slabs worn smooth by many floods and the porters had often to steady them-selves by holding on to branches of the brushwood which grew on the steep bank. After a short stretch the Panior turned at right angles, disappearing behind a cliff that forced us up many hundred feet above the river level. I admired the porters as they climbed the rock-face with their heavy loads, never putting a foot wrong or losing their balance. But hardly had we topped the ridge than we embarked on an equally steep descent that brought us once more to the bank of the river.

For the next few hours we continued to wind along the valley bed, following it in general direction, but compelled to climb many a minor ridge as the swirling waters, rushing through a gorge, left no leeway along which to pick a path.

Towards dusk a rising wind whipped the steady drizzle into heavy rain which clattered on the banana leaves and beat upon our backs. We had grown accustomed to wading through water and plodding ankle deep in the thick yellow mud and our only concern was the sudden chilliness of the evening. At last we reached the Dafla village of Joyhing, and could warm ourselves by a fire. There seemed to be no point in taking the Dafla and the Apa Tani porters any further in such weather, for here they had excellent accommodation and could spend the night in comfort. But Betty and I with the Gallongs con-tinued on our journey, racing through the darkening forest with the thought that inspires all travellers on the last lap, the thought of a dry roof and a change of clothes.

Arrival in the Plains

When we came to the edge of the gardens, where the tea bushes begin, we each made our separate ways, the Gallongs to their camp on the edge of the forest and we to the manager's bungalow. Through a confusion of alleys we came to the lights of the front door, and calling out found ourselves stared at by two servants rendered speechless by our appearance. But Mr. and Mrs. Farmer received us with open-armed hospitality and when a few minutes later we lay stretched out in a hot bath we felt that the age of miracles had not yet come to an end.

7

TRANSPORT AND POLITICS

AFTER OUR first visit to the Apa Tani valley, I went to Shillong and discussed plans for the following season. We hoped to be back in the hills by the beginning of October and to remain there until the end of May 1945. My proposals included an expedition to Licha, which I considered necessary if the relations between the Apa Tanis and their neighbours were to be stabilized, as well as an extensive reconnaisance through the area of the Upper Khru and the Upper Kamla, believed to be inhabited by tribes that maintained trade relations with Tibet. The use of an armed escort on the visit to Licha seemed unavoidable and this coincided with Government's intention to establish military outposts at several points in the Subansiri area.

Mills forwarded the proposals to New Delhi and in August I was informed that the Government of India had decided to establish a provisional base in the Apa Tani country and at least one military outpost in the Dafla country. Political control was to be extended not only over the foothills and the Apa Tani country, but also over the hitherto unexplored valley of the Kiyi river. The immediate objective of these measures was to check the raiding of the Daflas of both Licha and Likha, and their long-term aim was the establishment of a rule of law and the gradual suppression of tribal feuds. One and a half platoons of Assam Rifles, a total of seventy-five men, were to be employed in the pursuance of this policy, and a Survey Party was to carry out a ground survey of the Apa Tani and the Kiyi valleys in conjunction with an air survey of the whole area.

The preparations for this extensive programme, which involved the movement of hundreds of loads and the provisioning of sepoys and porters in advanced areas throughout the winter, fell almost entirely to me, and from an anthropologist on special duty I turned, much to my dismay, into a kind of glorified quartermaster-general. During Sep-

96

tember and October supply and transport problems held me up in the plains, and even a large part of November was mainly spent in building up supply dumps on the line of communications and in establishing a base in the Apa Tani valley.

The circulation of rations required by the porters at the various points of the route was in itself something of a nightmare, and it was only due to Betty's flair for organizing this enormous and far flung ' household' that none of the many parties moving through the wild hills of the Subansiri during the following months ever found themselves in a lonely camp without adequate provisions. Even the Assam Rifles, who brought their own army rations, were mere passengers in so far as transport was concerned. We were told how many loads would have to be moved with each unit, and it was for us to find the necessary porters.

The discussions in Shillong had been based on the assumption that the bulk of the provisions for the operations would be dropped from the air in forward areas at regular intervals. I had also asked for two hundred permanent porters as the minimum transport force with which to assure the mobility of such large numbers. For it seemed improbable that in an area over which Government exercised little or no control, and where some of the tribesmen were suspicious and even hostile, an expedition could rely for long periods on large numbers of locally recruited porters. I had no sooner returned to North Lakhimpur, however, than I was informed that the lack of transport planes would exclude the possibility of air-droppings, and with the following post, I received the news that the heavy demand on Abor porters for war work made it impossible to provide more than one hundred Gallongs, and even these would be three weeks late in arriving. This created an entirely new situation ; it left me almost entirely dependent on the local recruitment of tribal porters in the unadministered hills of the Subansiri region.

To make work for Government more attractive I introduced very considerable improvements in the conditions of men recruited on a temporary basis. Each was to be loaned a warm blanket and a waterproof sheet, so that they would be comfortable even when camping in places where no building material for shelters was available. Moreover, all porters employed for more than a day were to be supplied with rations of rice, pulse or potatoes, fat, salt and tea.

The route to the Apa Tani valley which we had used during the first season was impracticable for an expedition moving with hundreds of porters and relying on the recruitment of increasing numbers of local

97

tribesmen. As closer relations with the Daflas was one of the aims of the second year's operations, and the movement of Assam Rifles along the route seemed likely to deter hostile elements from interfering with our communications, I decided on a path which led for three stages along the right bank of the Panior river, then crossed the river by a suspension bridge yet to be built by men of Potin and Sekhe, and finally passed through the Dafla village of Mai to the southern end of the Apa Tani valley.

The first stage camp on this new route was Selsemchi, a Dafla village some ten hours' march from Joyhing, and using seventy foothill Daflas as porters I went there on the 15th of October, and installed a ration dump with one section of Assam Rifles to guard it.

The Daflas of Selsemchi welcomed the arrival of the Assam Rifles. They set great, and I regret to say, exaggerated store on the sepoys' ability to deal with the wild pig and deer that were ravaging the ripening crops. They were disappointed that every evening only one or two men were permitted to go out hunting; for they evidently considered an outpost failing in its purpose if at night the entire force could not be dispersed over the village land to guard the outlying fields. But they readily took to the use of new commodities. On the first day two tins of boot polish disappeared from the sepoys' camp, and I later heard that some Daflas, mistaking the waxy substance for a novel type of cooking fat, had filched the tins from under the sepoys' noses.

Selsemchi was the home of Bat Heli, a young Dafla of good standing, whom I had added to my staff of interpreters. Though not of the mental and moral calibre of Kop Temi, Heli was an efficient and energetic man, with a sense of humour and a pleasant manner. He could explain customs with which he himself was familiar, but he did not equal Temi in impersonal translation of enquiries on subjects of which he was ignorant.

The weather was now delightful with clear, cool mornings and from the spur of Selsemchi I had an excellent view of the Naga hills. I was impatient to move up to the Apa Tani valley, but further delays in the arrival of the Abor porters recruited from Sadiya forced me to return to Joyhing once more. It was not until the last day of October that we finally left the plains, and by that time the fine weather had come to an end.

Illness among the porters interfered with carefully prepared schedules, and treatment was often made difficult by the Daflas' conviction that

an Apa Tani patrician of Hari village.

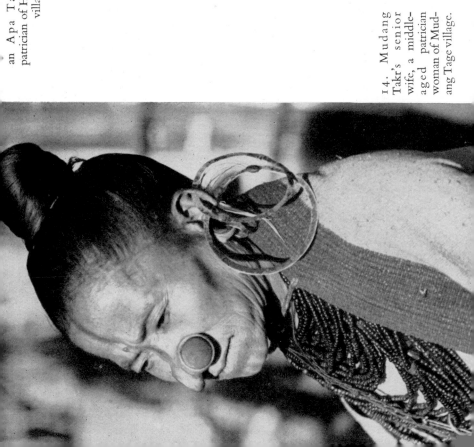

14. Mudang Takr's senior wife, a middle-aged patrician woman of Mudang Tage village.

15. Miri warrior of Rute-Hate village in the Kamla valley.

16. Apa Tani men on a hot day: red cane belts ending in curved tails is their basic dress.

every illness is caused by spirits. Like Apa Tanis they believed that a cure by sacrifice and offerings could not be combined with the taking of medicines, and men who had been given quinacrine for two days, refused further doses as soon as a priest performed propitiatory rites. One evening we were discussing this problem in the house of Bat Heli's kinsman, Pekhi, a charming, soft-spoken man who was convalescing from an attack of malaria. It was growing dark and someone brought a kerosene lamp from the camp and set it down beside me. I had hardly lit it when Heli jumped to his feet and carried it to a far corner of the house. It should not be placed near the patient, he explained, for Pekhi's illness was a sign that he was in the grip of a god and Dafla gods would certainly object to the smell of kerosene. "They are like sahibs, who eat only very good and clean food, and they dislike all bad smells."

We left Selsemchi on All Souls' Day, taking with us one section of Assam Rifles, and leaving the other in charge of the dump. The first day's march led over the 4,000-foot ridge of Tasser Puttu. Rain caught us on the summit and we ate our lunch in the shelter of a giant tree with water dripping down our necks and leeches converging on us from all sides. The descent that followed was an unbroken drop of 3,000 feet, and then we climbed steeply up a short incline to a site called Lichi. The Daflas of Potin had made an ample clearing in the forest and the scattered trunks of felled trees provided firewood and plenty of building material for shelters. There is a very special and unforgettable quality in the atmosphere of a large jungle camp, when relaxed after a long march everyone has settled round the fires, and the smell of cooking food mingles with the rich fragrance of freshly cut bamboo, fading leaves and recently dampened earth.

The next march brought us to Potin. We approached the settlement through the lower lying fields where part of the rice and millet crops had already been reaped and the ears were spread out on the threshing floors. I noticed that some of the rice had been cut in the ear, whereas the more usual Dafla practice is to strip the grain from the standing crop. Both rice and millet (*Eleusine coracana*) are thrashed under foot, a method very different from that used by the Apa Tanis, who beat ears in bundles against small wooden boards held slanting inside the reaping baskets.

On a flat-topped ridge the Potin men had cleared a good camp site. The view was magnificent. Looking ewastards the eye plunged into the deep, narrow valley of the Panior, and then soared up to Mount Lai, towering high above us on the opposite side of the gorge. To the north-west the river ran between hills rising to 7,000 and 8,000 feet, and half-way between the ridge line and the river, the villages of Chod, Sekhe and Yoijat stood on spurs divested of forest. But it was the mountains in the far distance, those lying on the left bank of the Panior, which aroused our greatest interest. For there lay Likha, and through our field-glasses we could just see the yellow patches of ripening crops.

In this part of the outer ranges Likha was as much a source of fear as was Licha in the Apa Tani country, and when I called on Tabia Nieri, the undisputed leader of the small community of Potin, I was inundated by complaints. Nieri's house stood on piles on an open hill slope and climbing the notched log to the verandah, we found ourselves in a long and not very broad room with five hearths at spaced intervals down the centre. The one nearest the entrance served as Nieri's parlour and there he received visitors; the next three were those of his three wives, and the last hearth belonged to his slave, Tabia Tömö. This was an elderly man whom Nieri had inherited from his father. Nieri addressed him and referred to him as ' elder brother ', and I was told that it would give offence if one talked of him as ' slave '.

Daflas are a hospitable people and they do not share the Apa Tanis' disconcerting prejudice against strangers entering their houses. Nieri's wives entertained us with excellent beer, hard-boiled eggs and pieces of sugar-cane, and the whole house was soon filled with people anxious to join in the conversation.

Nieri himself was a middle-aged man with an incipient goitre, and a scanty black beard. He was not blessed with a charm of manner, but even the most cheerful Dafla might well have been embittered by the blows that fate had dealt him. Until two years before, he told me, he and his people had lived at Lichi and it was there that the village had been raided by a party of thirty Likha warriors, who attacking at night, caught the villagers unaware. They had killed eleven men, carried off fifteen captives and looted property to the total value of some twenty mithan.

After long drawn-out negotiations Tabia Nieri had secured the release of eight men by paying sixteen mithan, fourteen Tibetan bells and many other valuables; another three captives had been ransomed by their own kinsmen, but one of Nieri's wives with her small son as well as a man and a woman from Sekhe, who had happened to be visiting Lichi at the time of the raid, were still held prisoner in Likha.

The people of Potin were not the only victims of this powerful village and from a nearby ridge I was shown the sites of several settlements on the neighbouring slopes which had been abandoned as a result of Likha's repeated attacks.

What was the secret of Likha's power? Why did hundreds of tribesmen tremble before this one village like birds petrified by the mere gaze of a cobra? I asked the men in Nieri's house why so many people, all thirsting for revenge against Likha, could not combine in a retaliatory raid on the common foe. Likha was not only strong, they answered, but had built up a network of ceremonial friendships and marriage relations with so many families in different villages, that no offensive could be discussed, much less executed, without intelligence reaching Likha. Dafla warfare depends for success almost entirely on the element of surprise, and no force would dare attack so powerful a foe who had been forewarned.

Tribesmen from many surrounding settlements had assembled at Potin, and as day after day I listened to the tales of survivors from villages that had suffered at Likha's hands, I gradually came to the conclusion that, without curbing this aggressive spirit, peace could not be established in the Panior valley. While the scope of our task seemed to grow with every day and an ever-deepening tangle of local politics and feuds threatened to frustrate all hopes of the exploration of distant areas, our transport and rationing arrangements were thrown into confusion by the sudden defection of the greater part of the Gallong porters. They had brought us to Potin with close on a hundred loads from the Selsemchi ration dump, and while we halted, they had returned to make the second of the four journeys necessary to transfer the whole dump from Selsemchi to Potin. Instead of the expected convoy, however, came the news that sixty-five of the men had returned to the plains, saying that they would not work in such difficult country and so far from their homes.

Without air-droppings and without Gallongs we were now wholly dependent on the local tribesmen. The Daflas of the outer ranges had rendered excellent service, and many of them were prepared to continue working on the Potin–Joyhing route. But the journey from Potin to the Apa Tani country would have to be completed with the co-operation of the Apa Tanis. The days passed, however, and no message came from Haja, nor was there any news from our Apa Tani interpreters. If the transport problems had not been so pressing the delay would not have been altogether unwelcome, for it enabled me to learn something of

Dafla custom, and to talk at leisure on subjects not directly linked with war and slave-raiding.

It was pleasant to sit in the evenings at the hearth of a Dafla house, eating sweet potatoes roasted in the red-hot ashes and drinking the strong clear millet beer. Nearly all the Daflas' large crop of *eleusine* millet is used for brewing, and only when rice is short is millet ground and made into unleavened bread.

The beer we were given in Tao Kara's house loosened the tongue of my interpreter Bat Heli, and he began to hold forth on the respective merits of Dafla and Apa Tani marriage customs. Heli thought the Apa Tanis' practice of premarital freedom rather convenient. Apa Tani youths could amuse themselves with unmarried girls, while with Dafla girls you might do no more than joke ; if you were caught in any more intimate relationship the girl's father would force you to marry her and at the same time demand double the bride-price.

Adultery was a most serious matter. If he were to find that his wife had been unfaithful, he would be so upset that he would be unable either to eat or sleep. He would not hesitate to kill her lover, tear him limb from limb and show her the dismembered parts ; then, roasting the flesh, he would stuff it in her mouth. This, I thought, was rather a drastic method of resolving marital triangles, but I wondered to what an extent such intentions were likely to be carried into effect. The faithless wife, Heli said, he would treat harshly ; but he would not drive her away, nor would he kill her, for would this not involve the loss of the bride-price he had paid for her ?

The position of an attractive young slave who found favour in the eyes of one of his owner's wives must be particularly unenviable. Heli knew of rich men who had killed slaves for interfering with their wives, and as it needs two for adultery, one can only assume that some young wives of polygamous elderly men are not averse to adventure with their husbands' young slaves.

A son inherits a right to all his father's wives except his own mother, and he is entitled to receive the bride-price for those who wish to remarry outside the kin-group. One day Tangum, the son of Nieri's brother, a small boy of perhaps eleven (Pl. 28), who had made himself indispensable by carrying the cat-basket, came and lodged a formal claim to one of his father's wives. I was recording cases which the Daflas wished to submit to arbitration, when the boy suddenly stepped into the ring of headmen and elders, and in the most self-possessed manner argued his right to his father's widow. With folded arms and head held high he began : In the raid on Lichi, his father had been killed and he himself had been captured and taken to Likha. After some time his father's brother had paid his ransom, and he returned to his own house. There he found that his father's younger wife had married again, and that the bride-price of five mithan had been paid to her brother who lived in Nakripila. Tangum claimed that the woman belonged to him. He would not have given her up, but as in his absence she had already married another man, he should at least receive the bride-price. When I suggested that he was rather young to take over a wife, he answered firmly and unhesitatingly that in three or four years he would be quite old enough to keep the woman himself, and that his age had nothing to do with the bride-price.

The assembled elders agreed that in principle this was so, but no one thought that in the circumstances he stood a chance of recovering the price already paid to the woman's brother.

It is such grievances which, harboured and recounted over the years, finally lead to bloody feuds and raids. The cause of Likha's enmity against the Tabia people, I was told, and thus the pretext if not the reason for the raid on Lichi, was a Tabia man's default over a marriage contract. Two generations ago, Likha Piji is believed to have paid a Tabia man sixty mithan as the combined price for his two daughters and a very precious Tibetan bell. But the partner in this deal—Tabia Tekhe, the father of a man now over seventy—gave him only one daughter in marriage and never delivered the Tibetan bell. Likha Piji's descendants held the Tabia clan responsible for this breach of faith, and two generations later took revenge on Tabia Nieri and his family.

The transport situation improved with the arrival one morning of Koj Karu and about forty Apa Tanis. I was still in bed when Temi put his head through the tent door to tell us the good news. A few minutes later we were up and watching a long file of men winding its way through the ravines below our camp. Soon they stood before us, laughing and chattering, and quite unconscious of the inconvenience they had caused us by their long delay. They had been nervous, they said, of coming to Potin, an area they had not dared to visit for many years, until they were certain the Assam Rifles were with us.

We left the next day and crossed the Panior river at a place called Pite. The Potin men had rebuilt the cane suspension bridge cut down many years ago when Likha began raiding the villages south of the

Panior. After a long march, first along the left bank of the Panior, and then up the valley of the Pangen, we cleared a camp-site on a piece of level ground near the river-bank. We were now within raiding distance of Likha, and took the precaution of surrounding the camp with a perimeter of bamboo and wooden stakes.

After supper Karu and Rika came to sit by our fire. They told us the harvest was over in the Apa Tani country. The crops had been good. Yes, they said in answer to my enquiries, we would be able to buy plenty of rice in Pape. But there was bad news too. During the rains six Apa Tanis had been captured by Licha men. Licha was in a truculent mood, and had threatened to attack any Government party that approached their village. The attitude of the Likha Daflas appeared to be equally discouraging. They had declared, it was rumoured, that they would massacre us if we came within striking distance, cut up our bodies and throw the pieces into the Kiyi river to be washed down to the plains whence we had come.

We had intended to take the route that leads to the Apa Tani country through Mai, but hearing these tales, I thought it politically advantageous to take the longer route and pay an unannounced visit to Jorum, a large Dafla village reported to be on friendly terms with Likha.

As we left the Pangen valley and entered Jorum land, the character of the landscape changed. The forest receded and tree growth was confined to narrow ravines. The hill-slopes, long since cultivated to the point of exhaustion, were covered with high dry grass, and the Jorum Daflas deprived of their use, had turned from shifting cultivation on hill-slopes to the growing of rice on terraces in the valley bottoms. These irrigated fields lay between knolls and hillocks, and on one we found a possible though somewhat damp site for a camp. The village of Jorum was perched on a high spur far above.

We sent a message to one of the notables and waited to see what the response would be. Night had fallen and we were warming ourselves with a cup of tea, when a long line of torches was seen moving down the hillside. Soon we were surrounded by a crowd of men, shouting and pushing in their eagerness to see us. The sepoys, faced by hundreds of fierce-looking tribesmen bristling with swords and daggers, grew nervous lest the flood of visitors overwhelmed the camp, but the Jorum men had come with the best of intentions. Jorum Kamin, whom I had met in the Apa Tani country, had brought a welcome gift of rice-beer and a fowl and he invited us to visit his house next morning.

This we did and after climbing a long shoulder, found a large building which, like a mediæval watch-tower, commanded a wide view over the surrounding country. The interior was so dark that only the glow of the eight fires down the centre allowed us to judge the dimensions of that huge undivided hall. We sat down at Kamin's hearth and his entire household, and presumably a good many people from other houses, gathered round. Hot from the steep climb, we gulped the excellent rice-beer we were offered. Having hung under the eaves all night, it was as cold as if it had come out of a refrigerator and the enormous size of the mugs encouraged us to take large draughts. The atmosphere was most cordial and we left Jorum refreshed and hopeful of winning the Daflas' confidence. But the effect of this early morning refreshment proved disastrous. From Jorum we had still to climb 2,000 feet up a treeless slope to the 6,000-foot range which separates the Apa Tani valley from the Dafla country. On the top of several pints of rice-beer this was too much for Betty ; her steps grew slower and slower ; she stopped to look at the view, then sat down, and finally rolled over and went to sleep in the warm grass. So we all sat down, the sepoys with their rifles and the porters with their loads, and waited for the worst effects of Kamin's beer to wear off. It did not take very long and half an hour's sleep and a little prodding soon brought Betty back to something very near her old form.

On top of the ridge we entered the high virgin forest which covers the hills surrounding the Apa Tani valley, and an easy march of a few hours brought us out on the open bracken-covered slopes above the fields of Haja, bright yellow with the coverage of newly reaped rice-stubble.

Our arrival in Pape produced one of those anti-climaxes with which one must reckon when dealing with unsophisticated people, but which can nevertheless be deeply disappointing. After the splendid reception we had been given in the spring, and the friendly relations we had had with scores of Apa Tanis, we had expected a warm welcome. Only four men, however, waited to greet us at the approaches to Haja, and not one of them evinced any pleasure at seeing us. There was no rice-beer, and the village, we were told, was barred to all strangers ; a sacrificial rite was in progress and none might enter until it was concluded. At Pape the houses of our old camp were dilapidated, and although we had paid for a watchman to look after our interests during the monsoon, there was not a scrap of firewood.

After a little Nada Chobin hurried up. He had the good grace to apologize for his tardy appearance, but he, like the small groups of men who began to collect under the pines, seemed only interested in the sepoys and their equipment and paid no heed to our requests for firewood and bamboos to rig up the porters' tarpaulins. Karu had disappeared soon after our arrival and as it began to grow dark we grew anxious about the prospects for fires and a cooked meal. Fortunately Karu reappeared at that moment at the head of a line of men from Duta carrying all the wood we were likely to need that night.

Next morning I summoned the leading men of Haja and Duta and explained Government's policy. I reminded them that in the spring they had prayed for protection against Licha, and I told them that as Government had now decided to meet their request for assistance, they must play their part by providing sufficient porters to bring up the main body of the Assam Rifles and the large quantities of provisions and trade goods that were assembled in the plains. We also needed timber and bamboo to enlarge our camp, and would pay for everything at generous rates. As money was of little use to them, we would open a shop at Pape where they could exchange the wages they earned in our service for such commodities as cloth, iron and salt.

The elders listened politely and promised co-operation, but it seemed to me that there was little determination to translate words into action.

Days passed, and only a handful of porters presented themselves for dispatch to Joyhing where hundreds of loads awaited collection. What was to be done? To accept the Apa Tanis non-co-operation in the matter of porters would have been disastrous for the prestige of Government, and I had specific instructions to bring home to the tribesmen the necessity of complying with reasonable demands for transport. But compliance with any order was as novel a procedure for Apa Tanis as it was for the Daflas, and with only twenty-four Assam Rifles at my disposal it was hardly practicable to exert much pressure on villages of several thousand inhabitants.

Yet with a large party of Assam Rifles, officers and surveyors assembled at Joyhing it was essential to recruit several hundred porters by a definite date. The cautious and considered approach of the anthropologist had to give way to the impatience of a harrassed transport officer, charged with the distressing task of moving a large expedition through roadless and potentially hostile country without permanent and dependable transport. Regretfully I pondered on the peaceful and comparatively carefree circumstance of our first visit to the Apa Tani valley.

A Miri Delegation

Fortunately, just when the tension created by my demands and the non-co-operative attitude of the Apa Tani headmen had all but reached breaking point, a diversion occurred which, if it did nothing else, distracted attention temporarily from the transport problem. One day returning from a visit to Haja I found a crowd of exotically dressed men waiting for me under the pines at Pape. They were Miris from Gocham, Biku, Ratam, La and Chemir, villages which lie in the rugged hills to the east of the Apa Tani valley. This group of Hill Miris were the only hillmen in the Subansiri area over whom Government exercised some influence, for they had long been the recipients of annual cash payments known as *posa* (see page 182). Their feud with the Apa Tanis of Hari had prevented them from visiting me in the spring, but now they had come in response to my messages calling upon them to submit their dispute for arbitration.

Most of these Miris had never before been to the Apa Tani valley, and while they complained of the long and difficult way, they marvelled at the fertility of the country, and the size of the villages. There was no doubt that seeing the Apa Tanis in their own homeland, they looked with very different eyes at their neighbours and trade partners.

I sent word to the *buliang* of Hari inviting them to come and discuss their differences with the Miris. But it was several hours before Gat Tadu, Hage Gat, who had recently been held captive in Chemir, and several other Hari men arrived for the negotiations.

Under the pine-trees of Pape the men sat down facing each other; to one side the Miris, stocky warriors in barbaric costume, with headdresses of bear-skin, enormous silver-trumpet ear-ornaments and heavy necklaces of multi-coloured beads, no man dressed quite like his neighbour; to the other the uniformly elegant Apa Tanis, beautifully groomed figures in white cotton cloaks, with their sleek, well-oiled hair neatly contained by narrow metal fillets and their long Tibetan swords all tilted at exactly the same angle. Somehow the scene conjured up a picture from classical times. Such must have been a meeting between a delegation of ancient Romans and the representatives of some barbarian tribe of the north.

The first to speak was Gat Tadu, and he began the long story with events lying back two or three generations. He illustrated his eloquent speech with the usual bamboo tallies, sticking some upright into the soft earth and laying others horizontally on the ground. These tally-sticks represented not only the men and valuables figuring in the account, but marked the outstanding events in the long-standing relationship between the Apa Tanis and the Miris.

From time to time Guch Tamar, the headman of Chemir, who sat opposite Gat Tadu, muttered in agreement, or made a gesture of dissent. Gat Tadu did not extend his argument to the recent murder of a Miri by Hari men or to Guch Tamar's capture of his kinsman Hage Gat, the acts which had caused the break between Hari and Chemir, but he ended his speech on a historical note and then motioned Guch Tamar to reply.

Tamar also started his narrative in the distant past, and Gat Tadu listened silently, half stretched out and leaning on his arms, while both Miris and Apa Tanis threw in short comments. After recounting a long sequence of alliances and disputes, Tamar came finally to the incident in which Taia Tara, his wife's younger brother, had been killed by two Hari men ; to obtain compensation for this act he had, he claimed, been fully justified in detaining the person of Hage Gat.

Hage Gat himself was the next speaker, and he laid out the tally-sticks which recorded the expenses he had had to incur to effect his own release. But his attempts to justify the killing of Taia Tara left the Miris unconvinced. Taia Tara, it appeared, had engaged some Hari men to capture a mithan belonging to a Hang villager against whom he had an old grievance. These men double-crossed Tara. When he went with his brother to the appointed meeting place to receive the mithan the accomplices killed him and captured his brother. Hage Gat asserted that Guch Tamar had used an equally treacherous trick to attract him to Chemir, where he was captured and imprisoned for many months.

I knew that the statement of claims and counter-claims would continue for several hours and that the question of compensation and a peace treaty would not be considered until every phase of the feud had been discussed from every angle. So I interrupted the proceedings by saying that obviously both sides had committed acts of violence and had suffered injuries. There was no point in perpetuating a feud which profited no one, and paralysed all trade between the Apa Tani valley and the Miri country. Government expected peace to be established as soon as possible. The trade partners should work out a settlement and compensate each other for real and undeserved losses. When they had agreed on a settlement they should let me know the details. Guch Tamar said at once that as a friend of Government and frequent visitor to the plains, he was prepared to make peace with Government's friends

108

and pay compensation to Hage Gat. I took this as a hopeful sign and optimistically imagined that as the parties had now come together some sort of settlement would emerge. The Miris and the Hari men went to Bela village where they spent the day discussing the dispute, but in the evening the Miris left abruptly for their own country, and a formal peace settlement seemed no nearer than when they had arrived.

The next day I turned my attention once more to the porter problem. I had heard rumours that Dümpre Dübo, a Hari man of slave class, was openly boasting that it was he who had dissuaded the Hari men from enlisting as porters ; without his assent, he was reported to have said, not a man would carry our loads. This personal animosity, if such it was, was difficult to understand, but at least it gave me an individual person with whom to deal. I could have sent for Dübo or gone to his house in Hari, but I decided to bide my time and wait for Dübo to come into the open. One morning I saw him holding forth among the crowd of spectators on the edge of the clearing not far from our house. I took two sepoys, walked across the grass and putting my hand on his shoulder, said that I was well aware of his attitude towards Government ; as he was the cause of the trouble I was having, he must remain at Pape until Hari village furnished a fair share of the porters I required.

Dübo did not seem in the least surprised. He grinned broadly and calmly walked back with me to the sepoys' camp. It was the first time that I had used Apa Tani methods in dealing with an obstruction and I was surprised that the bystanders took so little notice of the incident. They were familiar with the principle of capture to right a wrong and did not seemed astonished that Dübo's challenge had landed him in trouble.

These tactics produced immediate results. That evening one of the Hari *buliang* brought fifteen young men to effect Dübo's release. They enlisted as porters for a trip to the plains and the *buliang* promised to collect enough men to meet my demands. Dübo, when he heard he could go home, asked me for the blanket which I had lent him for his night's detention. My refusal to part with Government property did not disconcert him in the least. If I would not make him a gift of such value, would I not give him a few boxes of matches ?

Far from bearing me a grudge, Dümpre Dübo became from that day our most loyal friend, and in the months to come his resourcefulness, energy and reliability accomplished many a task before which a lesser man would have faltered. His story was interesting. His father, a man of slave class belonging to Haja, moved to Hari where he lived on agricultural labour and ultimately acquired a small piece of land. But Dübo, realizing that within the traditional pattern of Apa Tani economy a quick rise to prosperity was impossible, employed his unusual energy in trading expeditions to the plains. Soon he became the leader of those Hari men who went regularly to Assam and, acquiring a smattering of Assamese, he was useful to those who had no experience of the outside world. Gradually he gained prestige and acquired a fair measure of prosperity, and eventually, even the patricians of Hari had to recognize his influence with the people of lower class. He was appointed *buliang* and represented the people of slave descent in the village assembly. I never discovered why Dübo had at first opposed co-operation with Government, but his attitude was perhaps explicable if he felt that the recruitment of Apa Tani porters for Government service threatened his position as the ' foreign trade expert '.

The Hari men had hardly left the camp when we were startled by a series of long drawn-out cries. It was a dark night, and standing on the verandah, we saw the fields alive with lights moving in our direction. Was this a surprise attack by Apa Tanis resentful of being harassed by the recruitment of porters ? We held our breath, but the suspense did not last long. The lights passed the camp and following them with my eyes I saw that Haja was on fire. The shrill cries in the night had sounded the alarm, and the moving lights were the torches of those answering the call for assistance.

Soon a great pall of reddened smoke hung in the air above the north end of Haja, the sharp reports of exploding bamboos echoed over the valley, and huge flames shot into the sky and lit the surrounding landscape. I thought the village with its six hundred houses already lost. But I had reckoned without the efficiency of the Apa Tanis. Rapidly they set to work cutting down the houses that surrounded the burning buildings and, saturating the débris with water, created an effective fire-line. Only three houses were burned to the ground and fifteen were demolished, but the rest of the village was saved. I was anxious lest the Apa Tanis ascribed the disaster to the spirits' displeasure at our presence in the valley. Next morning, however, Chobin came and told me quite casually that the fire had been started by the red hot ash from an old man's pipe falling on some old clothing.

Though I was relieved that a major catastrophe had been averted, the necessity to rebuild the eighteen houses occupied the time and energy of a good many men of Duta and Haja, the two villages which so far had been nearly the only source of porters. To add to my troubles a message arrived from Mills asking me to come down to Joyhing to join a reconnaissance flight over the area of the Upper Khru.

This meant that I would have to leave Pape on November 23rd and left me only a few days to assemble the porters to bring up the large Government party already waiting at Joyhing. Day after day I made desperate efforts to recruit men ; first I tried at village level, holding each village responsible for the recruitment of fifty men ; with seven villages in the Apa Tani valley this would have given me three hundred and fifty porters. When this failed I approached the *buliang* asking them each to furnish four or five men from among the members of their own clan ; this would have brought in a wealth of porters and four or five did not seem an excessive number to demand from each clan. When this appeal also produced no results, I hit upon the method which eventually enabled us to maintain our communications throughout the season. Profiting from my experience with Dümpre Dübo I appointed *sirdars* or gang-leaders in each village from among those who were known to go to the plains of Assam on trading expeditions, and I paid these men a small retaining fee during the whole season on condition that they produced twenty men to carry loads whenever required. It took some months to perfect this system, and the need for porters was immediate and pressing.

Indeed it was so pressing that in an attempt to assert Government's authority by a show of force I nearly precipitated a crisis in our relations with the Apa Tanis.

Two days before my departure for Joyhing there was still no sign of the necessary porters, and I heard that some of the clans of Hari not only refused to co-operate, but had started a new agitation, this time against Gat Tadu and Dümpre Dübo who were now aiding the recruitment of porters. To leave the valley and allow this agitation to gather strength would have been fatal, and so I decided to bring the issue into the open. Accompanied by four sepoys I went to Hari and demanded that two kinsmen of the un-co-operative clan heads should return with me to Pape and remain there as hostages until the villagers changed their attitude. The demand was, of course, pure bluff, for had they refused I could not have carried them off by force. But the bluff succeeded. One principle in the game of kidnapping and raiding is never to resist superior force. If you give in you are at the worst taken prisoner and your kinsmen must arrange your ransom. If, on the other hand, you resist, you are likely to be killed. In Hari superior force was not really on my side, for what are four sepoys against hundreds of men in the labyrinth of an Apa Tani village? But the magic of fire-arms was still a myth and the reputed inexhaustible resources of Government gave me the advantage. Two down-cast patricians, still carrying their long Tibetan swords, tamely walked back with me to Duta.

The next day brought no change in the situation. The Hari men remained in camp and their womenfolk provisioned them with food and rice-beer. No one came to negotiate and no porters enlisted. Late that evening I announced that if no porters were forthcoming one of the patricians would have to accompany me to Joyhing, but that as soon as Hari provided a company of porters both would immediately be released.

On the morning of my departure for Joyhing only a handful of Haja and Duta men arrived and it was nearly midday before enough porters had collected to carry me and one section of Assam Rifles to the plains. We had not gone more than five hundred yards when shrill cries went up from every village within sight, and as we skirted Duta men came running out of the village shouting to the porters that they should drop their loads. My Dafla interpreters Heli and Gogoi picked up and translated the threats and taunts flung at us by the men now lining the path. The Apa Tanis would make war on us—not in daylight when they could not prevail against the rifles of the sepoys, but at night when the Apa Tanis would have the upper hand.

The position was absurd. For these were the same Duta men who six months previously had implored me to bring sepoys to the Apa Tani country and launch an expedition against Licha. Had I been on an anthropological journey I would have called off the trip to Joyhing and tried to discover the reasons for the Apa Tanis' sudden *volte-face*. Alas! There was no time for argument, I was committed to a programme laid down by Government and hampered by set dates. I could not delay.

However, worse was to come. Hardly had I reached the open ground between Duta and Michi Bamin when I saw men streaming out of Hari. Long lines of figures ran along the rice-bunds and looking through my field-glasses I saw that they all carried spears and shields, and wore the peculiar black rain-cloaks used in hunting and in war.

Once clear of the village the lines of men converged and a great block of warriors advanced up the valley. This was a hostile demonstration if nothing worse, and I did not think it wise to continue on my way and leave the camp protected by only twelve men.

So I walked back across the rice-fields with Temi and a rather shame-faced Karu to see how the situation had developed at Pape. Everywhere the paths were lined with men, some glum and silent, some shouting and truculent. It was clear that I would have to revise my plans. After discussing the various alternatives with Betty, we decided that she should stay in charge of the camp with both sections of Assam Rifles, while I proceeded to Joyhing without escort. The risk of interference by Daflas seemed small, and I hoped that twenty-four well-armed sepoys would be enough to guarantee the safety of the camp. In these circumstances it seemed best to leave both hostages with Betty. Without an escort I could not very well take a reluctant Hari *buliang* to Joyhing, and if he remained within the confines of the Apa Tani country perhaps the tinder would be removed from the smouldering fire.

Once more I set out. I sent the sepoys and the Hari headman back to camp, and continued on my way with the interpreters and the porters who had strangely enough almost doubled their numbers while I re-arranged my plans. More and more porters joined our party as I walked down the valley, and by the time we passed Hang I had close on a hundred men following in my wake. Having lost half a day we had to spend the first night in the forest above the Dafla village of Mai and the Apa Tanis seemingly forgetful of the morning's disturbance, proved the most pleasant and cheerful companions.

I reached Joyhing in the record time of five days and found the new Additional Political Officer, a Captain in command of three more sections of Assam Rifles, and a party of the Survey of India under Mr. W. M. Kalappa all waiting for transport to the Apa Tani valley. Fortunately there were also sixty-seven newly recruited permanent porters, fifty-two Gallongs from the Sadiya Frontier Tract and twelve Gurkha porters from Charduar. Added to the Apa Tanis whom I had brought down with me they formed a porter contingent adequate to move the entire expedition and a considerable amount of supplies to the Apa Tani valley.

The reconnaissance flight was to take place on November 29th and we prayed for good weather. A clear sky would allow us to see the unmapped area that lay between the Apa Tani country and the main

Himalayan range, and this aerial view would be of immense value in planning the exploratory tours which we hoped to make after our visits to Licha and Likha, and it might even solve the question of the sources of Khru and Kamla. Did these rivers break through the Himalayan main range or did they rise on the southern slopes?

A single-engined plane met us on an air-strip near Joyhing and we took off at 10 a.m. After gaining height we followed the line of the Panior river and, flying high above Selsemchi, passed within a few minutes the densely wooded country through which on foot we had struggled for four days. Here the cultivated land appeared as small patches amidst the vast forests covering hill and valley. But soon the picture changed; below us spread the open hilly grasslands of the Jorum area, with only here and there a streak of forest in the ravines and river-beds. We crossed a wooded range and saw a valley running at right angles to the Panior. This we took for the valley of the Kiyi. Here too we saw a great deal of grassland and many cultivated slopes as well as three settlements laid out in typical Dafla style, which must have been the houses of either the Likha or the Licha group.

Further west on the left bank of the upper reaches of the Panior several large villages appeared in the distance, but before we could reach them clouds began to gather and the pilot climbed to 14,000 feet. With no maps to guide him he dared not fly blind over unknown mountain country at any lesser altitude. The sun shone brightly in the upper air and above the clouds which blotted out the ground we had a magnificent view of the snow-ranges, a continuous chain of dazzling peaks rising out of a milky sea.

The deterioration in the weather and our premature return was a great disappointment, but even the glimpse we had had of the Dafla country on the Upper Panior convinced me that Jorum, Talo and Likha were only the outposts of a large population who inhabited the open valleys between the Apa Tani country and the snow-ranges. From above the Kiyi valley we had looked northwards and there too we had seen traces of heavy cultivation on most of the ranges in view. A large area, apparently densely populated, lay before us. Unknown and unexplored, it was a land of promise for the anthropologist, but for the administration anxious to carry India's rule to the mythical McMahon line, it posed a number of problems of which means of access and methods of control were not the least.

I was relieved to find on my return to Joyhing a messenger from

17. Chigi Nime, the seer of Duta, invoking the gods before sacrificing a mithan.

18. Apa Tani war-dance on the morning of the departure to Licha.

19. Kirum village, a Licha settlement, with long-houses and granaries scattered over sloping s

20. View over the Lower Kamla valley from Chemir village.

Betty with a letter written two days after my departure from Duta. She had had a busy time negotiating with Hari, first through go-betweens from Haja and Duta, and then with Hage Gat and other kinsmen of our two hostages. Some phases in the negotiations seem to have been both tricky and humorous. Describing the final phase, she wrote :

Up to this time the hostages had behaved fairly well, but at about two o'clock, fortified by enormous quantities of rice-beer brought by relations from Haja and Hari, they became restive and garrulous. The Naik,[1] fearful of their escape, ordered the hostages to be bound and disarmed, arguing that he was responsible to you for their safe custody. This created a great hue and cry. It is apparently a great dishonour for an Apa Tani notable to be subjected to such treatment in his own country ! Karu was in tears because one of the hostages is his maternal uncle and he considered himself slighted by the dishonour done to his kinsman. Nime began to shout and his voice was soon joined by many more. Even when I tried to explain why the men were disarmed, the scene did not quieten. I said that if only they would stay in one place and not scoot about near the perimeter we would be prepared to loosen their bonds and return their weapons. It was a very difficult position. Then I had a bright idea. I asked Karu and Chobin whether they were prepared to guarantee that the two men would remain in camp. They accepted this responsibility and I explained the situation to the Naik who agreed, though rather reluctantly and only because Karu was a Government interpreter. Actually my idea was as much to raise Karu's prestige as to stop his tears.

Finally the hostages were released because Hari furnished a reasonable number of porters and made amends for their hostile demonstration by rebuilding our house. This had been pulled down on the first evening after my departure to provide material for a perimeter. In the emergency the Assam Rifles had declared that they must have a camp that could be defended and they had enclosed a large space with a stout fence made from the houseposts to provide safe sleeping quarters for all the camp personnel ; only Betty, confident that she could handle the Apa Tanis, had pitched her tent outside the perimeter.

Last night [she wrote], the valley resounded with the most deafening noise. From every village rose shouts and yells, which after about half an hour trailed away into the hills as though hunters were out on every slope. We in the middle of the valley were the only silent patch. Having heard Hari's war-cries

[1] The Gurkha N.C.O. in charge of the two sections of Assam Rifles.

the day before the Naik grew anxious, and our 'island' was literally dotted with sentries who challenged every passer-by and had orders to shoot any who failed to halt. Actually all the shouting and noise was connected with the final celebrations of the *lapang* building in Bela. The cries continued at intervals during most of the night, ending in some really lovely chanting just before day-break. I imagined a wonderful scene, and longed to join in the festivities, but I was kept so busy jumping out of bed every time a sentry's challenge rang through the night—I feared a nervous sepoy might shoot some unsuspecting villager drunk from the celebrations—that I did not dare either to go to sleep or to leave the camp. Oh ! to be alone again, and to be able to enjoy the life of the tribesmen !

This cry of exasperation with the troublesome apparatus of sepoys and huge porter convoys found an echo in my heart ; I too felt frustrated at having to neglect unique anthropological opportunities for the organiz-ation of a huge expedition over whose policy I had little control as soon as the Political Officer took over.

Thanks to Betty's diplomacy more and more Apa Tani porters flowed in to Joyhing, and on December 1st the whole expedition set out with rations and barter goods for several weeks. By now the rest-camps and the transport arrangements were so well organized that the journey to Duta was almost in the nature of a pleasure trip.

We halted a day in a camp at Pite, and there many Daflas came to see us. Among them was Chera Tasso, a young man recently released with other prisoners by a Likha growing nervous at the prospect of our visit. He was a miserable-looking youth, the most pitiable victim of slave-raiding I have ever seen. His face was drawn, his body emaciated and his legs were weak and spindly. Five years before, he said, Likha Tasser had raided his father's house in Sekhe and captured both him and his mother. Tasser, however, sold his captives to Nich Topu for five mithan. Topu was a rich man who bought them on speculation, hoping to extract from their kinsmen an even higher ransom. But Tasso's father was too poor to pay the required price for his wife and son, and ever since the woman had worked as a slave and the boy had been imprisoned in stocks. In vain had Tasso pleaded to be freed of the log in which his foot was encased, promising to work for his captor if only he might move about unfettered.

Even with the chance of a ransom it seemed strange that any man should feed a captive for five years without at least obtaining the advant-age of his labour. Tasso's mother and several other Sekhe villagers were still held prisoners in Likha and their kinsmen left no doubt that they were looking to us to secure their release when we visited the village.

We reached Duta on December 6th, and found the camp in good order. The excitement which had accompanied my departure had died down and Betty had not only restored good relations with Hari, but had rebuilt the camp with one house for us and one for the Additional Political Officer.

8

CRUSADE AGAINST LICHA

THE ARRANGEMENTS for the expedition to Licha were now complete. One and a half platoons of Assam Rifles were assembled at Pape, and the store was packed with provisions, salt, cloth and other barter goods. But on the diplomatic side the preparations had been less successful. All attempts to establish direct contact with Licha had failed. We had received no reply to the messages which we had sent through Daflas of neutral villages, but indirectly we had heard that the Licha men scoffed at our intention to intervene in their feud with the Apa Tanis, and openly threatened to destroy any party who entered their territory. During the rains they had committed another act of aggression ; six Apa Tanis had been captured and all negotiations for their release had so far failed.

But on the day after my return from Joyhing one of the captives, Rade Lalyang of Bela, arrived in camp. He had escaped from Licha under cover of darkness and came to relate his experiences. Some two months previously, he said, he and several of his friends had gone hunting : they had been cooking a meal in the shelter of a large rock when they were attacked by thirty Licha warriors. Some of the Apa Tanis got away, but Lalyang and five of his companions were overpowered and carried off to Licha, where they were put in stocks. One night, however, he had managed to free his foot from the wooden block and making his way by unfrequented paths, he had crossed the hills to the safety of the Apa Tani country.

Lalyang said that in Licha our prospective visit was the main topic of conversation. From the remarks he had overheard, he gathered that several stratagems were being debated. Some advocated the killing of all Apa Tani prisoners as we approached and a fight to defend their village. Others favoured cunning : they would give us a friendly reception and then fall upon us when we were off our guard. This

118

had a familiar ring, for many years ago, when I accompanied Mills on a tour through the Assam-Burma border area, we had found ourselves in a very similar position. There the tribesmen were Nagas and in making a surprise move they had nearly caught us on the wrong foot.

Oddly enough the Apa Tanis' enthusiasm for the expedition to Licha seemed to cool off the nearer it came to the date of departure. Men who had clamoured for action in the spring now admitted that they were too frightened to accompany us. The prize in unashamed timidity went to Nada Chobin, Haja's most influential *buliang*, who earlier in the year had sent messengers to the plains with the purpose of enlisting Government's support against Licha. When I chided him for his chicken-heartedness, and jokingly suggested that he should accompany us dressed as a woman and thus avoid all risks, he laughed and said that this was an excellent idea, but that to stay in Haja was even safer.

On the evening before we set out for Licha, Chigi Nime came to our camp to perform the rites considered necessary for the inauguration of any martial undertaking. He wore full war-dress and led a small black dog on a leash. To him and to all Apa Tanis the projected visit to Licha appeared as a raid, and this despite the fact that we had sent Daflas of the neutral village to announce our arrival. If you went to a village with a large armed force, you were on the war-path; for if you wanted to negotiate you went in the company of one or two go-betweens. There was, according to Apa Tani custom, no third alternative and they could not at this stage be expected to comprehend the nature of a Government mission.

Chigi Nime therefore busied himself with the magical preparations for our joint venture. He set up his spear on a grassy plot and tied the dog to a small peg driven into the ground. Then, facing towards Licha, he and his assistant squatted down and started the diaphonal chant that is the preliminary to most Apa Tani rites.

He invoked the spirits of heaven, forest, water and earth, calling on them to bear witness that the fault of the quarrel lay with Licha and with no one else. "May no evil befall the Apa Tanis participating in the expedition, may their swords and spears be sharp, but may the swords of Licha be blunted and their arrows miss their mark." Gradually warriors and spectators gathered at the ritual place until the crowd watching the rites was several hundred strong.

Night fell and fires were lit, but the priests continued the ceremonies and when I woke at four-thirty next morning they were still chanting.

Now the invocations were interrupted from time to time by shrill war-cries and a strange humming sound, which reminded me of nothing so much as the angry buzzing of a swarm of bees. I dressed and went out to join the ritual circle and found that it was the young Apa Tani warriors who hummed as they danced round a large sacrificial structure of wood, bamboo and leaves; spent arrows quivered in the cross-bars and chickens, both large and small and all still alive, hung head downwards from the bamboo staves which bent under their weight. The final rites were now performed; the dog was tied at the foot of the 'altar' and Chigi Nime and his assistant waved kite feather fans before its nose, calling on the gods to give the Apa Tanis victory and protect them from all dangers.

After a short while the warriors set on the dog and slashed at it with their swords. It died instantly and Nime cut off its head. Then he severed the heads of the chickens. The warriors shouted and brandished their swords and danced with great hopping steps round the ritual structure. The morning mist, still hanging low, blurred all outlines and the men in the black fibre rain cloaks and cane hats leaping about with spears on their shoulders and swords in their hands were a fantastic sight. Once more their yells alternated with the peculiar, ominous, low humming drone, and I wondered at the strange ways in which courage is instilled into different peoples. At last Chigi Nime cut the dog's head in two and tying the nose and jaws to a warrior's shield, set the remainder of the head at the foot of the 'altar'.

In the meantime the porters had arrived in camp. They all wore their war-and-hunting outfits, and carried long spears. Of the prominent men Nada Tomu and Tano Tasso appeared dressed for the trip, but Padi Layang disappointed us by declaring—a little shamefacedly—that he was going to stay behind.

There was still some wrangling about loads and it was well after eight before we set out. Bhattachariya, Rajoni and Temi and three interpreters were to accompany us, but to her great regret Betty had to remain at Pape, for this was considered something of a military expedition, and the two captains responsible for military and political affairs would not hear of having a woman in the party. As a matter of fact she could ill be spared from Duta; the Surveyors were to map the Apa Tani valley in our absence, and the difficult task of finding porters for their trips up the various mountain-peaks fell to Betty, the only person left at Duta who had any influence on the villagers.

Heading almost due north we climbed the bracken-covered slopes that enclosed the valley. Our column consisted of a band of tribal guides, a platoon of Assam Rifles, one hundred and forty Apa Tani porters and a good many hangers-on—Dafla as well as Apa Tani—all of whom hoped to settle their own private accounts with Licha. Although we left the valley in brilliant sunshine, the mist drew down as soon as we entered the area of sub-tropical forest, and visibility dropped to no more than ten yards, dangerous weather for a marching column when an ambush might lie round any corner.

On the crest of the hill we came upon a well-trodden path, running in moderate gradients along a ridge of some 7,000 feet. Resting places and traces of burnt-out fires showed that we were still in country frequented by Apa Tani hunters, and Karu explained that even such distant hunting grounds were owned by individual Apa Tani clans. It was in this kind of country that the Apa Tanis had so often been ambushed by bands of Licha Daflas.

Early in the afternoon we reached a stream running through a narrow marshy valley. Our guides told us that this was the last source of water before the Pai river, nearly a day's march ahead. So we camped on this moist and inconvenient spot, where the tents had to be pitched on uneven ground between boulders and trees. In the evening it began to rain and though there were enough tarpaulins to rig up shelters Chigi Nime decided that my tent would prove far more comfortable sleeping quarters. He came with two Dafla companions soon after dinner and as Betty was not with me there was plenty of room for the four of us.

Next morning Chigi Nime and our other Apa Tani guides told us of two possible paths ; the shorter one was more difficult going for the porters but more frequently used, the other was longer and lonelier. Thinking it over, we came to the conclusion that Licha would expect us to take the more usual path, and we consequently decided on the round-about route. But at the first resting-place it was evident that Licha had taken no chances ; Karu trod on a *panji*, and looking about we found many newly cut spikes embedded in the grass. These *panji* slowed up our progress considerably, for the scouts and porters had to tread warily.

When we came to the end of the country frequented by Apa Tani hunters, Chigi Nime stepped aside. He drew an egg from his basket and, invoking the protection of gods and spirits, smashed it on a convenient rock. The long file of porters passed him without a glance but no doubt they drew comfort from this appeal to supernatural powers.

121

Chigi Nime may have been a good priest, but he was a poor guide. He had assured us that we could easily reach the Pai river before nightfall, but as the afternoon drew out it become increasingly evident that our progress was too slow for us to arrive that day ; in many places the path had to be newly hacked through secondary jungle of bamboo, bracken and thorny cane and in the late afternoon we began looking about for a suitable camp-site. It was five o'clock when, with only half an hour of daylight left, we halted on a level stretch. The porters set down their loads and began to clear the undergrowth.

It was astonishing how quickly the Gurkhas and the Apa Tanis managed to carve a camp-site out of the forest and how rapidly confusion resolved into some kind of order. But nothing could quite make up for the lack of water. We had emptied all our bottles in the nine hours of a long and tedious march and as none was available we could not even brew tea, and worse still neither porters nor sepoys could cook.

We had not been long in camp when we heard long-drawn-out shouts coming from the direction of the Pai river. Obviously the men of Licha were well informed about our movements. In the failing light it was impossible to build a perimeter, and we hoped that the surrounding jungle was sufficiently thick to prevent the Daflas making a surprise attack.

The night passed without incident, however, and breaking camp at seven next morning we set out without either breakfast or a wash. In less than an hour we reached the Pai river and found a level stretch on the further bank where, well protected by a bamboo stockade, both sepoys and porters could prepare their first freshly cooked food for twenty-four hours.

It was decided that some of the porters and one section of Assam Rifles should remain with the baggage in the camp of the Pai river, while we moved on to Licha with three sections and the rest of the Apa Tanis and Daflas unencumbered by loads.

We had to break a way through grass and scrub to reach a path leading towards the settlements of Licha. But once it was reached the going was easy and we travelled between hills that bore patches of both old and new cultivation. We had expected Licha to post look-outs to watch our progress, and it was not long before we saw the grass stirring, and caught a glimpse of a man moving parallel with us on a nearby hill.

In some places the valley narrowed and there was plenty of opportunity for an ambush. Ignorant of Dafla tactics we feared that Licha would make a surprise attack before we reached the open ground near the village. Nagas might have done so and I could not help thinking of an occasion in the Naga hills when in just such country as this I had been chased by a roaring crowd of Kalyo Kengyus. The Political Officer, on the other hand, who had served on the North-West Frontier and was accustomed to dealing with Pathans, thought the famous bow-men of Licha might snipe at us from concealed positions.

But on this occasion at any rate, the Daflas had neither the boldness of Nagas nor the determination of Pathans, and they relied on magic to bar the way. In a gully leading up a steep slope the path was blocked by a bamboo fence that carried the heads of a pig and a dog, both fresh from the rites on the previous day. Temi explained that Daflas perform such sacrifices when seeking to ward off raiders, and we wondered whether perhaps the Licha warriors had not originally intended to add poisoned arrows to magical charms, and had only lacked the courage to attack when they saw the size of our column.

At last we came into the open, and standing on a spur we overlooked two settlements of Licha known as Tabia and Bagi. The houses, flanked by granaries, were scattered over broken ground, and both villages looked deserted except for a few pigs still moving about between the houses. Kirum, the third and largest settlement of Licha lay, we were told, hidden behind a ridge. It was these three settlements which were collectively known as Licha, a name which is in fact that of the clan dominant in the area.

Nearest to us lay the settlement of Bagi, and as we approached a man began shouting across the ravine. He was recognized as Licha Tara and two of our Dafla guides volunteered to go and talk to him. They called out, bidding him stay where he was, but he shouted some derisive remarks and vanished before our guides could reach him.

As the afternoon was well advanced and there seemed little likelihood of contacting any of the headmen that day, I suggested that we should stay where we were, camp in one of the houses of Bagi with our Apa Tani and Dafla guides and half the sepoys, and send the others with the porters back to the Pai to bring up the luggage.

But the Political Officer did not like the idea of splitting the small force of Assam Rifles and thought it too risky to bring up the luggage after nightfall. He decided—perhaps rather rashly—to give the Apa Tanis a free hand in dealing with Bagi and then to return to the camp

123

on the Pai river. This decision was popular with the Apa Tanis, who set about spearing pigs, catching chickens and searching the houses for eatables.

Chigi Nime maintained the fiction that this was a raid by throwing the head of the dog sacrificed at Duta over one of the thresholds, and as we returned to the camp on the Pai he again invoked the gods, praying that the spells of the Licha men should recoil on their own heads, and that the Apa Tanis would be able to eat of Licha's pigs without suffering harm.

Next day we moved the whole party from the Pai river to Bagi and camped on an open spur in the highest part of the village. We had just got the tents up when Karu announced that four men could be seen approaching from the direction of Kirum ; I looked through my field-glasses and recognized one of the four as Likha Rebla, an old man who had visited me in Duta last season. Then he had come to complain about the raids of his own clansmen who had forced him to leave Likha and seek asylum in Licha. He arrived in camp protesting friendship and said that ever since he had heard of our coming he had tried to persuade the Kirum men to treat with us. But none would listen. Kirum, he explained, had now put the responsibility of negotiating a settlement with Government on Bagi, because, they held, it was Bagi men who were responsible for the more recent incidents in the feud with the Apa Tanis. He was a new-comer in Kirum and had nothing to do with this feud, but he had come to visit us as a friend and would gladly carry any message we wanted to send.

We demanded the release of the two Apa Tanis still held captive, and explained that Government did not want to fight Licha or any other Dafla clan, but that we insisted on direct negotiations with responsible men of the village. Kirum could not disclaim responsibility for the quarrel with the Apa Tanis, for many of the raids had been led by Kirum men and all had shared in the many ransoms paid by the Apa Tanis.

The morning passed without further developments, but late in the afternoon a party of Licha slaves brought one of the captured Apa Tanis into camp. He had just been released, and as he had had no opportunity of washing during the three months of his captivity, he was incredibly dirty. He told us that in the confusion that had followed our arrival two out of the four remaining Apa Tani captives had escaped ; he himself had been taken to Kirum, but Nani Lali had been carried off to the forest where the Bagi men were in hiding.

After a cold night we woke to a fine morning and watched the sun rise out of the white clouds that hung about the high peaks. As no negotiators appeared we decided to go to Kirum. We climbed for forty minutes up a steep slope, until we reached a ridge from which we looked down on the village of Kirum.

The Apa Tanis had always described Kirum's position as impregnable and indeed for people armed only with spears, swords and bows there was little chance of pressing home an attack against determined defenders familiar with the difficult terrain.

From a semicircle of high hills grass-covered shoulders led down, like the fingers of an outstretched hand, into a depression whose only outlet was south-eastwards through the deeply cut valley of the Kiyi river. Perched on open spurs stood nineteen large long-houses, each surrounded by its own suite of well-built granaries.

As we descended the open slope, cries rose from every part of the settlement. Our guides and interpreters called for the Kirum notables, asking them to come and meet us, but the villagers shouted back that we should remain where we were and not enter the village. We halted, and I looked through my field-glasses at the confusion caused by our approach. From every house men and women could be seen running to the granaries with baskets on their backs, then out they came and staggering under huge weights made for the nearest patch of jungle.

What now followed was largely in the nature of a farce and showed how little superiority of arms alone can achieve in settling tribal disputes. With the fire power at our disposal we could have killed every man in sight; our intention was, however, not to wipe out the Apa Tanis' enemies but to persuade the leaders of Licha to come forward and discuss a peace settlement and in doing so indirectly acknowledge Government's authority. Unfortunately the men of Licha had not the slightest intention of making peace on Apa Tani terms; they considered Government's sudden interest in their affairs as only a temporary embarrassment. No Government party had ever before visited the Kiyi valley, but the inhabitants of Licha had heard of Government incursions into other parts of the Dafla hills and they were familiar with the customary behaviour to be expected of punitive expeditions: the burning of a village followed by a quick withdrawal to the plains. They considered therefore that their best policy was to delay matters as long as possible and allow both Government and the Apa Tanis to spend their wrath. If the village was burnt and they had to rebuild their houses these were of infinitely less value than the compensation the Apa Tanis were demanding.

When it became clear that the people of Kirum were directing all their efforts to removing their valuables from the village and doing nothing to further negotiations with us, we moved down from the high ridge to the house of Licha Sera, a man notorious for his part in recent raids on the Apa Tanis. This action was followed by the immediate withdrawal of all the inhabitants and our interpreters shouted themselves hoarse in proclaiming our desire for a peaceful settlement and calling for negotiators to come and talk things over.

Slowly an old man with a wrinkled weather-beaten face came up the hill. His hair was white and his step faulty. He wore an old cloth but no ornament of any kind, and instead of the usual *dao*, he carried a kind of wooden sword. This signified that its bearer had come to talk peace. We welcomed him and asked him to sit down. We were told that he was Licha Saha, in his youth a great warrior and now one of the brains of Licha. Many years ago he had led the raid which had wiped out Soli, the village of Temi's father.

Now he played the rôle of injured innocence. He squatted on the ground, sucking his long-stemmed pipe and pretended to know nothing of the whereabouts of the other Licha notables. Neither did he know what had happened to Nani Lali. He sat before us sullen faced, staring at the ground and answered every question with a contemptuous ' tse ma ' (' I don't know ').

Although Temi suppressed all emotion when facing his father's old enemy, and spoke as gently and reasonably as he would have done to an honoured visitor in his own house, the net result of the conversation was nil.

After more than an hour of useless interrogation, we moved one spur forward and, taking Licha Saha with us, went to sit in the empty houses of Toko Panior and Licha Teli which stood together on the edge of a gulley. Here a very old man with white hair and a fine nose and profile joined Licha Saha. He had the manner of an ambassador of the old school, and the Political Officer nicknamed him Sir John Simon. He was Toko Tatam. Though the owner of the largest house in the village, he was as poorly dressed as Licha Saha and he too carried a wooden sword. But the smoothness of his manners did not get us any further than the gruffness of Licha Saha, and there seemed to be no end to argument and evasion.

At last a third and much younger man strode up the hill. His arrival brought some life into the conversation. He was Nielom Tami. With violent gestures and raised voice he proclaimed that he understood the necessity of negotiating with Government and had done his best to persuade the men of Kirum and Bagi to meet us, but they had preferred to run away and hide in the jungle. Again we explained our aims and he relayed whatever we said sentence by sentence to the men collected before the houses on the spurs below. He swaggered and gesticulated and his voice carried over the hills in fine ringing tones. But it was all for show. He enjoyed hearing his own voice and was not seriously persuading the other Licha notables to come and treat with us.

Throughout these ' negotiations ' we were watched by men, women and children gathered on the platforms of the more distant houses, and by groups of young warriors sitting fully armed on the edge of the jungle. There was little point in visiting any other house in the village, for at our approach the people faded away, only to reappear at another vantage-point, which being unfamiliar with fire-arms, they judged to be out of our reach.

While the Licha people underestimated the range of fire-arms our Apa Tani friends had altogether exaggerated ideas of a rifle's effectiveness. More than once they pointed excitedly at a piece of jungle close at hand begging us to order the sepoys to shoot the particular ' villain ' believed to be in hiding there. When we retorted that not a soul was to be seen, they considered our insistence that the target must at least be visible as unnecessarily pedantic. To them it seemed sufficient to know in which direction you should fire for the bullet to find its victim. If magical spells could harm a victim irrespective of distance and visibility, surely the miraculous weapons of Government could also do so.

After endless and inconclusive arguments with the gruff old warrior, the polished elder statesmen and the spluttering orator we closed the proceedings, saying that, if by that evening Nani Lali had not been released, the men of Kirum would regret their defiance of Government. Then we returned to the camp at Bagi.

In the afternoon a man and a small boy from Nielom, a village within sight of our camp, arrived with a present of chickens and eggs, and professed a great desire for friendly relations. It seemed inexpedient to ignore even the smallest gesture of goodwill, and accepting the gifts we promised to visit their village on the following day. As a matter of fact we were running short of rations, and it had already been decided that we must move camp whatever attitude Kirum adopted on the morrow.

That evening, long after dark, we heard shouts from a great distance and saw lights moving through the valley below us. Karu and Nime declared that the voices were those of Apa Tanis calling for guides, and two scouts were sent to bring up the party. Shortly afterwards nine men of Haja, carrying heavy loads of rice, arrived in camp and we were horrified to hear that, bringing relief rations for their kinsmen, they had walked with their conspicuous torches through the valley where the Daflas of Bagi were in hiding. For the Licha warriors it would have been the easiest thing in the world to capture the nine men and we would have looked pretty silly if instead of recovering one prisoner, we had lost nine men.

The next morning saw a repetition of our farcical negotiations. Again we went to Kirum and again we were cold-shouldered by the inhabitants, who at our approach retreated to more distant places whence they could view our doings without endangering their persons. One old woman, described to me as 'the owner's mother', however, greatly daring, appeared in the house of Licha Sera, and there she was later joined by a boy of about ten, the son of the famous warrior Toko Panior. It was obvious that the Licha people credited us with a code of honour higher than their own, and assumed that we would harm neither women nor children. To the Apa Tanis, however, our behaviour was inexplicable, and Padi Layang, who had joined us the previous day, nudged me again and again, each time throwing significant looks at the boy, who appeared to him as an ideal subject for a swift grabbing action.

There were more arguments with Licha Saha, and a great deal of shouting from one group of spectators to the other, but nothing concrete emerged. The Political Officer considered that the only way he could convince the people of Kirum that they were not as clever as they thought themselves, was by burning the village and he announced that unless they changed their minds and set Nani Lali free within half an hour, he would destroy the houses of the most important men.

He ascertained the houses of those responsible for the more recent raids on the Apa Tanis, and when half an hour had elapsed, ordered five of them to be burnt. Even when smoke began to rise from the doomed buildings, groups of people on more distant verandahs stood watching in silence and seemed as unperturbed as they were unapproachable.

128

By the time we returned to the camp above Bagi, the luggage had been packed and we were able to leave for Nielom without further delay. The path dropped sharply into the valley of the Kiyi and for several hours we walked along the river's edge, crossing and recrossing the water by many make-shift bridges.

In Nielom we were well received. The envoys of the previous day, supported by some men from Talo, came to meet us and suggested a reasonably suitable site for the tents.

While sepoys and porters settled into camp, we went to the village with Temi. The few people who were about seemed pleasantly surprised that we were not ferocious raiders bristling with arms, but studiously smiling visitors who presented them with cigarettes and matches and declared that their only desire was to see peace established between all Dafla villages. On the majority of the inhabitants of Nielom, however, our attempts to produce a favourable impression were lost. For most of them had thought caution the better part of valour and had absented themselves on urgent business.

As we walked down the path an amiable woman virtually dragged us into her house and there we found quite a large gathering round the fire. There was, no doubt, an element of anxiety in the solicitude with which the Nielom ladies treated us to millet beer, but they were anything but shy and the senior lady of the house grasped me by the arm as she spoke with emphatic urgency of her desire for friendship. Soon our hosts were reassured that they had nothing to fear and they produced quantities of eggs, welcome gifts after many puddingless days in hostile country.

In the evening a deeply disturbed Chigi Nime called us out into the dusk, and pointed to a great pall of smoke hanging over Bagi. Licha, it seemed, was indulging in the empty triumph of burning our abandoned camp.

"The place where I slept for two nights," Nime lamented, "where I sat and ate my food, this place is now being devastated by those wretched Daflas. How they will jump in triumph on the ashes of our huts. What a disgrace for me, and for all of us!"

He could not explain exactly why he took the burning of the abandoned camp so much to heart, but his reactions suggested that the burning had some magical purpose; perhaps he believed that the destruction of a person's leavings spells misfortune if accompanied by the appropriate ritual.

But on this as on so many other occasions on this tour, I was unable to gather all the relevant facts; for informants as well as interpreters were too busy with practical arrangements to indulge in lengthy discussions on belief and custom.

Next day we crossed the wooded ridge which separates the Kiyi valley from the Talo-Jorum area. At its highest point it must be well over 7,000 feet, and from there a well-trodden path drops steadily on to the open grass-lands surrounding Talo. Most of the hill-slopes had been cultivated to the point of exhaustion and we were told that the crops they yielded were poor. But the people of Talo, like those of Jorum, had taken to wet-cultivation, and though not as skilled in the building and maintenance of terraces as the Apa Tanis they relied on their rice crops for a substantial part of their food supply.

Talo was the largest and most prosperous-looking Dafla village I had yet seen, each long-house with a group of pile-borne granaries standing on its own hill-top. Toko Bat, the richest and most influential man of the village, had a reputation for great political shrewdness. This had led him to eschew a warrior's rôle and content himself with backing and sometimes financing raids undertaken by his allies in other villages. In his relations with us he played the game of wait and see. Just as in the spring of that year he had avoided all direct contact with me by sending his wife to visit our camp at Pape, so now he sent Yoyum, recognizable a long way off by her enormous goitre, to meet us at the village boundary with the customary courtesy of mugs of millet beer. She pretended that her husband was away on business in Pei, a small and unimportant village near Mai, but as a matter of fact we knew that he had been conferring in Likha, and suspected that he was reluctant to meet us until he knew how matters stood and how much we knew of his connections with Licha.

Deciding to ignore the absence of Toko Bat for the time being, I went that evening to visit his cousin Toko Tekhi who lived in an enormous long-house on a nearby hill-top. I was received most cordially, and the old and grey-haired Tekhi went out of his way to be pleasant. He declared that the Licha men were rascals, who had stolen many mithan belonging to him and to other Talo people, and that he only wished we had killed or captured the whole lot.

There were fourteen hearths in Toko Tekhi's house, and its single room was filled with innumerable men, women and children. Now they crowded round me, and, showing little respect for the old patriarch, chattered happily irrespective of the conversation he was trying to conduct.

In the course of his long life Tekhi had married nine wives. Five were still alive, and two of them were young and uncommonly pretty. It seemed doubtful, however, whether the aged husband could take more than a platonic interest in these lively young girls, whom he may have married to further some political end. But his ten sons, some of whom had wives and children of their own, all shared in the life of this enormous house. Apparently there is little harm if the sons, the heirs to a father's wives, anticipate some of their privileges, and deputize for an ageing parent. This system certainly makes for contentment among junior wives, and prevents the development of tensions which might otherwise jeopardize the harmony of a giant household.

The days in the peaceful atmosphere of Talo gave us all an opportunity of reassessing the political situation. The Apa Tanis had seen the futility of relying on force to press their claims on Licha ; they began to talk about parleys on neutral ground, and their friends and trade-partners in Talo seemed to encourage this idea.

The dispute between the Apa Tanis and Licha was not the only political question to be considered. Equally grave was the tension between the Dafla villages of the foothills and the war-leaders of the Likha clan settled in villages on the north bank of the Panior. Though lending Government's moral support to the threatened villages of the outer ranges we hoped that it would be possible to initiate negotiations between the opposing parties and thus obviate the necessity of recourse to arms. What we had in mind was a kind of general gathering of the tribesmen where Government guaranteed to hold the peace and grievances could be ventilated and compromises discussed.

The tribal institution of peace councils known as *mel* seemed capable of being harnessed to Government's purpose, and we decided to call such a meeting for the first week of January. Messengers were sent to all the tribesmen concerned, bidding them to come to Talo, a village which seemed eminently suitable for such a concourse.

Meanwhile we had to return to Duta to organize the transport and purchase of provisions for the coming months. During our absence constant relays of Apa Tanis had brought up considerable quantities of salt and cloth to Pape, and it now remained to us to begin the large-scale purchasing of rice, with which our porters, our staff and ourselves were to be provisioned for the remainder of the season.

With Chigi Nime I walked at the head of a long column of Apa Tani warriors and porters, and soon we crossed the wooded ridge, and looked down into the lovely bowl of the Apa Tani valley. Nime was not in a cheerful mood and the other Apa Tani notables were gloomy faced. The expedition to Licha had been a great disappointment. Compared to the lengthy preparations and the numbers of men employed the result had been ridiculously small. One small mithan calf, which the Apa Tanis had caught near Kirum, was the only booty they had been able to bring back, and Nani Lali, the last of the Apa Tani captives, was still in the hands of the Licha Daflas.

"How can I hold up my head," moaned Nime, "when we appear in Duta with neither killed nor captive? Will not the people laugh at us when we return empty handed? How can I show my face to Yelu? Won't she be disappointed if we bring her neither trophies nor prisoners?"

Yelu was the Apa Tanis' pet-name for Betty, and Chigi Nime seemed genuinely worried that he could neither place before her a Dafla's hand nor offer her a few fettered slaves.

But his laments gave way to the business of the hour. As we approached Pape, he and Karu collected some bamboos and split them into small sticks. They sat down on either side of the path leading into camp and, putting down a stick for each man, checked the number of returning Apa Tanis as they filed in. I had expected some kind of rite to mark the men's homecoming. But though an impressive ceremony had initiated the start of the expedition, the returning warriors as well as the porters made their way quietly and unceremoniously to their own houses.

During our absence wild rumours had reached the Apa Tani valley. Several Apa Tanis had been reported killed in battle with the Licha Daflas and others were said to be without food. Some of the *buliang*, fearing a triumphant Licha, had even suggested posting scouts on the hills surrounding the valley to sound the alarm if the Daflas counter-attacked. With our return all these rumours died a natural death, but Betty had had to exert all her powers of persuasion to maintain the morale of the camp and provide Kalappa with sufficient porters for the work of surveying the valley.

9

A TRIBAL PEACE CONFERENCE

A SHORT STAY in Duta was a welcome change from the constant moving from one jungle camp to the other, and our small bamboo house with its cheery fire and clean floor seemed luxurious after the tents pitched on sodden and often uneven ground. A cooked meal, however simple, was also preferable to the uninviting alternatives of bully beef and spam. Eggs were never a difficulty in the Apa Tani country, and the Apa Tanis are such skilful gardeners that even in mid-winter with temperatures close on freezing point we were always able to barter fresh vegetables, coarse spinach, spring onions or tiny new potatoes.

We celebrated Christmas in good spirits and prepared the itinerary of our next tour. If the peace conference at Talo went well, we intended to travel through the Kiyi valley to Likha, and then make our way up the unexplored valley of the Upper Panior, visiting the villages on the north bank.

On New Year's Day came the welcome news that Nani Lali, Licha's last Apa Tani captive, was on his way home and that negotiators from Licha were preparing to attend the conference in Talo. So next day we set out with a band of Apa Tani notables and after an agreeable march arrived in Talo where we pitched our tents on a small hillock outside the village. From there we had a fine view over houses and granaries, and across the wide hilly grassland stretching as far as the Panior. That evening the 8,000-foot range south of the river appeared as a solid wall of deepest blue, its knife-like edge silhouetted sharply against a yellow sky, which in the moment of the sun's setting was streaked with pinky clouds.

Talo was thronged with Daflas from nearly every village south of the Panior, all clamouring for redress of their grievances against the people of Likha, Licha and—unfortunately—also of Talo. There was

Tabia Nieri, our friend of Potin with his men, hoping for the liberation of his wife and relatives still held captive in Likha. And a large party had come from Piliapu led by Nabum Epo, who had chosen the opportunity to assert his claims against Likha Teji of Likha and Toko Höli of Talo. Moreover there were numerous other men from the foothill villages, all eager to press claims resulting from trade transactions and feuds. Few of them would otherwise have dared to venture as far as Talo or Likha, but emboldened by the presence of Government officers they were now pressing for reparation of losses suffered during the last eight or ten or even twenty years.

Though from a long-term point of view it was a good thing that under our protection enemies of long standing should meet and discuss claims and counter-claims in an atmosphere of equality, the presence of so many people out for the blood—or rather the mithan and Tibetan bells—of the men of Talo and Likha did not facilitate our work of establishing friendly relations with the Daflas of this area.

The Talo people were obviously appalled by the invasion of these yapping claimants. Their real opinion of all the litigants crowding our camp was expressed in a remark overheard by Temi : " The livers of all these men have grown to colossal size and now they are swollen with courage ; but wait till the sahibs and sepoys have gone, and you will see that they will shrink to nothing."

To comply with the demands of the Daflas from the foothills and ' hear their cases ' was an obviously sterile procedure in territory where, theoretically, Political Officers had extensive magisterial powers, while there was in practice no machinery for the enforcement of their decisions. It was awkward to come for the first time to a manifestly friendly village only to lend Government's support to a lot of claims against our hosts. Such influence as we had we used therefore in initiating individual *mel*, referring the details of the settlement to arbitration by small councils of prominent tribesmen. As Daflas love arguing and displaying their remarkable powers of oratory, the fullest advantage was taken of this opportunity, and soon large and small groups of conferring Daflas were seated on every level space in Talo village. Claims and counter-claims were staked with the aid of tally-sticks and the fate of countless mithan, bells, cloths and swords were recounted as claimants delved into the past, resuscitating events that had occurred in previous generations.

Listening to the proceedings of some of these councils we learnt a great deal about the principles of Dafla justice. One of the peculiar aspects of their legal system and one which is baffling to the new-comer, is the ruling that an aggrieved person, such as a man captured or robbed of his mithan, is entitled to compensation not from the man who injured him, but from the person responsible for his suffering. This was clarified for us by a claim made against Pil Nyei of Talo. A long time ago Nyei had sold a slave girl to Jorum Hago but she escaped from her new master and eloped with a free-born man of Jorum. On their flight the run-away lovers passed through Teipu, and Jorum Hago, presuming that Teipu had given them shelter and food, retaliated by capturing Tao Heri, a Teipu villager. Heri was ultimately ransomed, but his brother Taram, who had paid the price, claimed compensation, not as one would suppose from Jorum Hago, but from Pil Nyei, who —to his mind—had caused all the trouble by selling a ' bad ' slave. Most of the Daflas present agreed that this was the right approach and that Jorum Hago was not to be blamed as he had only recouped his losses.

In those days in Talo I also learnt that a little discrimination was necessary when it came to the ' freeing ' of slaves at the insistence of interested kinsmen. One morning Mai Heli came to our camp and lodged a complaint against Toko Bat. Five years ago, he said, an epidemic had swept through Mai, Talo and the vicinity. The Talo people blamed Mai for having brought the disease, and in retaliation captured six Mai people working on their fields. Four of these were subsequently ransomed, but the youngest wife of Mai Heli's late father was still in Toko Bat's house. The woman in question appeared. Small and pert, she argued not in support of her stepson's plea for her release but in protest against any suggestion that she should return to Mai.

"Why should I leave Talo?" she exclaimed. "True, I was the daughter of a rich man, and now I live with one of Toko Bat's slaves ; but my former husband is dead, and here I am happy. Does Mai Heli want me ? No, he only wants my price. Why should Toko Bat pay ? "

If one views the stories of captures and slave raids from a western standpoint one is easily shocked at the violence and denial of personal liberty in Dafla life. But Daflas seem to have so great a capacity of fitting into almost any household that except when people are detained in stocks, lovers separated or small children torn from their parents, there is perhaps less hardship and suffering than one would be inclined to assume. I have seen several captives, men as well as women, who refused to return to their home-village when given the opportunity of doing so, and I do not believe that their reaction was exceptional.

Of course there are other cases too, and in Talo we witnessed the reunion of a man and his wife who had been separated for twenty years. One day the Licha people, perhaps as a conciliatory gesture which cost them little, sent an elderly woman to our camp. Years ago she had been captured from Talo and ever since had lived in Licha, first as a slave and later as the wife of Likha Takap. But recently Likha Takap had been killed in a fight with Tasser people, and being old and lonely she was quite pleased to return to her original husband even though he had since married another and younger wife.

After a few fine days there was a sudden deterioration in the weather. In heavy rain we sat shivering in camp or sought the warmth of a Dafla's fireside. One night the wind was so violent that we feared our tents would be blown off the hill-top, but in the morning the storm abated and the parting mist revealed a circle of hills covered in snow. Even the 6,000-foot range between Talo and Duta was quite white and on the hill above Nielom, where a survey party was working, the branches of many giant rhododendrons broke under the weight of the sudden fall. In the Apa Tani valley too, we heard, the ground was covered with hard, crisp snow.

A week had passed since our return to Talo, but there was still no sign of the leading men of Licha, and we began to doubt whether we would ever see direct negotiations between the Apa Tanis and their Dafla enemies. But every day more and more Daflas from the Likha area arrived in camp declaring themselves willing to talk things over with their enemies. Then one morning Temi brought the news that Likha Teji, one of the leading men of the Likha clan, had arrived in Talo and was prepared to negotiate a settlement with the Piliapu people, whom his men had raided four years before.

Knowing how easy it is to be adversely reported to suspicious tribesmen, I decided to outstrip all rumour and with Temi hastened to Toko Bat's house, where Teji was said to be. At that time I did not know that Teji was married to one of Toko Bat's daughters, but like everybody else I was aware of Toko Bat's good relations with most of the Likha leaders.

Stepping from the bright sunlight into the dimness of a large Dafla house one distinguishes at first little except the long line of fires, but as I groped my way to the nearest hearth I saw that it was surrounded by a large circle of men. They made a place for us by the fire and as I sat down I looked round expecting to pick out some elderly headman with an enormous head-dress and countless necklaces. But Temi pointed to the man beside me : a youth of hardly more than twenty-five, very handsome and well built, and in that first moment just a little nervous. This was obviously a personality very different from those hard-faced Licha men we had met at Kirum. A few amiable words, undoubtedly translated by Temi with superb tact and courtesy, produced a charming broad smile. I handed him a packet of cigarettes, but he said he did not smoke and would keep them for the people of his house.

After the exchange of a few polite phrases, Teji declared that he was a young man, who had never been to the plains and had never met any outsider. But he had received our messages and had come to hear what we wanted of him. He would do his best to satisfy our demands, for he wanted peace and friendship and would try to reconcile his enemies.

Teji's whole manner was delightfully simple and frank, and I felt at once that here was a man whose friendship would be valuable. Even the presence in Toko Bat's house of Nabum Epo, the Piliapu leader on whom he had made war, did not irritate him, and his attitude was as dignified as it was conciliatory.

It seems strange that in an atmosphere of perennial feuds and danger character and personality could yet develop to such early maturity and human dignity could blossom amidst savage warfare. How many civilized young men of twenty-five would face the strange emissaries of a foreign power of unknown resources and intentions with such composure and courtesy ?

I explained shortly Government's desire for peace and good relations between all villages, and by the time Betty and the Political Officer joined the party, there was an atmosphere of general cordiality.

Likha Teji invited us to visit his village and assured us that he would discuss matters with Nabum Epo, and let us know the result of the negotiations. So we left them to themselves, cheered with the thought that at least one troublesome feud was likely to be settled and that on our visit to Likha we should have at least one powerful friend.

Preliminary negotiations ' in secret session ' seemed to last all day, but the next morning the *mel* between Likha Teji and Nabum Epo was held in the full publicity of a large gathering on an open level space between great outcrops of granite boulders.

When we arrived the parties were already present. Likha Teji sat

137

cross-legged in the centre of a rough semicircle of his followers, and opposite, beyond an open space on which the tally-boards were arranged, sat Nabum Epo and his men, backed by a large crowd of sympathizers from the villages of Sekhe, Chod, Potin and Selsemchi.

Likha Teji opened the proceedings with a long oration. Flushed with excitement he spoke vividly and well : never hesitating or searching for a word, he handled the tally-sticks as an expert, exactly synchronizing the disposition of these symbols with the relevant phrases of his speech (Pl. 11).

Though I did not understand Dafla and Temi was hard pressed to keep pace with his running commentary, it was a pleasure to listen to Teji, to hear the skilful modulations of his voice and to watch the well-balanced gestures of his right hand and the smile with which he wooed the approval of the listeners. So continuous was the flow of words coming effortless to his lips, that he had not even time to swallow, and now and then ejected bubbles of saliva with a jerk of his head. Youthful and handsome, his cheeks rosy and his eyes bright, he was the very opposite of Nabum Epo, whose yellow mask-like face—more mongoloid than is usual among Daflas—betrayed no trace of emotion.

Likha Teji was recapitulating the history of his raid on Piliapu. Disease had come to the country and in the settlement of Likha Tablia and Likha Ekhin, separated from his own house only by a narrow gully, several people died. Tablia and Ekhin blamed Teji's people for having brought the disease, and—though of the same clan—raided his settlement and captured seven men and women. To ransom them Likha Teji had had to pay fifteen mithan, but he did not feel guilty, and cleared himself by ordeal of the accusation of disease-carrying. He had had a large pot of water heated to boiling point and into this he thrust his arm up to the elbow. When the arm was withdrawn it was found to be unscathed and everyone admitted that he and his people could not have been guilty of spreading the disease. The epidemic had obviously come from elsewhere and it was not long before people agreed it was Piliapu who had brought the disease from the plains.

" All of you," exclaimed Likha Teji, turning to the Likha and Talo men in the audience, " blamed Piliapu and talked about making war on the bringers of disease. You all encouraged me when I came forward to organize the raid. Why should I alone have to answer for it ? I had my losses when Tablia and Ekhin raided me without cause, why should only I pay for the damage done to Piliapu. You, Likha Rebla "

—and he addressed the old man—" you took two of the mithan paid as ransom for the Piliapu men. If I have to pay compensation why should you not disgorge your share of the spoils ? "

Likha Teji continued to describe how he had planned the raid and provisioned the warriors, but how as the organizer and a man of wealth and position he had not taken part in the expedition. He had ordered his men to capture Piliapu people, but not to kill them, and if in the mêlée Epo's mother had been slain, her death had not been foreseen. His intention had been to capture some people and thereby force the leading men of Piliapu to attend a *mel* and compensate him for the losses which he had suffered because the spread of the epidemic had been laid at his door. But of the eighteen Piliapu people originally captured only one had been ransomed ; all the others had been set free unconditionally when Government showed an interest in their fate.

Teji ended by saying that he was prepared to compensate Nabum Epo for his mother's death and to conclude a treaty of peace and friendship which would enable him to go to Epo's house and Epo to receive his hospitality. As a sign of goodwill he had brought with him to Talo one Tibetan bell worth five to six mithan, as well as three large mithan.

The next speaker was not Nabum Epo himself, but his sister's son Tabia Hakh, a rather insignificant youth and a poor orator who had difficulties in speaking and arranging his tally-sticks at the same time.

He was followed by Likha Teji's mother's brother and then Nabum Epo summed up his demands. He would be content with the return of the ransom paid by Piliapu and compensation for the murder of his mother. No one could fully repair his loss ; if it had been a wife he could marry another, but never could he find another mother. She had been famous for her beauty, being light of skin, almost like the sahibs, and his father had paid for her twenty mithan because she came from a great house. As *wergeld* for her he did not want mithan or many small bells and other valuables, but one very large and precious Tibetan bell, which he knew to be in the possession of Likha Teji. Then he would be prepared to forget the past and conclude a *dapo*-pact with Likha Teji.

He was speaking well and with animation, and while before he had seemed sullen and gloomy, the tone in which he addressed Teji was not unfriendly.

Epo had hardly ended when Teji jumped to his feet. " I am going back to my village," he declared, " and I shall collect the mithan and valuables due to Epo. I shall prepare myself for the reception of the sahibs and before their eyes I shall pay compensation to Epo and perform the rites of peace-making."

With these words he stepped out of the circle, and strode away. His two wives, who had watched the discussions, departed with him. It was a dignified and dramatic exit, and we all felt immensely pleased.

We had hardly returned to the camp when we were accosted by Selsemchi Daflas who came to seek our intervention in a marriage dispute. The claimant Pil Leji, a mild elderly man without much sense of humour, complained that many years ago he had given his sister together with a large dowry to Tod Rekha, on the understanding that in return he would receive Tod Rekha's sister in marriage. But the marriage never took place, for on the eve of the ceremonies Tod Rekha's sister eloped with Gem Pumbo, one of the leading men of Licha.

Tod Rekha, a man of about forty with a thin face, shifty eyes and not too good a reputation as a debtor, was one of the Daflas resident in Haja. He did not deny the truth of Pil Leji's story. He had intended, he said, to give his sister to Pil Leji; he had taken her to Leji's village with a rich dowry, the details of which he enumerated, describing after a lapse of perhaps twenty years the exact colour and value of every bead and ornament. But then things had gone wrong; for while they were staying with friends the girl, wearing all the ornaments of the dowry, ran off with Gem Pumbo, a man as notorious for his success with women as he was famed for his exploits in war.

"What could I do against a man like that?" exclaimed Tod Rekha. "Not only did he run off with my sister, but he tricked me over the bride-price. It should be a proper marriage, Pumbo had promised, with the payment of a bride-price in full; but first I should complete the girl's dowry. So, fool that I was, I gave her in addition four bronze plates and another string of beads, but did I get a single mithan out of Gem Pumbo? No, not a thing. Who can realize a claim from Gem Pumbo?"

The idea that the miserable Tod Rekha so heavily indebted to Apa Tanis that he was practically their slave, could challenge the great Licha leader was indeed absurd.

"This is not my affair!" screamed Pil Leji. "I gave you my sister and she is still your wife, but I have received no girl from you. Your sister is gone, well and good. But now you have a daughter old enough to be married. Give me your daughter and I shall be

content. My wife is getting old, and a young girl will do me very
well. Otherwise pay me two mithan as my sister's bride-price."

Tod Rekha scratched his head. He would not give his daughter.
Not that he would have minded marrying a young girl to an old man
—over-sensitiveness was not one of his failings—but for his daughter he
hoped to get a fat bride-price which would enable him to pay off some of
his debts, and the obvious anxiety of his Apa Tani friends and creditors
lest he dispose of his only asset convinced me that they shared his view.

"I cannot give you my daughter," he said at last. "But I do not
want to be unreasonable. I owe you a girl, and a girl you shall have.
Take my son's wife, she is young and a hard worker. You can have
her to-morrow."

Pil Leji looked non-plussed. This offer was one he had not expected.
But Tod Rekha was a slippery customer and no one knew better than
Leji how low Rekha's credit stood. Never would he get a single
mithan out of Tod Rekha, and here was a concrete offer : a young
girl, not very pretty perhaps, but undoubtedly a sturdy wench.

Still he hesitated. But the Apa Tanis pounced on him, using all
their powers of persuasion to make him accept the bargain.

"Take her, take her," they cried. "She is young and strong, just
right for an old man like you. You are lucky to get her. Don't
think twice but say yes."

No one enquired what the girl's husband would say, but Koj Karu
reassured me in a whisper : "The boy will not mind. He does not
like her and anyway he never sleeps with her."

"You can have her to-morrow. See her for yourself and then say
whether you like her or not. Anyhow, try her for a night and pound
her as much as you like !" And here they used the word which
describes the pounding of rice in a mortar.

Pil Leji was wavering and we left it at that, advising him to take
the girl offered rather than clamour for compensation in mithan, which
a poor man like Tod Rekha would never be able to pay. Privately I
wondered how long Tod Rekha would be able to meet his obligations
by giving away his relatives, for only the previous day I had been shown
a sister of his whom he had sold into slavery. She had been the price
he had paid for rice bought from Hari village and his Apa Tani creditor
had later resold her to Toko Höli for three mithan. Now she lived
as a slave in Talo, the village in which she had been born as the daughter
of a free though impoverished man.

That evening several of the leading men of Licha arrived in Talo, and the news of the impending conference brought many prominent Apa Tanis to Talo.

There was general excitement when, next morning, the Licha delegates and the Apa Tani *buliang* faced each other in brilliant sunshine at the *mel* which we hoped would determine their future relations.

Chigi Nime, as the principal spokesman of the Apa Tanis, opened the sitting with a short statement, pointing out which of the Licha men were present and which notables must still arrive before any final settlement could be negotiated.

The next speaker was Licha Taga of Bagi who embarked on a long tale of the injuries allegedly suffered by the Licha men at the hands of rapacious Apa Tanis. Very much in contrast to the aristocratic looking, well-turned-out Likha Teji, with his clean cloth, rich outfit of beads and rakish feather in his hat, Licha Taga was wrapped in a coarse dirty cloth and wore no ornaments.

Here was a ruthless rogue if ever there was one, but I could not help liking the rough joviality with which he addressed his opponents. He and the men of his party did not look like the warriors who for years had terrorized thousands of Apa Tanis but rather like a band of tough desperadoes.

When Licha Taga had laid out a formidable array of bamboo tallies, each representing some claim against the Apa Tanis, he began a new series to reckon the damage we and the Apa Tanis had inflicted during our visit to Licha : the houses burnt, the granaries despoiled, the mithan captured and the pigs and chickens eaten. But here we intervened ; the burning of houses was Government's punishment for Licha's intransigence, and could not be debited to the Apa Tanis' account. The idea that Government's actions should not be reckonable in the whole system of claims and counter-claims did not recommend itself to Licha Taga, but he was too shrewd a politician to press this particular claim, and the relevant tallies were removed.

The first of the Apa Tanis' spokesmen was Chigi Nime, and he began with a passionate indictment.

"In past years," he exclaimed, "many of you Licha men found refuge and hospitality in Apa Tani villages, and we lent you rice when you did not know from where to take the next meal. But how did you repay your hosts ? By treachery, by robbing our mithan, and by capturing our men. Did not the sahibs send you messages through

142

Talo ? Did you not have ample time to come and talk things over ? It was your own fault that you rejected all pleas for negotiations and thus drew misfortune upon your heads."

Chigi Nime then enumerated the many claims of Haja and Duta against the various leading men of Licha, and to this Padi Layang added the demands of Bela village.

Having privately warned the Apa Tanis not to drive too hard a bargain and thereby jeopardize the chances of an agreement, we left the parties to work out a settlement. And when after some hours we returned the atmosphere seemed relaxed and almost cordial. Instead of two opposing parties facing each other like cat and dog across the tally board, Dafla and Apa Tani leaders sat side by side arguing about mithan and Tibetan bells. They had now assumed the attitude of old business associates and discussed the gap between their respective positions with many a laugh and good-humoured joke. Negotiations of such kind, the wrangling over mithan to be paid, the assessment of injuries, the valuation of specific Tibetan bells or strings of beads, is to the tribesmen a kind of national sport. The higher the stakes and the greater the values involved, the more exciting is a *mel* and the greater the opportunity of showing off gifts of oratory, exactitude of memory and skill in diplomacy. No doubt after a few days of inconclusive discussions the participants can get just as tired and disgusted with each other as delegates to the Security Council, but the first day is great fun, and a brilliant match such as the contest between Likha Teji and Nabum Epo, which we had watched the day before, is thrilling for actors and spectators alike.

By the evening of that first day the Apa Tanis had stated an endless list of claims and then with a great gesture of realism had reduced them by three-fourths. They now demanded only the return of the Tibetan bells and bronze plates recently paid, and a total payment of thirty-six mithan, of which sixteen would go to Bela and ten each to Haja and Duta. The Licha spokesman promised to consult his fellow villagers and send for those of the leading men who had remained in Licha. Though the gap between the positions of the two parties was great we expected further concessions on both sides and deluded ourselves with the hope that a negotiated settlement was well within sight.

But early next morning came the anti-climax. We were at breakfast when Temi came running up the hill with the news that at sunrise all the Licha men had slipped away. He had been told that some men

of Talo had tried to detain them, but that the Licha men had drawn
their swords, threatening to strike at any who stepped in their way.
In how far this story was true, we never discovered, but it is not unlikely
that the details were invented by those anxious to prove their innocence
of the negotiators' hurried departure. Several weeks later I heard two
conflicting versions. Toko Tekhi, who had always been far more
friendly than Toko Bat, told me that the stampede had been caused by
the rumour that next day the Assam Rifles would seize all the leaders
as they sat at the *mel* and that rather than be captured they had bolted
taking with them the Tibetan bells and other valuables which they had
brought as an initial payment to the Apa Tanis. A more likely story
was, however, that Toko Bat, seeing how well the *mel* was progressing,
and fearing to lose his influence with Licha, advised the negotiators
not to part with their valuables ; he had pointed out, the story claimed,
that Government would not stay in the hills for more than a few
months and that its officers would never be able to enforce the Apa
Tanis' demands. However this may have been, everybody agreed that
the Licha delegates had come with the intention as well as the means
to satisfy some of the Apa Tanis' claims, and that their sudden *volte-face*
was due to some extraneous influence.

With all hopes of a speedy settlement of the Licha conflict shattered
there was no point in staying on. We decided to leave outstanding
quarrels that concerned Talo to settle themselves and move on to
Likha, from where we hoped to explore the Upper Panior valley.

While the participation in two major *mel* had taught me a great deal
about tribal ideas on right and wrong as well as about the customary
methods of resolving disputes, I had had little opportunity for systematic
work with individual informants. Our three Dafla interpreters had had
their hands full reporting on the progress of the various negotiations
and it was only now and then that I could spend a few hours in consecutive anthropological enquiries. Yet even under these conditions
the stay in Talo helped to clarify certain points not directly linked with
the political problems of the day.

One morning, for instance, as I walked through the village in search
of porters willing to take the Survey Officer's kit up a nearby peak,
I came upon the preparations for a mithan sacrifice. A large animal
was tied to a post in front of the house of Licha Butu and a priest stood
beside it chanting invocations to gods and spirits. When some time
previously the owner of the house had fallen ill, the priest and seer,

discovering that a certain spirit was trying to kill him, had appeased it with the promise of a mithan. It was this animal which was now being prepared for sacrifice, and when I returned late in the afternoon I was just in time to witness the slaughter and the subsequent rites.

Many guests had arrived for the ceremonies, and Licha Butu, wearing several necklaces of considerable value, did the honours of host. Judging from the appearance of his house, and the general style of the ceremony, I took him for a prominent man of good class, and I was not a little surprised to hear that until some ten years before he had been a slave in Toko Tekhi's house.

Butu himself told me the story of how he had managed to gain the position of a respected freeman. His father, who had lived in Korlu, a now deserted settlement of Licha, had been killed in a drunken quarrel with Licha Tale. Butu was then still a small child and Licha Tale had sold him to Toko Tekhi of Talo. For many years Butu lived in his master's house, and when he grew to manhood Toko Tekhi paid the bride-price for a free-born wife.

Then, while still living in Tekhi's house, Butu began cultivating a field of his own and in the off-season went to work in the plains. With his earnings he bought bazaar cloth and beads, and these he traded for pigs. From the owner of pigs he became the owner of mithan and finally Tekhi allowed him to build a house of his own. He married three more wives, and also bought a slave-woman, who together with her free-born husband now lived under his roof.

Butu's rise to wealth and respectability illustrates the fluidity of Dafla society. The slave of to-day may be the affluent householder and owner of other slaves of to-morrow and even a slave still living in his master's house may marry a freeman's daughter. The classes are not as rigidly divided as among the Apa Tanis; the Dafla word *niera* (slave) has not the same connotation as the Apa Tani *mura*, indicating an incident of circumstance and not an immutable membership of a social class.

But despite this great social mobility there is the firm belief that conditions in the next world are an exact reflection of life on this earth; rich men are again rich and slaves are again slaves. The Land of the Dead is called Nilitu and is believed to lie under the earth. On the road to Nilitu the departed must pass Porotado, a male deity, and his wife Uli, who have a very big long-house standing close to the path. Porotado first questions the departed on the verandah of his house, asking them what they have done in their life on earth, how many enemies they have killed, how many slaves they have bought or captured, how many wives they have married, and how many mithan and bells they have possessed. Success in war and slave-raiding as well as the acquisition of wealth are appreciated by the guardian of the Land of the Dead. The heroes of many raids and the husbands of many wives are invited to Porotado's house and entertained for several days. Poor men without martial achievements, on the other hand, are scornfully turned away. "You have done nothing of any worth," Porotado tells them, " Off with you to your place." Equally invidious is the fate of those who die unmarried. They remain single even in the Land of the Dead where they live apart from all the other departed. People who are killed in war or lose their lives in an accident cannot enter Nilitu, but go to a place in the sky known as Sukhutegiguir, where they lead a life similar to that on this earth.

For future administrators, intent on weaning the Daflas from war and slave-raiding, these eschatological concepts present a very real difficulty. The mild inoffensive man who neither engages in war nor captures slaves and cattle, has little chance of a friendly reception from the guardian of the Land of the Dead, while the man of valour is entertained by Porotado and gets a good start in Nilitu. In view of these beliefs the average Dafla can hardly be blamed if he evinces little enthusiasm for a life of peace and universal brotherhood. For he knows that in the world beyond there is a premium on quite different ideals.

10

THE SOURCE OF THE PANIOR

A DEARTH OF porters, rather worse than usual, delayed our journey to Likha. On the morning of our departure we were still eighty men short of those required to carry the cumbersome equipment of three sections of Assam Rifles, the Surveyor's instruments and tents and our own modest requirements. The transport of large convoys in unadministered territory had never proved a more delicate business. Our meagre band of permanent porters, men who drew a monthly wage and could be deployed as we chose, were hardly sufficient to bring up essential supplies from the plains and the extensive operations in the interior of the hills, involving many thousands of man-days, had to be maintained by the casual recruitment of tribesmen to whom the idea of carrying loads for Government was entirely foreign.

The Apa Tanis had, after initial difficulties, responded to the lure of wages. For these enabled them to secure hitherto unheard-of quantities of salt, cloth and iron, commodities which they required not only for their own consumption, but which helped them to extend their trading operations with other tribes. The problem of Dafla recruitment was much more complicated. Not only had we marched against the powerful warriors of Licha and dealt a severe blow to their prestige, but our avowed intention of instituting a rule of law and the settlement of disputes by negotiation and compromise had roused the latent opposition of those leaders of Dafla opinion whose wealth and status depended on the manœuvring of alliances and the power and spoils to be derived from raiding. Even those who had no personal stakes in the scheme of current feuds hesitated to offend powerful and potentially dangerous neighbours. To entertain the officers of Government with rice-beer was one thing, but to aid and abet their intervention in Dafla politics by carrying their loads to neighbouring villages was another.

The men of Talo and Jorum, the two villages on whom we had

reckoned for porters to carry us to Likha, decided therefore to sit on the fence, and no amount of persuasion would make them change their attitude. There was nothing to do but to split the camp and move to Likha in two parties. The Political Officer, Kalappa, and Betty and I would proceed to Likha with half of the Assam Rifles and stores for a few days, while the remaining sections and the bulk of the provisions would follow as soon as porters could be found.

This involved some repacking of loads and it was late in the morning before we began the ascent of Pad Puttu, the 7,000-foot ridge which separates Talo from the Kiyi valley. That evening we pitched our camp on a ledge just below the summit, well sheltered by giant forest growth. Curiously enough this forest camp, though 4,000 feet higher, was warmer than our previous night's lodging on the grassy downlands of Talo.

Next morning we were up long before dawn. We sent the porters ahead while we made a short detour, hoping to catch a glimpse of the snow-ranges from the hill-top where Kalappa's men had previously cleared a view-point for the survey operations.

We climbed quickly through a short stretch of dark forest and came out on the summit just as the first rays of the sun touched the peaks of the distant snows. Deep shadow still veiled the intervening country, but the great giants of the Himalayan main range stood out in clearly delineated splendour. Gradually the snow-caps turned from delicate pink to luminous gold and then to dazzling white, until the whole crescent of snow-covered mountains stretched out in shining glory against the dawn sky.

Soon the ridges and valleys of the lower country began to take shape and our Dafla guides could point out the salient features of the land-scape ; the low saddle behind Kirum, the Palin valley with its great patches of cultivated hill-sides, and the course of the Khru, running due east from the mountains from which it was said to spring. North of the Khru rose a steep ridge, and beyond, still confused by blue haze, we could see four or five ridges before the rise of the snow-mountains. From where we stood the Great Himalayan Range seemed tantalizingly near.

The porters were already well down the hill and we hurried after them lest they reached Nielom before us. On the outskirts of the village the inhabitants had gathered in great numbers, and many of them carried large bamboo mugs of rice-beer with which to refresh

148

their friends among our porters. The influential Nielom Takr too had come to greet us and it seemed only diplomatic to spend a short time in his house, where we found a large gathering of notables.

The path from Nielom to Likha dropped fifteen hundred feet to the level of the Kiyi river and then rose equally steeply on the other side. We waded the river, and as we were toiling up the sunny slope, we came upon two obsequious slaves. Their masters, Likha Horku and Takhe, they said, had sent them to show us the way.

This was a reception very different from that presaged by the blood-curdling threats circulating earlier in the year. The Likha messengers even spoke of a prepared camp some way ahead, but when the sun began to sink we thought it more prudent to halt where we were. We found an open spur a little way from the path, and there, protected by hill-slopes too steep to be rushed, we set up a tolerably comfortable camp.

The night was cold and clear, and in the crisp morning air we saw the blue silhouette of the Naga hills on the distant horizon : a mirage-like phenomenon known as ' dawn reflection ' had conjured these hills from behind the ranges that separated us from the Brahmaputra valley. We were now close to the group of settlements known collectively as Likha, a name which, like Licha, is that of the clan predominant in the area. Each settlement has its own locality name and as we waited for the luggage to be packed the Likha slaves pointed out the various groups of houses. The nearest was Müdo, the village of Likha Takhe and Horku, and close by was Pelü, while on the other side of the ridge, we were told, lay two more settlements.

We struck camp early and within half an hour reached the site cleared by the men of Müdo for our reception. With this sign of good will tangibly at hand we decided to leave escort and porters behind and to stroll casually into the village. These tactics took the Müdo people by surprise. We found them gathered near the largest house in the settlement, uncertain and suspicious. But very soon men and women were crowding round eagerly accepting cigarettes and matches. After a while we went up to the long-house belonging to Likha Horku and Takhe and climbed the shaky ladder on to the verandah. Two women, who were hastily sweeping the surrounds of the hearth used for the reception of guests, invited us in, and we sat down on the mithan skin mats which in wealthy Dafla houses serve as seats. Soon the house was thronged with people. We exchanged polite remarks with the

most talkative in the group round the fire and ignored the absence of
Horku and Takhe, assuming that these formidable warriors were somewhere holding council and would appear when they had decided on
an attitude.

Suddenly a slave shouted to the people to make way. There was
a scuffle, and a moment later two young men rushed in and sat down
in the places that had been vacated for them. I could hardly believe
my eyes and ears when Temi whispered that here were Horku and
Takhe. At last we were face to face with the bogey of many tales,
but instead of some battle-scarred old warriors, we were faced with
two handsome boys, neither of whom could have been more than
twenty years old. Both were unusually fair-skinned and well dressed
in new silk cloths and a good many strings of beads. Though clearly
nervous, they smiled pleasantly at our overtures and showed a childish
delight in cigarettes and matches and the gift of two large safety pins,
for which they enquired and which luckily I happened to have in my
pocket.

Horku and Takhe were half-brothers and their mothers, dignified
but still youthful ladies, offered us rice-beer and from time to time
whispered advice to the boyish warriors. We began the conversation
by saying that we had come to promote peace between the various
Dafla villages. The men of Likha clan need not be nervous about our
intentions, but they should settle their feuds by negotiation and try to
reconcile the Daflas of the Panior valley who had for so many years
suffered at their hands. We realized, we said, that at the time of the
raid on Lichi when the men of Likha had wiped out half of Tabia
Nieri's family, Horku and Takhe could have been little more than
children. Nevertheless, they should do their best to see that friendly
relations were once more established between Potin and Likha. The
two boys eagerly took up this line ; their father, they explained, had
been a great war-leader and from him they had inherited many feuds
and enemies. They themselves would be glad to settle things and satisfy
the reasonable claims of their enemies if that was our wish. But, they
added, if we were really so anxious to establish peace would we not
help them to deal with the raids of Tasser, an aggressive village in the
Palin valley ?

What were we to make of this overture ? Were these boys really
trying to gain our support or was their suggestion intended merely as
a diversion ? We were all rather taken aback. For nothing could have

been more distasteful and nothing more damning to our plans than to appear as the champions of Likha or indeed of any particular Dafla clan in an area from which we hoped to travel unescorted into the region of the Upper Khru.

I do not think that either Horku or Takhe noticed our discomfiture. They seemed to be more interested in our persons and clothing than in high politics. Each in turn tried on my sheepskin waistcoat and there was general laughter as one after the other had difficulties in extricating himself from the armholes. But the smiles and laughter changed to frowns when we announced our intention of camping near the village. The boys made feeble attempts to distract us, emphasizing the advantages of their prepared camp in the valley far below, but we set out firmly to reconnoitre the surrounding hill-slopes. After clambering over slippery paths for about half an hour we found a reaped field on the shoulder of a hill mid-way between Müdo and the neighbouring settlement of Pelü and a messenger was sent to bring up the sepoys and porters who had waited all morning in the shelter of the forest.

Transport arrangements occupied most of our first day in Müdo, largely because few of the Daflas who had carried for us from Talo were willing to do a second trip. Even the payment of wages in salt and cloth proved insufficient inducement, for it transpired that these Daflas had only carried for us in the belief that to enter Likha in our company would give them an advantage over their enemies. They now swarmed over the various settlements of Likha in bands of ten and twenty calling on their foes to come out and settle their claims for ransoms and compensation.

At the news of our approach Horku and Takhe had freed all the members of Tabia Nieri's family who were still held captive, but notwithstanding this gesture our hangers-on from Potin, Piliapu and other foothill villages were not prepared to forgo their temporary advantage. They were unanimous in demanding huge compensations for the damage wrought by Likha's raids on the villages south of the Panior, and soon groups of seasoned warriors, heavily armed even while talking peace, were assembled on every open space. Gratifying as it was to witness this sudden recourse to negotiation, we were again embarrassed by the necessity of having to recruit porters from a village in which we had just arrived and on whom our coming had let loose a stream of litigants.

One afternoon, weary of the crowds and the arguments, I was walking through the village with Temi when I saw an engaging-looking old couple sitting on a verandah. They smiled at each other and at me so invitingly that I went up and sat down beside them. The little white-haired man said he belonged to the Nabum clan. No, he was not of Likha. He had come with his wife from Lebla, which, using the Aya dialect, he called Labā. The journey took four or five days and the path ran through Kirum, Tasser and Blabu. In Lebla there were many villages, " more than he had hairs on his head ", and the surrounding country was flat like the Apa Tani valley or the plains of Assam. At the time I wondered whether I was not perhaps on the track of another Apa Tani valley, but on reflection I realized that too much emphasis should not be placed on topographical descriptions. Daflas who have never left the hills cannot imagine a real plain, and when they speak of flat country, they mean open country, generally hillocky grasslands with here and there a level expanse in the valley bottoms.

But the chatty old man led on from one excitement to the next. He fingered my clothes and especially my sheepskin jacket. These, he said, were like the clothes of the Tibetans who came to Lebla every year. They brought salt and swords and ornaments which they exchanged for furs, dyes and rice.

" The people of Nime come down from the white country," explained the old lady, " and they have their loads carried by Daflas from the villages close to the snow-ranges, just as you have your luggage carried by the Daflas here. But they don't live as you do in tents. They sleep in Dafla houses. Most of them can speak our language, but when they speak their own we do not understand them. They never stay long in Lebla, but some of the Lebla Daflas travel to the land beyond the snow. It takes them at least seven days to get there and the path is dangerous and difficult."

The visits of the people of Nime coincided approximately with the time of the harvest in the months of September and October, and from the fact that they used porters rather than pack animals, I deduced then that their route must lead across a pass too difficult even for yaks. It was only years later, when I travelled in the high regions on the Nepal-Tibet border, that I began to doubt this interpretation. High passes are less likely to prevent the use of yaks than the narrow gorges, which lie at altitudes of 8,000–12,000 feet ; it is in such areas that Tibetans may have to use local porters to transport their baggage.

The news of these trade contacts led us to revise our programme. If Government wished to establish its influence up to the McMahon line, it was essential to know more of the areas affected by Tibetan infiltration, and it now seemed that here in the Kiyi valley we were only five or six marches from a region which regularly attracted traders from Tibet.

That night over dinner we recast our plans. After a short trip up the Panior we would set out for the Khru and try to reach Lebla. The nearest route seemed to lead through the Palin valley, but there remained the question of Licha. Would an expedition up the Palin valley be practicable as long as an unreconciled Licha lay at our backs? Regretfully we came to the conclusion that it would not, and that the most urgent problem was therefore a settlement between Licha and the Apa Tanis.

Messengers were dispatched to Joyhing with instructions to direct the next ration convoy to Kirum, the starting point of the route into the Palin valley, and Karu was sent to the Apa Tani valley to inform the *buliang* that they should attend a peace conference in Kirum in the middle of February. Two sections of Assam Rifles, who had arrived on the 20th of January with two months' rations, were to man a temporary outpost in Müdo which—it was hoped—would keep the Likha clan out of mischief. Rajoni too was to remain at Müdo and lend his experience of tribal affairs to the commander of the outpost.

When we had completed these arrangements we were left with only a fortnight in which to explore the unsurveyed valley of the Upper Panior and to visit Mengo, a village which was said to have direct trade connections with Lebla and other regions close to the snow-ranges.

We made it clear to the local tribesmen that on this trip we would travel without escort and would not concern ourselves with local disputes and feuds. Such Daflas from the foothills as had claims on villages through which we happened to pass could go there in their own time and at their own risk, but we would not include them in our party or associate ourselves with their cause.

This attitude was certainly capable of misinterpretation, but it was in tune with the policy of Government to exert direct control only in a limited, though gradually expanding area, and to explore the adjoining country without immediately taking on the responsibility for the maintenance of peace. In the Naga hills the same policy had been in force for years ; beyond the fully administered territory there lay still a zone where the tribes could indulge in feuds and head-hunting without risking immediate intervention by Government. Only a violation of the border or an attack on Nagas normally resident in administered territory was considered cause for punitive action. In the Subansiri region we were still feeling our way, and no one knew in how large an area Government would ultimately be able to exert effective control.

The first day's march brought us to Takho, the settlement of our handsome young friend Likha Teji. There we found Nabum Epo and his men encamped near one of the granaries. Their negotiations with Teji had reached the final stage, and everyone expected that the *pakhe* rites, which were to end the old feud, would be performed the next day. But the most essential act, the handing over of the compensation for the death of Epo's mother, had still to take place, and the following morning we went to Teji's house to witness the reconciliation of the two adversaries. There we found the parties ranged on both sides of the principal hearth with Tana Kuli between them acting as mediator. The atmosphere was tense. Epo, grim-faced and unyielding, seemed determined to press his claims to the utmost, and Teji was by no means a beaten foe bent on making peace at all costs.

"It is all very well for Likha Teji," began Epo in a clear, hard voice, "to provide mithan for the *pakhe* rite, but before I can agree to end this feud, I must receive the full compensation for the loss of my mother : for each limb of her slaughtered body, I must be given the appropriate price."

To this Likha Teji gracefully acquiesced. He was ready to pay compensation. Bending over a conical-shaped basket, he drew out a Tibetan sword and placed it before Epo : this was the price for the ribs of Epo's mother. Then he proffered a Tibetan bell as the price of her knees, a cornelian bead for her eyes, two strings of yellow Tibetan beads for her bowels, and a bronze bracelet as the price for her arms. Finally he drew from the bottom of the basket the Tibetan bell which earlier in the negotiations Epo had specifically demanded and set it down beside the other objects.

Epo and his party scrutinized the gifts in silence. They turned over each article and viewed it from every angle. In the Tibetan sword they could find no fault, but the bell offered 'for the knees' was rejected. The cornelian bead was declared cracked and the bracelet which seemed to me a very ancient piece was pronounced valueless. Teji tried to substitute a bell-metal plate for the despised Tibetan bell, but Epo scoffed at the plate as inferior and of Assamese origin. There was deadlock. The parties turned their backs on each other and the hall was filled with gloomy silence.

Ending a Feud

After perhaps five minutes Tani Kuli cautiously intervened: it would be a pity, he remarked in a seemingly detached manner, if the negotiations were to break down at this stage, for assuredly the prestige of both Epo and Teji would suffer.

"Cut my throat," shouted Teji, flashing a look first at us and then at the go-between. "I can do no more."

Yet he must have been prepared for such a contingency; after a little he held whispered consultations with his wives who went meekly to the end of the hall and drew an enormous mithan horn from a store hole in the roof. From this Teji extracted a larger bracelet, a bead the size of a pigeon's egg, and a Tibetan bell which glowed with the lovely lustre peculiar to the most valuable of such *maje*. Carefully the new gifts were scrutinized and when after a little more argument Teji replaced the Assamese plate by a genuine Tibetan specimen, Epo declared himself satisfied. Earlier the Piliapu men had talked of a cloth as the price for 'the skin' but this claim they did not press.

Though the acceptance of these gifts was as good as the signing of a truce, there was no demonstration of cordiality and the Piliapu party packed up the valuables in a matter-of-fact way and left the house. Outside they delayed only long enough to receive the mithan that went with the price, and then they retired to the granary where they were encamped.

The payment of the death price was followed by the sacrificial rite of *pakhe*, which ended the feud of many years' standing. I was surprised at the lack of formality in the performance of so important a ceremony. Epo looked on from a distance, but Teji was not even present when the two mithan were tied to a forked post for slaughter. A priest in leopard-skin hat and ceremonial cloak, invoked the god Potor-Met, calling on him to avenge any breach of the pact; the mithan were swiftly dispatched with a sword and the blood of the slaughtered animals was smeared on the forked posts.

Epo and his men could now have accepted hospitality in Teji's house, but they preferred to cook their share of the sacrificial meat in their own camp. We too received a share of the mithan, and we ate it in the spirit in which it had been slaughtered, trusting that it would also seal our friendly relations with Teji and Epo.

The *pakhe* rite was the first step in the reconciliation of the two enemies. Later Teji would take a mithan to Epo's village, where it would be sacrificed with similar rites; and if the one-time opponents

155

wished to replace their former enmity with a pact of mutual friendship, the more elaborate ritual of *dapo* would be performed on the path midway between their two villages.

With the successful conclusion of these negotiations we considered ourselves temporarily free of political obligations. Next day we set out on a short tour of the Upper Panior valley with porters whom Teji had collected for us. Turning westwards we left the valley of the Kiyi and, after crossing a high ridge covered in virgin forest, came at midday to the village of Dorde, where a kinsman of Teji's received us with a show of the greatest friendliness. Studiously we avoided any reference to feuds and captured slaves. Whatever our dealings with other branches of the Likha clan may have been, to the villages of the Upper Panior valley we had come with no other purpose but to pay a friendly visit. The smallness of our party and the absence of an armed escort helped to allay suspicion and we were willingly set on the road to Likhipulia, a village lying midway between Dorde and Mengo.

The way to Likhipulia led through groves of wild lemon and across hill-slopes covered by a verbena-like shrub with scented leaves. Everywhere tall plumes of feathery-white rose from great thickets of elephant grass. Though beautiful to look on, this grass is the scourge of the agriculturist, for once it takes root it gradually and relentlessly steals the cultivable land from the tribesmen. In the evening we reached Likhipulia and set up our tents between two enormous long-houses. A few women came to look at us but the settlement seemed deserted of its male inhabitants. It was only after dinner while we sat round the fire that we were joined by an old man, a slave who was yet a priest, highly esteemed for his ritual art. He regaled us with tales of Likhipulia's past and glorified the prowess of his master, renowned for the many successful raids he had led.

The night was bitterly cold and in the morning we emerged from our tents to find the landscape painted white with hoar frost and the mountains at the head of the valley rising to 10,000 and 12,000 feet sprinkled with snow. To both sides of the Panior villages lay at spaced intervals on open ledges, half-way between the gorge and the crest-line, and considerable areas of cultivation extended over the surrounding slopes.

A narrow path running parallel with the Panior kept us well above the valley bottom on the whole day's march. But progress was slow. A succession of gullies, cutting deeply into the hill-sides, involved us in innumerable tiring descents and ascents, and as the day drew out even the porters began to doubt whether we would reach our destination that evening.

At last we climbed out of the last ravine and saw the houses of Mengo dispersed over a complex of knolls and spurs. We pitched our tents on a rounded shoulder and Khuike did one of his miracles, producing boiling water for tea off a slit trench fire in a remarkably short time. While we were still sipping this comforting beverage the first sightseers began to assemble. The appearance of these shy but curious men and women provided ample justification for our journey. No doubt they were Daflas and from the ease with which Heli, our interpreter, made himself understood it was apparent that we had crossed no major linguistic boundary. Yet there were many indications that we stood on the threshold of a new cultural sphere—a sphere strongly influenced by Tibetan trade and fashion. Most people wore Tibetan ornaments of heavy silver studded with coral, turquoise and jade, and their coarsely woven cloths were embroidered with red and black wool in the Tibetan manner.

We spent the next days in house-to-house visiting, combining long drawn-out conversations on family histories and trading connections with the drinking of much rice-beer. It was not long before we found the explanation for the Tibetan influence on Mengo fashions. Nearly all the families living in Mengo had come within the last two generations from an area on the Panyi river which, as it was described to us, appeared to be a tributary of the Khru. This area, locally known as Labā, was obviously the same as the Lebla of which we had so frequently heard. There was a steady traffic between Lebla and Mengo during the summer months when the snow melted on the high ranges over which it was necessary to pass, but even if we had had the time and the supplies it would have been difficult to do the journey in mid-winter.

The only habitations along that high route are a few settlements of Sulungs. Our acquaintance with this primitive jungle-tribe was slight. We had met only a few individuals, men of small stature and facial features rather more primitive than those of any Dafla. They lived in small groups said to be scattered over the higher hills between the upper courses of Panior, Khru, Kamla and Subansiri. Everywhere they are considered the oldest population, for there is the tradition that when the Daflas' ancestors first entered the area they found Sulungs already in possession. Unsurpassed in their skill in hunting and trapping,

Sulungs spend weeks and months moving about the forest. They live largely on game and wild jungle produce, and it is believed that originally they did not cultivate. Nowadays, however, most Sulungs till small clearings, where during the summer months they grow millet and vegetables. Their only domestic animals are fowls and dogs, and so few are their material possessions that they do not attract the attention of Dafla raiders. I have heard it said that no one would think it worthwhile to capture a Sulung; for no bonds were secure enough to hold for long so agile a prisoner and no kinsman could pay even a modest ransom. It seems indeed that this hardy and elusive people lives peacefully among the warring Dafla and Miri clans, sometimes trading game and jungle produce for salt, iron or cloth, yet remaining on the whole independent and self-sufficient.

The language of the Sulungs is not understood by either Daflas or Miris, but I was told that all Sulungs, wherever they may live, speak among themselves the same tongue. In addition most of them know the local Dafla dialect.

In the crowd of Mengo women who daily thronged our camp, bartering beer and eggs for our much-prized salt, I noticed a girl with an unusual head-dress. She came from Litlot, a village in the Lebla area. Recently she had married the son of Tara Nana and now lived with her parents-in-law in Mengo. This was exactly the informant I was looking for, and that evening we climbed the hill above our camp and paid a visit to her family.

Our unannounced arrival caused little surprise. Tara Nana invited us to sit down by the fire with his wife and children. He was a sick man, and as he talked he rested his arms on the firewood rack hanging above the hearth. So weak and tired did he look that at first I had little hope of profiting from this visit, but when I questioned him about Lebla he quickly warmed to the subject.

Living in small settlements and having little contact with any but their closest neighbours, Daflas enjoy visitors, and the spontaneous hospitality with which we were received in the remotest villages always filled me with warmth and renewed my belief in the fundamental friendliness of man. Nowhere was the atmosphere of an amiable and generous hospitality more marked than in this modest house at the head-waters of the Panior. Beer was offered and eggs baked in the hot ashes, and a little later our hostess, seeking yet another expression of pleasure at our visit, dragged a cackling hen from its roost and set it

158

in Betty's lap. I suggested that we should all eat it then and there.
And so we did. A little boy cut its throat, singed its feathers, and
removed the guts and then Tara Nana's wife put the carcass on the red-
hot embers to roast. Soon a pleasant and appetizing smell pervaded the
room and in an astonishingly short time the meat was cooked. It was
succulent and tender, presumably because it was cooked before *rigor mortis*
had set in. Indeed I felt that chicken *à la Dafla* would be a worthwhile
addition to Western cuisine. We were handed the choicest pieces and,
gnawing the bones, we continued the conversation in which the girl
from Litlot took a leading part.

Tara Nana told us that as a young boy he had come with his father
across the northern ranges from a village on the Panyi river. There
were many villages in the area known as Lebla. One of the most
important was Bur and beyond Bur there lay Nao and Buni and then
Puchilusa, the nearest Tibetan settlement. Puchilusa lay on this side of
the great snow-ranges and consisted of a huge building of stone, like a
great rock, in which were many 'houses'. Neither Tara Nana nor his
daughter-in-law had visited Puchilusa, but all those present had heard
of it from Dafla friends who had been inside when trading with Tibetans.
I had little doubt that this house of stone must be a Buddhist monastery,
comparable perhaps to such smaller monasteries on the south side of the
Great Himalayan Range as Thyangboche at the approaches to Mount
Everest.

Tara Nana and his family had no personal knowledge of Tibetans,
but they had all met men of the Boru tribe, a people inhabiting the
borderlands of Tibet and the Dafla country. Nana described the Borus
as people living in houses built like those of Daflas, but dressing in coats
and boots like Tibetans. They wore their hair in Dafla fashion and their
language was very similar to the dialects of the Northern Daflas. They
were warlike folk, often fighting amongst themselves and at times
attacking their Dafla neighbours. Of late, however, the Tibetans had
induced them to make peace and now it was said there was no more
fighting between Borus and Daflas. Recently, they had heard, peace
had also been established between the Ngas and the Tibetans. The
Ngas were a people with a language of their own, who built houses of
stone, wore woollen clothes and lived largely on the milk of sheep.
They did not grow rice and millet but wheat and maize. Armed with
muzzle loading guns they were a match even for Tibetans and in the
past they had often recruited Daflas as auxiliaries. Their fights against

the Tibetans had lasted for a great many years and had resulted in the killing of many Ngas.

This was news indeed. Nowhere had I seen so much as a hint that in the Subansiri region there existed such populations south of the Himalayan main range. The people to whom Tara Nana referred to as Nga—a name not to be confused with 'Naga'—are perhaps a group of Sherpa-like people living on the fringe of the Tibetan sphere of influence, while the Borus may well be Daflas tibetanized in the same manner as the Daflas of the Assamese plains are gradually becoming indianized. Though retaining their language and certain features of tribal culture these Daflas have adopted many of the material aspects of the Indian way of life ; similarly the Borus may have taken over Tibetan dress without abandoning their tribal pastimes of war and raiding.

Late at night we left the hospitable house of Tara Nana charmed by the friendliness and generosity of its inhabitants. We had little with which to reciprocate their hospitality but next morning we sent them a substantial present of salt.

For me this visit to Mengo had rounded off the picture of the Panior valley Daflas, and had provided additional evidence of the slow drift of populations from the northern regions towards the foothills. Here in Mengo we could trace the family histories of emigrants from Lebla over at least four or five generations. In the matter of genealogies Daflas have excellent memories and many men know not only the names of their forefathers but are aware of the fate and whereabouts of most branches of collateral kin. The dominant populations in every settlement on the north bank of the Upper Panior consist to-day of clans which have arrived within a traceable period from villages in the Panyi valley, and this southward movement is in the process of extension across the Panior river. There the newcomers are gradually displacing clans which, though themselves hailing from regions further to the north, have been settled in the area for several generations.

What is the explanation for this movement from the higher to the lower ranges ? Why should one Dafla clan after the other migrate from the valleys close to the snow-ranges to the hot and unhealthy foothills, where they dwindle and disintegrate, until clans once famous for their wealth and prowess are reduced to as few as three or four families ? Are the Tibetans exerting pressure on populations such as Ngas and Borus, so that, forced to give way, they encroach on the land of the highland Daflas? Until the country immediately north and south of the Great Himalayan Range is fully explored this question will remain unanswered. But the traditions of the Mengo people are interesting not only on account of their historical implications but because they throw a great deal of light on the mechanism of tribal migrations. Movements of populations are often thought of in terms of great waves of warring invaders. Yet in the case of the Daflas the southward movement appears to have been accomplished by slow infiltration rather than by mass migration. Marriage relations to clans in neighbouring areas have invariably paved the way for a clan's desertion of its ancestral land. First one man has left his home to settle near affinal kinsmen in a distant village, and later his clansmen have followed until within three or four generations the whole area would be dominated by an entirely different clan. Under the conditions prevailing in the Dafla country movements of whole communities are impracticable because large food supplies cannot be carried over long distances, and new settlers find it difficult to support themselves until the reaping of their first harvest, unless they can rely on the assistance of kinsmen or friends.

Physical barriers seldom stand in the way of trade and marriage relations. Our friends in Mengo had well-established alliances not only with Lebla Daflas but also with the people of the Kamen valley, six days' journey across the mountains to the south-west.

It is on these high hills that a plant used in the manufacture of arrow-poison is found. This bushy herbaceous plant, locally known as *omi*, holds poison in its small tuberous roots. The plant occurs only at high altitudes and a man is said to be lucky if he finds more than ten plants in the course of several days' search. The poison is therefore expensive and the trade value of a single tuber, sufficient only for one or two arrows, corresponds roughly to that of a silver rupee. But the effect of the poison is deadly and an arrow point remaining in a wound for more than a few seconds kills the victim almost instantaneously.

While the Mengo men are suppliers of arrow poison, and act as middlemen in the trade in Tibetan ornaments they depend on other villages for cotton goods. Little cotton is grown in their village and none in the Lebla area, but many men and women wear cloths made from the fibres of a shrub called *pud*. From cuttings planted near river-beds this plant grows to a height of about ten feet, and is cultivated both in Mengo and in the Panyi valley. *Pud* yields a coarse strong yarn which is woven into hard-wearing cloth.

It rained all through the days and nights of our stay in Mengo. I do not know whether the physical discomfort we endured in the mud and slush or the inability to use a camera was more depressing. But the gods saw fit to reward our patience. On the last evening the weather cleared, the hills towering high above us were coated in the powder-snow of a new fall and a glorious full moon lit the valley from end to end. The next morning I took my first and only photographs of the village and the upper part of the Panior valley.

We retraced our steps to Likhipulia where we found Tana Kuli embroiled in a *mel* with the representatives of one of Likhipulia's most renowned warriors. Flushed from the success of his mediation between Likha Teji and Nabum Epo he had decided to exercise his influence in a matter concerning his own kin. Two years previously two women of his village had been captured by raiders from Likhipulia and he was now trying to effect their release. But the captor of the women refused to come forward and his spokesman, the garrulous old slave who had entertained us on our first visit, had obviously been instructed to play for time and remain non-committal. We were annoyed, for although we had made it quite clear that on this exploratory trip we did not want to be involved in any dispute, Tana Kuli was now using our friendly visit to Likhipulia to further his own ends. Yet to leave the captives to their fate and move on without taking any notice of a trusted friend of Government was rather difficult, and reluctantly we did what we could to persuade the Likhipulia men to release the two captives.

But our intervention was not an unqualified success. As we left the village with the ' liberated ' women, loud wailing broke out on one of the high verandahs. It was, we were told, the wife of a Likhipulia notable bemoaning the departure of her sister. Such is the Dafla way of life ! One sister married to a highly respectable householder, the other detained next door as a prisoner of war !

It must be remembered, however, that among the Daflas the terms slave and prisoner of war do not necessarily denote a state of misery or servile bondage. This was borne out by an amusing scene we witnessed two days later in Bentam. There we found the space below the house of Likha Tablia crowded with warriors and once again it was the Piliapu men who were after their pound of flesh. They were demanding the release of a boy captured several years previously in one of Likha Tablia's raids on Piliapu. But the boy, grown now into a handsome young man,

..., one of the leading men of Jorum village.

22. Dafla woman of Talo village.

23. Dafla houses in Mengo village; in the background a 10,000-ft. ridge lightly sugared with new s[...]

24. The verandah of a Dafla house in Talo village.

stood before the assembly and gave no thanks to his would-be liberators. If they were so keen on having him back, he declared, they should have ransomed him years ago. Now it was too late to free him. Bentam had become his home and he had no wish to return to a strange village and live with relations he hardly knew. The men of Piliapu were furious. They suffered great loss of face, but in the circumstances they could hardly carry off the boy by force.

In Müdo we found the *mel* between the Potin people and Likha Takhe and Horku still in progress. The Potin men who, unsupported, would never have dared to set foot on Likha soil, exploited their advantage to the full and adopted an unyielding attitude ; while the Likha people, following delaying tactics, haggled over the payment of every mithan and every valuable.

We could not await the outcome of these long-drawn-out negotiations if we were to keep our appointment with the Apa Tanis in Kirum. So we left the matter in Rajoni's hands and on the 2nd of February started from Müdo with one of the three sections of Assam Rifles then stationed at the outpost.

For two days we walked up the Kiyi valley in almost incessant rain along paths often ankle deep in mud and slush. But I do not think Betty and I minded these discomforts half as much as the Political Officer who, accustomed to the gentle life of residency drawing-rooms, considered most of our journeyings in the Subansiri, even those under the best conditions, with about as much enthusiasm as a polished Roman would have viewed service in the hinterland of the Black Sea. Nevertheless, all things considered, we arrived in Kirum in good spirits and were pleasantly surprised at the welcome we received. In the village where two months previously Dafla warriors and Assam Rifles had glared at each other from opposite hill-sides and the houses of several prominent men had gone up in flames, we were now greeted with beaming smiles and mugs brimming with the clearest of all rice-beer.

The Apa Tani notables arrived in a body before we had had time to pay off our Müdo porters and at dusk the ration convoy from Joyhing filed into camp. It all seemed most beautifully timed. But we should not have given way to premature rejoicings. If the Licha Daflas greeted us with beer and a show of hospitality this did not signify a change of heart. It was just that they had learnt how to deal with a Government mission. No doubt we would pass on to the next village when we had eaten and drunk enough ! Nor were they keen on enabling us to open the route to the Palin and the Khru, for they were jealous of a trade monopoly which yielded them steady profit.

It would be tedious to recount the details of the negotiations which dragged on from day to day, fluctuating now one way and now another. Ultimately it became clear that a move towards the Khru through Kirum and the Palin valley was impracticable. Licha remained un-co-operative and potentially hostile, and their attitude was influencing the villages in the Palin valley. One by one the messengers we had sent to prepare the ground for a visit returned with stories of defiant headmen, who levelled threats against Government and declared they would oppose any move into their area.

What was to be done? Were all attempts at exploration to be sacrificed to the needs of a political settlement between the Apa Tanis and Licha? The Political Officer felt understandably that he must see through a matter in which Government was so deeply involved. But it would have been a waste of time for both of us to stay in Kirum and forgo the last two months when the weather still permitted a forward move. We decided to part. Betty and I, with one interpreter and the doctor, were to spend the rest of the season in an exploratory tour up the Kamla valley, while the Political Officer with the Assam Rifles and the rest of the staff was to devote his energies to the political settlement in the Kiyi valley.

We felt as free as birds as we left Kirum and sauntered lightly through the rain towards the Pei river and the Apa Tani valley. It was an enormous relief to be rid of the military trappings and the constraint which the very presence of an armed force imposed on the tribesmen. At the camp-site on the Pei, from which two months previously an expedition with hundreds of men had marched against Bagi, we pitched our tent in between the fires of our Apa Tani porters and enjoyed the intimacy and camaraderie of a small tribal party.

This feeling of exhilaration endured even on the next day's march through mud and rain. The path was bad and in the rhododendron zone it was blocked by a tangle of snow-broken branches. We all suffered in the icy wind that swept over the crest of the hills and feared being caught by a new snowfall on the pass. At mid-day we stopped to warm ourselves at a fire which the Apa Tanis kindled from the scraps of pine they always carry on their persons. It was then that Karu declared we could reach Duta that night if we took a short cut. As anything was better than another night in the dripping forest, we left

164

the main path and turned at right angles into a narrow swampy valley, and then Karu led us through a stream bed where we scrambled up the rocky course against the flow of cascading water. At last we reached the top of a ridge and came out on one of the well-trodden paths used by Apa Tani woodcutters.

Suddenly and unexpectedly we emerged from the forest and saw to our delight the rice-fields of the Apa Tani valley. Nothing in these hills can match the thrill of the moment when after a long trek in the high forest you look down on this heavenly valley. Whether in sunshine or in rain there is always magic in the scene. That evening it was painted in the most delicate colours, with no loud tone to confound the greyness of the mist, the pale ochre of the rice-fields, the blueish green of the pine groves and the dull brown of the bracken-covered hills.

It was a wonderful moment when we entered our house, and sat on the clean dry bamboo floor to kindle the fire at our hearth. After so many weeks in tents erected on damp and often muddy ground, we had now a chance of getting really dry.

11

A FEAST AND AN EXECUTION

AFTER THE weeks among the litigious Daflas it was sobering to
return to the smooth flow of Apa Tani life. A few rich patricians
and their henchmen might haggle over mithan and Tibetan bells
in Kirum, but the broad masses of the Apa Tanis were undisturbed by
the vicissitudes of the quarrel with Licha. On the eve of the new
agricultural year everyone was occupied in celebrating Morom, the
festival which engenders the fertility of man and field and at which
individuals raise their prestige by sacrificing mithan and feasting their
neighbours and friends.

We had arrived in time to watch the final two days of the celebration
in Haja, the last of the seven villages to perform the rites. That year
two rich men had embarked on the quest for social advancement : one
was performing a rite called *Un-pedo* which is high up in the series of
feasts of merit and involves the sacrifice of six mithan ; the other was
beginning his career as a donor of feasts with the minor rites that
necessitate the slaughter of only two animals.

As we sat at breakfast on the morning after our return from Kirum
we saw groups of men dressed in their best cloaks hurrying past our
house. They carried baskets of mithan meat which it is customary for
the donor of an *Un-pedo* feast to present to every household in the Apa
Tani valley. The distribution of this sacrificial meat—as indeed all Apa
Tani ritual activities—is organized with meticulous care and each quantum
of meat represented a just apportionment of the sacrificial animals on a
house to house basis.

Morom is essentially a festival of youth and later in the day the young
men and boys set out on a round of ceremonial visits which began in
Bela and ended with their return to their own village. Dressed in clean
white cloaks and laden with all the ornaments their families could
provide, they filed across the fields. The smallest boys came first,

166

beating large bronze plates like gongs, and the young men followed in groups of ascending age, brandishing swords whose flashing blades marked the rhythm of their staccato chant. In front and behind walked the priests wearing the head-dress, scarf and embroidered cloak of *hibu*. They fanned themselves with long feathered whisks and, intoning prayers as they strode over the newly prepared ground, scattered husked rice, thus magically reinforcing the fertility of the soil.

When, in the late afternoon, the procession returned to Haja it halted on an open piece of pasture outside the village; a long rod was rigged up on two posts and the young men showed off their skill at the high jump. Such competitions are as much a part of Morom as the rope-game is part of the Mloko festival. And so is the fertility dance performed by young men with bamboo staves held in the position of *phalli*. This dance began as a comic side-show during the jumping competition, but developed by the time the procession entered the court-yard of the donor's house for the final act of entertainment, into a riotous frolic. The girls and women wisely sought refuge on the high verandahs and from this point of vantage encouraged the performance with laughter and ribald comment. The four youths gambolled over the open space left by the crowds and tumbling over each other on the ground gave a most naturalistic imitation of the sexual act. Suddenly seeing Betty standing in the crowd they remembered her sex, and began to prance towards us with unmistakable movements; the girls on the verandahs greeted this sally with shrieks of laughter and Betty retreated to the nearest house and hastily climbed the stairway.

Feasting ended the festival of Morom and next morning men, women and children returned to the work on the fields which, until the Mloko, was to absorb most of their energies.

To have watched the Morom festival, even though I had only been able to see the end of the celebration, was an invaluable experience, and one which helped me to assess the Apa Tani way of life. The execution of the ritual within the social framework had stressed the cohesive forces that integrate the Apa Tani community and underlined the conceptual differences between the structure of Apa Tani and Dafla society.

When the delegates of the two tribes face each other at a *mel* and haggle over ransoms and compensation, mithan, Tibetan bells and slaves, this difference of social attitudes is blurred: material gain, the scoring of points and the enhancement of personal prestige seem for both the principal incentives. But in the Morom feast the striving for individual prominence is eclipsed by the expressions of tribal solidarity. A patrician may perform the rites in order to raise his own prestige, but the celebration of these rites is a communal undertaking, and all villages participate in the festival according to their sex, their age and their status in society. No Dafla village, not even the largest, is sufficiently well integrated to enact manifestations of social solidarity comparable to the ceremonial visiting of the Morom processions.

Nor does any Dafla celebration make so strong and so conscious an appeal to æsthetic feeling as that produced by those long files of gaily dressed men and boys, the low-voiced chanting and rhythmic swinging of swords, and the co-ordinated dance-like movements in the villages ceremoniously visited.

That the Apa Tanis have a highly developed æsthetic sense no one can doubt. They show excellent taste in the colour combinations and patterns of their textiles. Their clear strong dyes and their use of bright borders on white cloths, and their clever multi-coloured embroideries produce beautiful effects. The restraint in the choice of ornaments, which in both men and women are strictly limited to a few accepted types, seems also expressive of a developed æsthetic tradition which stands in great contrast to the Daflas' habit of loading themselves with a variety of miscellaneous and flashy finery.

On the other hand, their mediums of expression are limited. Wood-carving and painting are not Apa Tani arts, and when I provided pencil and paper and asked my friends to draw whatever they pleased, their efforts were astonishingly poor ; poorer indeed than those of the most primitive people of my acquaintance, the Chenchus of the Deccan. Yet, in potter's clay small Apa Tani boys mould charming figures of mithan and other animals which evince a striking ability to concentrate on essentials and are truly pieces of art. One of these clay mithan still stands on my mantelpiece and gives me pleasure whenever I look at it.

The main outlet for the Apa Tanis' manual skill lies in the field of such practical crafts as weaving, pottery and iron work. Their textiles are eagerly sought by the tribesmen of an area extending several days' journey beyond the Apa Tani valley, and the knives and swords of Apa Tani blacksmiths find a ready market among Daflas and Miris.

When I expressed the wish to see a blacksmith at work, I was taken into a side valley and then up a pine-covered slope to a small hut, standing in an isolated position amidst pasture land. The blacksmith's forge, I was told, must stand at some distance from the village, for his art is fraught with magical danger and the gods would be offended if iron were worked close to the houses and the sites of religious rites.

Nenkre Kechi, the smith I found at work, explained that he had learnt his craft from his father, but that anyone who chooses may practise at the smithy. I examined his tools, all of which he had made himself, and was struck by the peculiar type of bellows he used. These consisted of two wooden bowls covered with banana leaf cones ; they were let into the floor and were worked by a man pulling alternate cones up and down, thus pressing the air into the bamboo tubes that lead to the forge. The iron he worked came from Assam, largely in the shape of old or broken tea-garden hoes, which plains-going men obtained cheaply. From these he made knives, swords and axes, but he had never succeeded in making the large type of hoe which nowadays the Apa Tanis use for work on their fields. Usually his customers supplied the iron from which to fashion the implements or weapons they required. If a man brought one tea-garden hoe, Kechi would turn it into two swords and would receive one side of bacon and one basket of unhusked rice for his labour.

I was puzzled as to where the Apa Tanis could have obtained their supplies of iron before the establishment of tea-gardens close to the foothills ensured a steady supply in the shape of disused tea-garden hoes. A certain amount of Indian iron has probably reached the Apa Tanis for a very long time. Just as iron filtered into the Naga hills on the southern side of the Brahmaputra valley, so it is likely to have found its way by devious barter transactions into the mountains to the north of the Assam plain. But the great value attached to Tibetan swords, and their ceremonial significance in Apa Tani culture, suggests that in earlier times many of the iron weapons and implements used by the Apa Tanis may have had their origin in Tibet. Iron must then have been scarcer in the Apa Tani valley, and this is probably the reason why the Apa Tani blacksmiths have not developed a local type of hoe, and why wooden agricultural instruments seem to have been in use until two or three generations ago.

Indirect evidence of the former lack of steady trade connections with Assam is reflected also in other spheres of Apa Tani life. Their ability to produce a local substitute for salt by a process so laborious that it would never have been evolved had sufficient supplies of natural salt been readily available, provides further support for such a contention. This black salt, as it is called, is culled from water filtered through the ashes of burnt bracken and herbs specifically grown for the purpose. The fluid is then boiled and reduced until only the salty sediment remains in the bottom of the pot. It tastes rather bitter, but Apa Tanis still use it to flavour their food. In the old days, they say, it was also in great demand among their neighbours, who did not know how to make it themselves.

Although we were eager to be off to the Miri country I had to spend a few days in Duta in order to straighten out the supply position. This interlude brought many additions of my knowledge of Apa Tani custom, and I gradually began to understand how social controls operate within this remarkably well-integrated society.

One cold evening, while I tried to scrawl my diary with fingers barely able to hold a pen, our friend Chigi Nime appeared with a serious face. It was a welcome excuse to squat down by the fire, and together we shared some beer which I had been given earlier in the day.

" On the day you arrived back from Kirum," he began in a doleful tone, " those wretched Hang people killed one of my clansmen. Didn't you hear the singing in Duta this morning ? It was the funeral chants for Chigi Duyu. Alas ! We had no part of his body to bury, and only his clothes and ornaments could be placed in the grave. Was Chigi Duyu a slave, that he should be executed for the theft of a cow ? No, he was a young patrician of my own clan, and willingly would we have paid any reasonable ransom. Six days ago he was captured from an assembly platform in Mudang Tage. I almost wept with shame when visiting Hang with a Morom procession, I found him tied up to the Taliang *lapang*. I offered four mithan as ransom, but his captors refused to accept any price. Now they have killed him ! They cut off his hands and feet, took out his liver, and when we asked for the corpse they denied us even that."

I had never seen Chigi Nime so disturbed. His irrepressible good humour had carried him cheerfully through all the disappointments of the first expedition to Kirum and the wearisome negotiations at Talo, but now he was burning with indignation. Privately I thought that Chigi Duyu must have committed worse crimes than the theft of a single cow, but his clansman Chigi Nime was hardly the man to render an impartial account. Fortunately he did not ask for my intervention, and indeed he made it clear that this was a matter which concerned none but the Apa Tanis—a refreshing contrast to the Daflas' numerous attempts to make use of Government officers in the pursuance of their own ends.

Chigi Duyu's Crimes

Chigi Duyu's clansmen, said Nime in the first flush of anger, would accept no compensation for his death. They would ask a life for a life and be content only with the death of one of Duyu's slayers—the omens would decide on the victim. Quietly the Chigi men would enter his house, allow his wife and children to leave, and then kill their man. No other villager would intervene lest he too became involved in the feud.

Would the execution of Duyu be considered a breach of the *dapo* between Duta and Hang?

"No," said Nime, "this is a private quarrel. There will be no disturbance of the general peace. It is these *dapo* pacts which enable us Apa Tanis to live in peace; without them we would be like Daflas, for ever fighting among ourselves with none secure of his life or property."

I felt I should like to know more of the execution of Chigi Duyu and as soon as I had dealt with the most urgent supply problems, I made my way to Hang and paid a call on Hibu Takr, most prominent of priests and seers.

Takr was in his house when we arrived and after a long diversionary conversation on the rites of Morom I broached the subject of Chigi Duyu's execution. Hibu Takr replied without any hesitation, and I saw at once that there was no feeling of guilt on the part of the Hang people.

Chigi Duyu was a habitual thief. He had repeatedly stirred up trouble by stealing cattle from both Apa Tanis and Daflas. He slaughtered the stolen animals in the forest and sold the meat to the unsuspecting, thereby adding dissension and quarrels among the villagers to the material losses of the cattle owners. That he must die had been the decision of the prominent Apa Tanis of all villages but his own; and when at last he had been seized on a public platform in Mudang Tage no man stood up in his defence. He was taken to Hang and kept at the Taliang *lapang*; though he was fed with rice and beer, he ate little and did not answer those who accused him of his many crimes. Men of Bela, the most recent victims of his depredations, violently opposed the acceptance of the ransom offered by his clansmen and two days after his capture he was executed. The warriors had gathered at the Taliang *lapang* to tell Duyu that he must die for the crimes he had committed. It was his own fault, they said, and he should bear them no grudge. Then they cut off the hands, 'with which he had stolen', slashed him over the eyes, 'with which he had spied out other men's cattle ', and over the mouth, ' with which he had eaten stolen goods '. In a few moments he was dead. The Bela men took away one hand with which to perform their own *ropi* rites but the rest of the body was burnt in Hang. To-morrow the *ropi* rites would be celebrated in much the same manner as is done for an enemy slain in war. The men of Hang would dance at the *nago* shrine and a mithan would be sacrificed. Towards the price of the mithan every household had contributed rice, and with this rice they had bought four cows ; these cows were now to be exchanged for one large mithan belonging to a Dafla of Jorum.

I had a look at the Taliang *lapang*, the scene of the execution, and found it still heaped with the shields and spears of the men who had taken part in the killing. There these weapons would remain until the completion of the *ropi* ceremony.

The affair of Chigi Duyu's execution demonstrated the strength and efficiency of the Apa Tanis' system of justice. The men who had enforced the law that habitual thieves must die had acted according to the public will. By recourse to collective action in the punishment of recognized crime they obviated the need for private raids such as are the order of the day in Dafla society. And even Chigi Nime, after his first indignant protest, tacitly accepted the justice of the penalty. Nothing more was said about revenge or the possibility of demanding compensation from the executioners.

Meanwhile I continued my preparations for our move to the Miri village of Chemir and thence northwards up the valley of the Upper Kamla. The feud between Hari and Chemir was not yet settled, but the first conciliatory steps had been taken and after the visit of the Chemir Miris to Duta in the autumn, no further violence had occurred. I hoped therefore that I would be able to persuade both parties to end the feud by concluding a formal peace treaty.

Anxiety as to whether sufficient porters would turn up was the prelude to every tour in the Subansiri hills. But this time we need not have worried. Before the sun rose on the day of our departure sixty men from Hari and Bela arrived in camp fully provisioned for the trip to Chemir. They included not only slaves and poor men but also a number of young men of good family, who would never have enlisted for a journey to the plains. They appeared to welcome the opportunity of re-establishing contact with their traditional trade partners in Miri villages, and had provided themselves with an abundance of exchange goods such as knives, chillies, and cloth which they arranged picturesquely on the top of our loads.

Our small party consisted of Betty, myself and Kop Temi, the only one of our interpreters with a good knowledge of the Miri dialect. Bhattachariya who was still in Müdo looking after a sick sepoy, was to join us later in the Miri country. Except for two Apa Tanis from Haja who had volunteered to accompany us on the whole tour we had no permanent porters. This facilitated our rationing arrangements, but it meant that our movements would be entirely dependent on such local porters as we could recruit. The tribesmen of the Upper Kamla valley could not be paid in money, rupee coins and indeed any kind of coinage being unknown to them, and such services as we would require would have to be paid for in salt and cloth. Sufficient quantities of such bulky commodities for a two months' tour required far more porters than the transport of our tents and personal equipment.

Through the pine and bamboo groves of Hari, where large stacks of firewood stood ready for the Mloko festival, we made our way up a side valley drained by a clear, swift flowing stream. The grass and the bracken on the hill-sides were still dead and brown, but the valley yet breathed an air of spring. Early budding willows lined the waterside and here and there the first mauve primulæ raised their lovely heads.

12

PAYING INDIA'S TRIBUTE

FOR TWO days our way led through the belt of forest which surrounds the Apa Tani valley on all sides. The first night we camped on a narrow wooded ridge, where the blood red blossoms of giant rhododendron littered the mossy ground; and the next we spent close to the Semla river on the deserted site of Sole, the village where thirty years before Temi's father had lived and died at the hands of raiders from Linia and Licha. On the third day we reached an open saddle that commanded a wide view over the Kamla country. There we found Guch Tamar, the elderly headman who in the autumn had visited us in Duta, and with him was a colourful crowd of Miris. They had come to welcome us with mugs of rice-beer of the best quality.

Guch Tamar suggested that we should camp at the nearby village of Bua, and the Apa Tanis, weary after three long and tiring marches, greeted the suggestion of an early halt with undisguised enthusiasm.

Bua was a small village, built according to a pattern which we soon came to recognize as characteristic of the Kamla valley. The houses stood in one compact cluster—not dispersed over spurs and knolls as in the Kiyi and Panior regions. The slope to which they clung dropped at an angle of perhaps thirty degrees, and above the village stretched a living barrier of thorny scrub. This, we were told, was a defensive device to break the rush of a surprise attack. Bua's immediate neighbours, Pemir and Rakhe, whose fields were clearly visible on the ridge to the west, were friendly, but the villagers lived in constant fear of the warlike inhabitants of Linia and other more distant Dafla villages.

Close to one of the larger houses several men were putting the finishing touches to a complicated ritual structure of bamboo to be used in a disease scaring rite. A prominent man of Bua was seriously ill and a mithan and a pig tied up nearby were presently to be offered to the disease spirits responsible for the affliction. Such scaffold-like structures,

174

decorated with tassels of bamboo shavings and incised staves, are essential for every sacrificial rite, but as soon as the rite is over they are abandoned and allowed to fall into decay. Unlike the aboriginals of Peninsular India most of the Assam hill-tribes have no shrines regarded as the permanent seats of gods, and the altars built of perishable materials are not treated with any degree of reverence once a rite is completed.

Talking to the men of Bua I tried to clarify a problem which had been worrying me for some time. Was it possible to draw a distinction between the populations currently known as Daflas and Miris? Both these terms seem to have originated among the Assamese populations of the plains, and they had been consistently used by our Dafla interpreters when speaking Assamese. Those tribesmen who came to the plains through the Panior valley or used paths to the west of it were described as 'Daflas'; whereas those who reached Assam by way of the Subansiri valley or across the hills between Subansiri and Panior were called Hill Miris. The members of the Miri Mission who had approached the Kamla valley through the villages of the Hill Miris, extended the use of this term to the tribesmen in the Upper Kamla valley. But here in Bua, a village lying seemingly on the borders of these ethnographic zones, I found no evidence that the tribesmen themselves recognize any such distinction.

The people of Bua intermarry with the 'Miris' of Chemir as well as with the 'Daflas' of Rakhe, Pemir and Linia. Similar bonds of blood and marriage link Chemir with the villages in the hills to the east and those on the north bank of the Lower Kamla, while Linia maintains marriage relations with the inhabitants of Licha and villages on the Upper Khru. In like manner, as I was later to discover, there is intermarriage between the various groups on the Upper Kamla, Sipi and Subansiri, and the web of connubial ties is thus spread over the whole of the tribal country south of the snow-ranges, a web unbroken by any clear tribal boundary comparable to that separating the Apa Tanis from all their neighbours.

This essential unity of the 'Daflas' and 'Miris' throughout the region watered by Panior, Khru and Kamla is reflected in a mythology which traces their origin from a common forefather known as Teni. He is believed to have had five sons, each of whom was the ancestor of a tribal group. It would seem that at one time these five groups had territorial associations, but the migrations of recent generations have blurred the picture, and to-day members of two or even three groups

175

may be found living in the same valley. The five groups that sprung from the sons of Teni are further subdivided into clusters of clans, and the members of such clans consider themselves so closely related that intermarriage would amount to incest.

Thus every Miri and Dafla clan has a definite place in a genealogical system which embraces the entire population within the Subansiri bend except the Apa Tanis and the Sulungs, that tribe of primitive forest nomads who dwell in scattered groups over an area extending from the Upper Panior to the higher mountain ranges north of the Kamla river.

In the interests of accuracy it would probably be best to drop the terms Dafla and Hill Miri and to refer to the entire tribal population claiming descent from Teni as Nisü, a term used by most of the tribesmen to distinguish their own race from the plains-people, as well as from the Apa Tanis and the Sulungs. But a travel book is hardly the place to introduce a new ethnographic terminology, and here I shall continue to use the terms Dafla and Miri, reserving the latter name for the inhabitants of the Kamla valley and the hills lying between the Lower Kamla and the plains of Lakhimpur.

As the crow flies it cannot be more than three miles from Bua to Chemir, but we, alas, were earth-bound. The path zigzagged over broken ground, plunging into one deep valley after the other. The day was oppressively hot and soon the Apa Tanis divested themselves of all their clothing and walked in nothing but their red cane-tails and their diminutive loin cloths.

It was five hours before we reached the open spur above Chemir and caught the first glimpse of the Kamla flowing in the valley far below. The grandeur of the mountains framing the Kamla and those extending east beyond the Subansiri dwarfed anything we had seen during that season's journeyings. Though of no great height, they rose from the level of the river in a single sweep of 7,000 to 8,000 feet with no ledge or break to interrupt the upsurge of their enormous masses. Comparing the picture I have retained of that view with the much more startling and magnificent scenery of the Nepal Himalaya and particularly the towering snow-peaks of Khumbu, I find it difficult to explain that impression of massiveness that the Kamla mountains created. It is possible that belonging to geologically older formations they lack any detail which would draw the eye from the main outlines of the mountain-ranges and relieve the feeling of colossal bulk.

Guch Tamar stood beside me on the hill above Chemir and as we looked out over the mountain country to the north and east he pointed out the villages on the surrounding hills. Lying at altitudes of 3,000 to 4,000 feet they appeared larger and more substantial than the habitations of the Panior Daflas. Nevertheless Tamar's rapid survey of recent Miri history left no doubt that this tract of country was in as unsettled a state as the Kiyi and Panior valleys. Within the span of the last three or four generations the whole area had been subjected to much savage raiding and there had been a complete transformation of the political set-up. Previously inhabited by the Gungü group of clans, clans to which the Miris living south of the Kamla belonged, the area was now dominated by the powerful Kabak clans. Having come from the upper reaches of the river some three generations ago these clans had first established themselves in Mingö, a village some four days' march north-east of Chemir, and had rapidly extended their hold over the whole of the neighbourhood so that now they occupied most of the villages in the country lying south of the Sipi and north of the Kamla.

My first task in Chemir was mediation in the old disputes between Guch Tamar and the Apa Tanis.[1] Gat Tadu and several other men of Hari were with me in camp, but were reluctant to make the first conciliatory move. Guch Tamar, the undisputed leader of Chemir, was equally proud and more or less ignored the Apa Tani notables. Each party convinced of the righteousness of their own cause stood on their dignity and neither side was prepared to approach the other with a plea for negotiations. Thus two days passed in a game of mutual avoidance, and it was not until I forced the issue and myself led an Apa Tani delegation to Tamar's house, that the opposing parties agreed to sit down and discuss terms for a settlement of the dispute.

Peace between Miris and Apa Tanis was clearly to the advantage of both tribes. Even the temporary security of passage created by my visit to Chemir had re-opened the area of Apa Tani trade, and not only the men who had carried for me, but many independent groups of Apa Tanis began arriving with their goods in Chemir, the western gateway of the Miri country, and soon dispersed to the neighbouring villages.

In speaking of Apa Tani traders, it is perhaps necessary to mention that these are not professional traders comparable to the hawkers of the Indian countryside or even the Tibetan traders who in other parts of the Himalaya come with their yak caravans across the high passes and

[1] See Chapter 7, pp. 107, 108.

sell salt and wool for cash or in exchange for goods to local merchants. To the Apa Tani, no less than to the Dafla and Miri, trade is a side-line. A man may take two or three cloths, a knife or a sword and perhaps a quantity of Indian salt on a visit to friends in a Dafla or Miri village, and try to barter these goods for local produce. He does not display his goods in a public place nor will he venture into a village in which he has no established contacts. Traditional friendships between individual households is the basis of all trade in the Subansiri area. Only the man who enjoys the protection of a friend will feel safe in a village far from home.

When a feud temporarily blocks his normal trade routes, he cannot easily switch to another area. Many of the Hari and Bela people, for instance, had friends and trade partners only among the Miris of the Chemir area, and their trading operations had stagnated ever since the feud between Guch Tamar and Hage Gat had made Chemir and its neighbourhood unsafe for Apa Tanis of these villages. Now they saw their chance. Bristling with knives and swords for sale, they arrived carrying rucksacks of plaited cane that bulged with cloth and leaf-parcels of salt. They had no difficulty in disposing of their goods. Soon we would see them returning, their approach heralded by the squeaks and grunts of small pigs which they carried on their backs in loosely woven bamboo baskets. Cocks and hens were transported equally humanely, and a varied array of fibre rain-cloaks and plaited hats, cane-belts, Tibetan ornaments and large gourds used as storing vessels, completed the loads of the first Apa Tanis to resume trade with the Miris.

Guch Tamar spent a great deal of time in our camp and Betty and I were soon captivated by his charm, his witty remarks and his naughty chuckle. He was then a man of about sixty with a small, pointed, white beard, excellent manners and a soft, quiet voice. Usually he dressed very simply in an Assamese silk cloth and a single string of outsize beads, but one day he appeared wearing a gauntlet of goat's hide with a long fringe of silky russet hair. It was made from the skin of a Tibetan goat, and when I admired it he pressed it on me, slipping it over my wrist like a bracelet (Pl. 27).

There seemed to be two sides to Tamar's character. His smooth manners overlaid a stern determination and tenacity of purpose in the conduct of trade and political affairs and he did not shrink from the use of force when the prestige of his house and village was in question. Yet, the forbearance he showed to an erring wife spoke of a broad-

25. Miris of Chemir village decorating a ritual structure with bamboo shavings.

26. A Miri girl of Rute-Hate village.

27. Guch Tamar, the leading man of Chemir village.

mindedness unusual among Dafla and Miri husbands. Some years before my visit the second of his five wives went to help cultivate the fields of a new settler, who had come from a village in the Khru valley. It was at Guch Tamar's behest that she had gone to lend a hand, but he had not foreseen that she would succumb to the charms of the handsome stranger. Before long the affair came to light ; instead of avenging the slight, however, Tamar invited his wife's lover to come and live in his house ; he allotted a separate hearth to the couple, and they became his dependents. This was a shrewd move, for by relinquishing his marital rights he not only retained the woman as a worker, but gained the services of the man who replaced him in the rôle of husband.

I doubt whether Guch Tamar or indeed any Miri would have viewed with similar equanimity the defection of a wife married with 'great rites' ; but the girl in question had been married to Tamar with 'small rites' and he had paid a bride-price of only two mithan.

Among the Miris there are several ways of concluding a marriage, and only one of them, known as *nieda*, establishes a lasting and socially significant bond between the families of husband and wife. A *nieda* marriage is solemnized with elaborate rites : the bridegroom pays a high bride-price and the bride's father is expected to match the value with a dowry consisting of ornaments, precious Tibetan bells and sometimes even a slave. The bride-price paid by Guch Tamar for his first wife comprised twenty mithan, and he recalled with pride—and perhaps a little exaggeration—that in the course of the celebrations and the subsequent visits he had slaughtered thirty mithan to feast his wife's kinsmen. This type of marriage union is upheld by supernatural as well as by social sanctions. Should a wife married by *nieda* rites elope with another man, the aggrieved husband may not accept her 'price' from the seducer, but must try to recover her and if negotiation fails 'make war' on his rival. For the Miris believe that a husband who by accepting monetary compensation 'sells' his *nieda* wife, will incur the displeasure of the gods and draw misfortune upon his house.

Only alliances between families of approximately equal status and wealth are solemnized with *nieda* rites. A wealthy man marrying the daughter of poor parents will pay a bride-price of only one or two mithan and there will be no question of a dowry. Such a marriage is called *tado hale*, and a wife married in this manner may be passed on to another man without arousing the wrath of the gods or the stricture of society. Indeed the usual way of dealing with the defection of a *tado hale* wife is to demand compensation equal to the bride-price originally paid to the girl's parents.

Yet another way of acquiring a wife is to abduct a girl without her parents' knowledge. Such a marriage is known as *nim-möli*, and when Guch Tamar had lost his first three wives, he married the daughter of respectable people of Rakhe in *nim-möli* fashion. She had been a willing partner to the elopement, and her parents, who had at first opposed the marriage, ultimately resigned themselves to the *fait accompli*. Over a period of several years Guch Tamar paid them a bride-price of eleven mithan, and they gave their daughter a dowry of four Tibetan bells and a string of valuable beads.

Though marriages are one of the principal methods of forging political alliances and often provide an occasion for the exchange of valuable property, parents have by no means the final word in the arrangement of matches. Miri girls are of independent mind, and Guch Tamar mentioned quite casually that his own daughter Yube had gone to live with a maternal kinsman without mentioning her intentions to her parents. The girl had remained single long after reaching marriageable age ; she had enjoyed a great measure of independence while living under the parental roof, cultivating her own field and cooking her food on a separate hearth. Every year she had called the men of the village to help her clear the jungle, and with the surplus of several years' crops she had bought two mithan and several Tibetan bells. Her father had allowed her to run her 'household' without interference and declared he knew nothing of the details of her transactions, until one day, dispensing with all formalities, she went to live with Meli Kokum in Pelrue. Soon after Pelrue, like all the smaller settlements on the north bank of the Kamla, was threatened by the rising might of the Kabak clan and the couple sought refuge in Chemir. To regularize his union with Yube, now that he was to live in her home village, and to reconcile her father, Meli Kokum paid him four mithan. He built a house of his own, and when I visited him I met not only Yube but Kokum's other two wives. The girl, who had shown so much independence in managing her own affairs, had no doubt exercised her talents in organizing her husband's life. With three pairs of hands to do the work in house and field, there was the prospect of a prosperous future.

Kop Temi told me that among Daflas too many a rich man's daughter married late and gained great independence even while living in her father's house. With the produce of her fields she could buy cattle, valuables and slaves, and ultimately she might marry the man of her choice, either taking him into the parental home or going to live in his house. Should father or brother demand a bride-price, she was likely to point out that since she was rich enough to dispense with a dowry her husband was under no obligation to pay a price for his bride.

Now that talks between the Chemir Miris and the Apa Tani negotiators were under way, I had little doubt that the self-interest of old trade-partners would lead them to a successful conclusion. It remained for me to make the annual *posa*-payment to the Hill Miri notables, and then we could set out on our journey towards the upper reaches of the Subansiri. These payments had never before been made in the hills. In previous years the Hill Miris had journeyed to the plains and there at some appointed place they had received their annual dues. With the extension of Government's influence beyond the Inner Line it seemed advisable, however, to alter the procedure and pay the Miris' *posa* in their own country. In response to my messages the *posa*-holders had all gathered in Chemir. They were a gay crowd, given to much laughter and the enjoyment of huge quantities of rice-beer. Foremost among them was Gocham Tapak, dressed in a faded red coat which years ago a Political Officer had given him in recognition of his rôle as a prominent headman. Though of smallish, stocky stature and unimpressive looks, he outshone all other *posa*-holders in intelligence, courage and spirit of enterprise. He spoke adequate Assamese and had far-flung connections with the tribesmen north of the Kamla. As a small boy Tapak had accompanied his father on the Miri Mission, and though he had never again ventured as high up the Kamla valley, he was the only South Kamla Miri with a first-hand experience of the country through which we would pass. I was delighted therefore when he agreed to come with us, and his value as a co-voyager increased as we journeyed north-wards into regions where Kop Temi had difficulties in understanding the local dialects.

Another delightful personality among the *posa*-holders, was Biku Yama, a tall, middle-aged lady of forceful character who had inherited the right to *posa* as well as the headship of Biku village. She took an instant liking to Betty, the first European woman to set foot in those hills, and declared that, like Tapak, she would accompany us on our journey.

One after the other the Miri notables produced their tattered *posa*-patents and received Government's ' tribute' in rupee coins, worth, owing to war-time inflation, only a fraction of their original value. How little attention had hitherto been paid to these border areas, remote and inaccessible from the centres of Government in Delhi and Shillong, was only too apparent from the almost unbelievable inadequacies of the *posa*-registers and documents. In the official records no attempt had been made to group the *posa*-holders by village or identify them by clan ; indeed their particulars had been treated with such levity in the official registers that recognition of the rightful recipients was sometimes difficult.

There seemed to be equal confusion as to the nature and origin of the payments themselves and it soon became obvious that there was a serious discrepancy between the official view and the tribesmen's attitude. By the officers of Government *posa* was generally considered as a form of tribute with which in the early days of British rule the hillmen had been bought off from raiding the plains. According to the tribesmen, on the other hand, the *posa*-payments were a kind of rent, paid by Government for the use of their ancestral lands in the Brahmaputra valley. Like many Himalayan people, the Miris of the hills south of the Kamla used to be semi-nomadic; in the spring and summer months, they explained, they cultivated their fields in the hills and during the winter they moved to the plains, where in the country between the foothills and the Brahmaputra each clan hunted and fished within the borders of its own clan territories. When Assamese peasants first settled on the north bank of the Brahmaputra, the traditional owners demanded and received rent from the new settlers for the use of their clan lands. At first this rent was paid in agricultural produce, but at a later date, presumably when the present system of land revenue was introduced, the Government of India took over the payment of this rent, which, assessed in Indian coinage, was paid annually in the form of *posa*.

Year after year the Political Officer of the Balipara Frontier Tract had paid the *posa* without making any demands on the recipients. But this time we were in need of their help and when sending word to the *posa*-holders about my intended visit to Chemir, I had added messages calling for porters to accompany us into the area north of the Kamla. Thanks to the good will and the local influence of the *posa*-holders an adequate number of porters had assembled in Chemir, but few of them were keen on going far afield, and I realized that we would be lucky if they carried for us more than two or at the most three stages beyond the Kamla river.

182

13

THE VALLEY OF THE KAMLA

HOW WERE we to cross the Kamla? This was the problem that had worried us ever since we had decided on this exploratory tour towards the upper reaches of the Subansiri. The bridge that had once linked Chemir with Pelrue had been cut down when the warlike Kabak clans had begun raiding the villages on the north bank. For those living south of the river had judged isolation to be their most effective defence and had destroyed all means of communication between themselves and their enemies. The only bridge still standing on the lower course of the river was several marches downstream, and whenever the Miris had occasion to cross at other points, they used rafts made from cane and bamboo. Such rafts, however, were not permanent features of the Kamla, and when I first discussed my plans with Guch Tamar, he said that his men would take several days to build a ferry strong enough to carry our loads.

During the week we spent in Chemir the villagers worked hard, cutting cane and bamboo and constructing the rafts, and when we arrived on the river-bank we found the ferry completed and our luggage in the process of being transported to the opposite side. The two rafts, broad based with pointed bows, slid smoothly over the water, propelled by men standing in the bows who hauled hand over hand on the ropes that spanned the river from bank to bank.

Our two Apa Tanis were horrified at the prospect of crossing the Kamla in this way. They had never been afloat before and did not know how to swim. In their own country there was no unbridged stream which could not be crossed by wading, and the swift current and the black waters of the Kamla, swishing over the floor of the raft, made them exceedingly nervous. But they comforted themselves with a thought that they were to voice again and again on this journey:

" If we die," they said, " we die in good company. We shall not travel alone on the path that leads to the Land of the Dead."

They insisted on making the crossing on the same raft as ourselves and we were flattered that our company should be considered so desirable on the journey to the netherworld.

We spent the night on a broad sandy beach on the further bank and enjoyed the friendly atmosphere of a camp that resembled nothing so much as a giant family picnic. The Miris were travelling with their womenfolk, and many had brought their children to carry the numerous bamboo bottles of rice-beer that they considered indispensable for a three days' journey. In the dusk the boys and girls played on the sand, and their laughter rang out over the gay chatter of the women who bent over the cooking pots preparing the evening meal.

We built a camp-fire close to the river's edge and sat in a semi-circle watching its reflection in the water : Tapak and Temi and the two Apa Tanis, the ever cheerful Bhattachariya and most of the *posa*-holders. The Miris warned us that a month later this low-lying sand-bank would be submerged by flood water, and that then it would be dangerous if not impossible to use this ferry. That evening, however, we were not inclined to consider the difficulties of our return. Instead we discussed the prospects of the outward journey and the immediate problems of to-morrow's march.

Tapak assured us that he was confident of a welcome in Dobom, the first village we would reach. There he had a trade partner, Yukar Terü, a rich and powerful man, who owned more than two hundred cows and mithan and commanded great influence in many of the villages on the north bank. But next day when we had climbed wearily up four thousand feet, descended two thousand, and climbed again another fifteen hundred, all the time uncomfortably aware of the sun on our backs, we arrived to find Yukar Terü's door closed to all outsiders. A religious rite, we were told, was in progress and none might enter until it was over.

We sat down on an outcrop of stone on the outskirts of the village and waited. The change in Tapak's attitude was disquieting. In Chemir, among familiar people from villages south of the Kamla, he moved with an air of authority. Here he behaved with marked cir-cumspection, careful not to obtrude on the villagers until he had spoken to his own friend Yukar Terü. The only members of our party who were not subdued by these circumstances were our two Apa Tanis who whispered and giggled over the current fashions of Dobom women. These ladies went sedately about their business in gay little ballerina-like skirts made of dried grass. In the cool climate of the Himalayas these flimsy garments, reminiscent of South Sea fashions, certainly looked a little incongruous (Pl. 35).

I soon discovered that no one in Dobom, or in any other village of the Lower Kamla valley, knew how to weave, and this was surprising because weaving is a craft practised by most of the surrounding tribesmen. Though the shortage of cloth must cause a great deal of hardship, no attempt seems to have been made to adopt a technique which provides so many of their neighbours with warm and substantial clothing. It is possible, of course, that neither cotton nor the fibrous *pud* which is used as raw material in the valleys of Panior and Khru, will grow in this particular area. The wealthier villagers wear Assamese bazaar cloths, which they purchase from Miris in touch with the plains and small quantities of handwoven cotton and *pud* fibre cloths are bought from the tribesmen of the Upper Khru valley.

But this was not the moment to investigate the distribution of weaving in the Miri hills. Before long Yukar Terü emerged from his house, followed by two men carrying great mugs of rice-beer. We drank the beer and explained to Terü the reasons for our coming. He did everything to appear pleasant, invited us to his house and offered hospitality to all our porters, many of whom had never visited Dobom before and had the status of strangers in the village.

Less welcome was Yukar Terü's solicitude for our safety. When Tapak told him that I wanted to visit the villages of the Upper Kamla valley, he expressed horror and disapproval. Up to Bidak, the village lying north-west of Dobom, we might safely go. There he had friends and relations, and he would send his son with us to show us the path. But on no account must we proceed further. The tribesmen in the Upper Kamla valley were warlike and treacherous, and a dangerous epidemic was raging in the villages beyond Bidak. This was water on the mill to our Miri porters whose one idea, now that they had reached Dobom, was to recross the Kamla and return home as speedily as possible. It was obvious, however, that this small village could not furnish sufficient porters to release them all, and while I was able to replace some of them by Dobom men, I had to persuade the rest to accompany me to Bidak.

Next morning we set out along a contour path and after an hour or two reached a crest some 4,000 feet high. Emerging from a grass thicket, we were suddenly confronted by a view embracing almost the entire area we were hoping to traverse. Before us lay the valley of the Upper Kamla, a landscape larger in its dimensions, and yet more friendly in character, than the scenery along the course of the combined Kamla-Khru. Rising steeply from a narrow gorge, the hillsides were broken at a level of about 4,500 feet by large grassy terraces on which we could clearly see the houses and fields of several villages. Our guides pointed out Bidak, the village nearest to us, Mingö, the home village of the Kabak clans, the twin settlements of Rute-Hate and, in the misty distance, beyond the junction of Kamla and Selu, the land of Sartam and Tali. Above the villages rose dark forested ridges, which culminated in conical peaks and massive humps close on 10,000 feet. The most prominent of these peaks was Pij Cholo, and the Apa Tanis pricked up their ears when they heard the name ; for tradition tells that the Apa Tanis reached their present habitat in three different groups, one of which passed Pij Cholo on their southward migration.

Between Pij Cholo to the north and the great mass of Mount Romta south of the river was a vista on which we looked with surprise and delight. Here in the triangle of the Selu valley appeared a chain of snow-covered mountains, dazzling white in the bright sun and wreathed with a delicate fluff of cloud. Was this the range that separates the Kamla from the upper course of the Subansiri, or was it a part of the Himalayan main range through which the Subansiri cuts its way in a series of deep gorges ?

The sight of this snow-range apparently so close excited our Dafla and Apa Tani companions almost as much as ourselves, and Kop Temi remarked optimistically that to reach the ' country of the snow ' by this route could only be a matter of days.

Below us on a low saddle lay Bidak and towards this village we now began to descend. The path lead through *jhum* fields, partly cultivated the previous year, and partly cleared and burnt in preparation for the new season's sowing. It was here that I noticed the variations in the systems of shifting cultivation practised by the Subansiri tribes. While the Panior Daflas are in the habit of clearing small patches of forest, each man being free to make his own choice of a plot in the area surrounding his village, Miri villagers prefer to cultivate a compact block of fields, clearing the jungle together, and then dividing the block into plots to be cultivated by the individual families.

Methods of Shifting Cultivation

The result of this system is that in some years the cultivated area will lie at a considerable distance from the dwelling sites ; for in order to allow sufficient periods of fallow, the village land is worked in carefully calculated rotation. In the borderlands of Dobom and Bidak territory we passed in quick succession a block of fields cultivated by the people of Dobom, a narrow belt of forest, and a similar block cultivated by Bidak men, the cycles of rotation of both villages having led them to cultivate that year on the periphery of their village holdings.

We reached the village late in the afternoon. There was no obvious place for a camp, but we found a knoll a little to the north of the village with a crown flat enough to accommodate our tents. The inhabitants though timid were quite friendly and we succeeded in persuading them to help clear the site. Yet, they were not entirely at ease and the reason for their malaise were soon discovered.

Chugdu Tagla, a leading member of the great Kabak clan, and the most important man of Bidak, had gone to attend a feast in Balu, a village lying on the opposite bank of the Kamla. In his absence the people of Bidak were unwilling to commit themselves to any definite course of action.

Would some of them carry our loads on the next day's march ?

Tagla might arrange for porters when he returned.

Did they have friends or kinsmen in Mingö, the village clearly visible at the foot of Pij Cholo ?

Tagla would tell us of Bidak's relations with neighbouring villages when he returned.

After a number of equally inconclusive responses I came to the conclusion that we would either have to await the great man's return or move on to Mingö with the porters we had brought. Our guides from Dobom agreed to accompany us to Mingö, but it needed a lot of coaxing to induce the porters from south of the Kamla to move any further into unfamiliar country. Tapak did his best, but it was Biku Yama, the adventurous lady with her large entourage, who finally rallied them. She said that where Betty dared to go she would go too, and her menfolk had little choice but to follow her lead. Reluctantly the rest of the Miris agreed to proceed. But only to Mingö. Further than that they would not go. While only that morning we had been told that Mingö was stricken with some terrible disease, which had already claimed two of the villagers, it was now discovered that Mingö was the last village still unaffected by the epidemic ; and once everything

187

was settled our Dobom guide suddenly remembered that his wife's three brothers all lived in Mingö.

Nevertheless one and all declared that Mingö was the furthermost place which we might safely visit. The people of Guchi and Sojam clans in the villages beyond Mingö were a dangerous lot ; with them no one in the Kabak group of villages maintained any connection. Moreover it was there that the mysterious epidemic was raging : in other words to venture beyond Mingö would be a particularly unpleasant way of committing suicide.

However, we were not to be deterred. We had won our point. Any further progress would depend on luck and diplomacy, and last but not least on our ability to barter rice for salt. For in order to keep all the South Kamla Miris with us we had had to feed them from our own supplies, and all that remained could be stretched for little more than a week.

Next morning we set out in the direction of Mingö. The path which we followed that day wound along the contours of steep slopes, but now and then it plunged into deep ravines, filled with rank-growing vegetation typified by several varieties of large leaved and heavy headed pink and white begonias, covering the damp ground in wonderful profusion.

At last we emerged on a grass covered hill-side and saw the scattered houses of Mingö. They were rather ragged and the village was disappointingly small for the parent village of the important Kabak clan, from which in the recent past not only Bidak but many other flourishing villages had been founded.

Our Dobom guides had gone ahead to reassure the inhabitants of our peaceful intentions ; they had taken with them small presents of salt, and soon they were seen returning with several men carrying mugs of millet beer. Here the people's dress was even more scanty than in Dobom and the little cloth they wore was dirty and torn. One young man had covered his nakedness with a banana leaf, and another sported a penis-cover carved from a bamboo root and attached to a waist-string.

Looking at these sparsely clad folk, I was reminded of the evening in Duta when Chigi Nime had laughingly demonstrated the use of just such bamboo penis-covers which he had seen on his travels in the Khru valley. From now on we were to become quite familiar with this peculiar article of dress, for in an area chronically short of cloth all manner of coverings are used as protection against thorns and spikes,

188

and of these the one made from the root of a bamboo is undoubtedly the most effective.

We found a camp site close to the village, and in a few moments were surrounded by sightseers. Our usual gifts of cigarettes and matches produced blank expressions : no one had ever seen a match-box ; no one had ever smoked a cigarette. What the women wanted was salt, and this they demanded by licking the open palm of their upturned hands.

Well satisfied with our reception in Mingö we reckoned that a stay of several days would be necessary before our relations could be sufficiently cordial to attempt a move, westwards or northwards, whichever opportunity offered. The Miris from south of the Kamla, however, were anxious to return home and the next morning we paid them off in rupee coins, which they fortunately accepted, thus allowing us to harbour our limited supply of exchange goods for regions where porters must be paid in kind.

Hardly had the porters left, when Chugdu Tagla, the great man of Bidak, appeared with a small party. He was short and stoutish, with a thin black beard and an impressive face, to which one drooping eyelid lent distinction (Pl. 32). His family, like other Kabak lineages, had sprung from Mingö, and his closest kin still lived in the village. He spoke with authority not only as the head of Bidak, but also as spokesman of Mingö.

He had heard of our coming, he explained, when he returned from Balu, and had immediately set out to overtake us. The people of Kabak clan, he went on to say, would give us all possible help ; I had only to let him know and he would provide porters. Would we like to go to Lapchi-Lapte or to Balu ? They were both on the other side of the Kamla but we could cross the river by means of a rope bridge below Bidak. I thanked Tagla. Yes, I replied, I would like to visit these villages next year ; this year I wanted to proceed up the Kamla.

That was impossible, declared Tagla ; no man of the Kabak group would go a step further north. Here in Mingö we were in the last friendly village. Further upstream lived warlike people who would endanger the lives of anyone rash enough to enter their territory.

Tagla spoke with such determination that I thought it useless to talk of my real intentions as long as he was in the village. So I took him and a few other men to a nearby hillock and got him to show me the surrounding country. The next village in the Kamla valley was a settlement of the Guchi and Sojam clans, but once again he was off on his old tack, the Kabak people never went there and did not even know the condition of the path.

Pointing to the high range overshadowing Mingö I asked whether there was any path leading north across those wooded mountains. Yes, Tagla said, beyond that ridge lay the valley of the Sipi river, containing many villages of which Deyi and Nilö were the nearest. They could be reached in three days, but the people were fierce and untrustworthy, and at present they had a feud with the people of Mingö. In dress and appearance they resembled the Abor tribes of the country east of the Subansiri, and were not at all like the Miris of the Kamla valley.

Tagla spoke also of the country lying in the fork between Kamla and Khru. There he had many contacts. Though Tagla himself had never ventured far up the valleys of either Khru or Kamla he had a fairly good knowledge of the character of trade that reached his village by the two trade routes, and what he told me threw new light on the possibility of a direct connection between the region of the Upper Khru and Tibet. Along the Khru route only valuables such as beads, bells and Tibetan swords filtered down to the Miri country, whereas bulkier goods such as salt and woollen cloth came from the region north of the Kamla river. Tagla had no explanation for the different character of trade goods current on the two routes, but venturing a guess I would say that a route along which only small but comparatively precious objects filter southwards is likely to be difficult and hence impracticable for men carrying heavy or bulky loads. Such an hypothesis does not fully explain, however, what equally light and easily transportable goods the tribesmen could offer in exchange for Tibetan beads and other valuables.

Tagla said good-bye with so many protestations of friendship that I could not doubt his good will, and I wondered what interest he could have in dissuading us from proceeding up the Kamla. When he had left the village I returned to the attack and was lucky enough to find a young man who was willing to carry a message to Rute-Hate, the nearest village of the Guchi and Sojam clans. I gave him a few pounds of salt to distribute among the friends he admitted he had in the village, and asked him to invite the leading men to come and see me.

Meanwhile I began calling in Mingö. In every house we were offered beer and in return we handed round cigarettes. In the gloomy interiors the lighting of matches startled and amused the people even more than it had done on the day of our arrival. Inveterate smokers, they quickly learnt to enjoy cigarettes, and during these long diplomatic visits it was lucky that there was no limit to the number of cigarettes Betty could smoke. A non-smoker myself I would have found it difficult to establish the easy fellow feeling so easily engendered between the addicts of nicotine.

Few of the Mingö people could have been called attractive. The Upper Kamla valley is one of the areas with a very high incidence of goitre and here more than half of the adults suffered from this disfiguring complaint. But Changmo Tachak's younger wife was a charming exception. She wore a broad belt of cane rings covering waist and hips and a breast-band of thin plaited cane. Three long strings of large white beads harmonized happily with this simple costume and a skin of warm coffee brown. Her black hair, held in place by a narrow fillet, fell on her shoulders and her broad, softly modelled face with its full mouth and strong white teeth wore an expression of smiling and satisfied sensuality.

Only ten days before, it seemed, her home village, Godak, which lies on the right bank of the Kamla, had been raided by men of Tumr. Five people were killed, ten captured and three wounded with poisoned arrows. The Mingö people related this in a matter-of-fact tone, and although their own kinsmen must have been involved, evinced neither indignation nor anxiety. Could it have been this incident which made our Kabak friends so nervous whenever we suggested advancing up the Kamla ?

The weather had changed. Heavy clouds hung on the high hills threatening rain and storm as one evening we hurried home from a visit to an isolated house. Half-way through a narrow belt of forest we were brought to a standstill by the sound of a crashing tree. The noise of tearing roots and breaking branches was followed by a melancholy chanting that floated eerily through the forest. We turned to Tapak, but he refused to speak ; he hurried us on out of the forest and into camp. Only when we were inside the tent did he start to explain that this was the work of a magician, who with the felling of the tree propelled the evil spirits towards his victim. To intercept such malignant powers was to endanger our lives.

Betty and I took little notice of this episode, but it made an impression on the rest of our party. There was an uneasy feeling in camp that night and as we sat round the fires everybody seemed to be waiting for something to happen. There was little we could do to reassure our companions and I suggested an early bed, hoping that a good night's rest would wipe out the evening's fears. We could not have been asleep more than an hour, however, when we were wakened by shouts from the tent occupied by Temi and the doctor. Both declared that they had heard sounds as of someone edging their way along the canvas of the tent wall, and both were certain that after they had raised their voices, they had heard rapidly retreating footsteps. We made a careful search of the camp but there was no sign of any intruder, and eventually we went back to bed ; but our Miri friends, and even Gocham Tapak, were so convinced that raiders or evil spirits were abroad that they sought shelter in a house in the village. If we thought that, sobered by the light of day, they would meet us next morning shamefacedly and full of excuses, we were mistaken. They did not consider it discreditable to flee the camp in the face of danger, indeed they explained rather proudly that had we been killed or captured, they would immediately have carried the news to the plains.

It was a bright and sunny morning when our messenger to Rute-Hate returned. With him came four impressive looking figures wearing huge yak hair head-dresses and attractive cloths narrowly bordered in black. Their long Tibetan swords were sheathed in scabbards made from the skin of grey monkey and hung on straps decorated with cowrie shells and the underjaw of the small Himalayan leopard.

These notables were accompanied by their wives, plump ladies with many ornaments, and several slaves carrying rice-beer and chickens in small baskets. After an exchange of courtesies we sat down on some convenient slabs of rock, and they listened quietly as I explained the reasons for my coming. I began by pointing out that we had travelled a long way to visit the only group of Gungü clans still living in the upper Kamla valley. I had recently spent some time in such Gungü villages as Bua and Chemir, and was anxious to pay a friendly visit also to their village. The reference to the common descent of all Gungü clans, now split into two groups by the emergent might of the Kabak people, was received with a nodding of heads. I continued by protesting our peaceful intentions and expressing the hope that they would help me to make the journey from Mingö to their own village of Rute-Hate.

The emissaries' reaction to this plea, translated and ably elaborated by Gocham Tapak, was surprisingly favourable. They would gladly welcome us to their village, and if we would be patient for another two

192

days they would return with porters to carry our loads as far as Rute-Hate. But this was the furthest point to which they could take us ; further up the valley lived people with whom they had few contacts and for whose attitude they could not answer.

To set their minds at rest, I replied that we would be well content to visit Rute-Hate, and indeed at that moment I was so grateful for this offer of a forward move, however limited, that I was prepared to let the future take care of itself. But a Mingö man chipped in with the tactless remark that this was exactly what I had said when we arrived in Mingö. There was a moment of uneasiness, but just then Betty and her friend Biku Yama returned from a visit to one of the Mingö ladies, and their appearance helped to dispel any lingering suspicion. Yama was loud in her support of my arguments: the white man had arrived with his wife as a friend and just as Miris did not take women on raiding parties, there would be no women in our party if we had any hostile designs. The logic of this argument impressed the envoys and we parted on a cordial note.

With the next move forward more or less assured, I urged Biku Yama and her party of South Kamla Miris to return to their villages. They had been pleasant camp companions ; and more than that, they had rendered me invaluable service by helping to establish informal relations with a people among whom I had arrived friendless. Now I felt it would be irresponsible to detain this charming elderly lady any longer in an area so far from her home. Yama wept when at last her loads were packed and it was time to say good-bye. Again and again she embraced Betty and begged her to come to Biku. " Come soon," she pleaded, " for who knows how long I shall live." Betty and I were deeply moved by this affection and felt that we parted from a genuine friend. Yama's helpfulness had been entirely selfless, she had provisioned herself and her party and had had no private reasons for travelling in strange regions.

The few days we spent in Mingö not only allowed us to stabilize personal relations with individual families, but it allowed the Mingö people to assess the tangible benefits of our visit. These were not inconsiderable, for in the short period of our stay we must have dispensed more salt than Mingö was accustomed to see in an average year. Everyone was anxious to trade and no hour of the day passed without some article being offered for our inspection. Edible roots, rice, chickens, eggs, smoked fish, legs of pork, Tibetan swords, hides, skins and precious beads all found their way to our camp, anything in fact that would gain for the inhabitants even the smallest amount of the much prized salt.

Once the people of Rute-Hate had consented to our visit, many Mingö men volunteered to carry our loads. But on the appointed day nearly a hundred men and women from Rute-Hate came to take us to their village and I had to explain to the Mingö people that their turn of earning wages in salt and cloth would come when we passed through on our return journey.

The village of Rute-Hate, where we arrived after a half-day's walk, was larger than Mingö and the houses standing in groups on an open hill-side had a substantial and prosperous look. Fenced-in fields, used mainly for growing maize, lay close to the houses and granaries with a curious sloping floor raised on piles, formed part of every homestead.

Nearly all the able-bodied villagers had carried our loads, but the older people and the children assembled to watch us prepare the camp. Some young men threw themselves into the task of levelling a hillock so that there was a space sufficiently level on which to pitch our tent, and others climbed the trees to cut branches for the cook shelters. But neither our persons, nor our tent and other belongings created half as much interest and excitement as our black cat, Chunki, and her six kittens.

Ever since Chunki had accompanied us on our first trek to the Apa Tani country, she had been firmly established as a member of our party. Whether we lived in Duta in our bamboo house, or moved from camp to camp in the Dafla country, Chunki was with us encouraging us to be comfortable with her soft purring. It must have been a fleeting encounter with one of the few Apa Tani cats that resulted in the birth of six kittens shortly before our departure for the Miri hills. Reluctant to leave her in Duta we had carried her and her kittens in a large basket and so far it had always been possible to find a little boy who was proud to carry this unconventional load. Whenever we arrived in a strange village Chunki and her gambolling offspring helped to lighten the first moments, and the further we moved up the Kamla valley the greater was the interest our cats aroused. Here in Rute-Hate the people had never seen a domestic cat, or even heard of such an animal. Fascinated they watched the kittens play.

"What kind of animals are these?" they asked. "They are not dogs, they are not pigs; what are they?"

28. Tablia Tangum, a Dafla boy of Potin village.

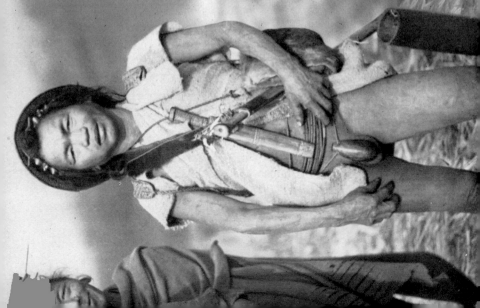

29. A Miri man of Göba village wearing a bamboo penis-cover.

30. Nilö Takhe, the leading man of Linkü-Rangpu in the Sipi valley.

31. Miri man of Rakhe village with fibre rain-cloak.

They grew even more enthusiastic when they realized that cats catch rats. The rats, like the human inhabitants of Rute-Hate, had never seen a cat and during our short stay Chunki must have made considerable inroads on the rat population. Every night she went hunting and our sleep was disturbed by the plomp, plomp, plomp of the six kittens jumping out of the high carrying basket each time their mother returned to the tent with a new victim. But the appetite of even six kittens is not insatiable, and in the morning the tent floor was littered with the mangled and dismembered bodies of rats the kittens had not been able to devour.

It is strange indeed that domestic cats have never found their way into the area of the Upper Kamla. Though not numerous in any part of the hills they are yet known to both Apa Tanis and Panior Daflas, and one would have thought that their usefulness in keeping down the rats would have led to their distribution throughout the hills.

Rute-Hate lies on the fringe of the economic sphere dependent on trade with Assam. Although none of the inhabitants had ever been to the plains, they relied on Indian salt obtained from such villages of the Kabak group as Mingö and Bidak, which in turn obtained their supplies through the Miris south of the Kamla. But no Indian salt reaches the villages beyond Rute-Hate. Göba, the nearest village in the Kamla valley, for instance, depended for salt as well as for all other imported goods on Tibetan sources. Cloth, as we had seen, was also in short supply and there was so little iron in Mingö and Rute-Hate that people tilled their fields with hoes made of the shoulder blade of mithan. Thus Rute-Hate, lying on the trade divide between India and Tibet, appeared an excellent base for any future exploration into the unknown regions to the north.

But for the moment I had to conceal my interest in this area behind a screen of questions on purely domestic affairs. The usual anthropological technique of enquiry into social relationships and religious practices served well to hold the people's interest and soon placed me on an intimate footing with many households in the village.

While elsewhere I had entered houses casually, I soon realized that here in Rute-Hate hospitality was no haphazard affair. People liked to prepare for a visit; when they wanted to entertain us they invited us a day ahead, or if they had not made sufficient preparations they asked us to defer a visit until they were ready for our reception. In a country where personal security and indeed the chance of survival depends largely on the number and standing of loyal friends, the ties created by hospitality are highly valued, and the first visit to a man's house accompanied by an exchange of presents is an act of great importance.

Entering a house we would be led to the principal hearth and offered mithan hides or deer skins as seats. While the chief lady handed us large bamboo mugs, the host usually busied himself with the preparation of pork snacks. Betty and I soon learnt to view this *pièce de résistance* with apprehension. Sometimes the pork, which was never more than lightly smoked, was comparatively fresh, and then we had only to combat our prejudice against swallowing huge lumps of unadulterated fat. But more often a putrid stench pervaded the house as soon as the cherished leg of pork was drawn from its hiding-place in the roof and we dreaded the moment when with a smile that brooked no refusal our host would offer us the glistening lumps lightly fired, but never properly grilled, on the end of a long bamboo skewer. It was easier to evince a proper appreciation of his hospitality if our host offered us a leaf heaped with salt with which to season this delicacy, but even then it was difficult to swallow with the expected show of relish.

During our whole time in the Miri country we were never invited to a full meal and it would seem that the customary way of entertaining such visitors as do not stay in the house is to offer them beer and a snack. At the end of the visit, when we rose to leave, the host usually produced a carefully prepared present. On one occasion it was a pig and on another a goat, but the less affluent were content to give us chickens or eggs. In return I gave small presents, such as a brass bowl or some salt and tobacco.

At a time when the Rute-Hate people were pretending that they had hardly any contact with the villages further up the Kamla valley, I discovered that a good many of the married women came from areas west and north-west of Rute-Hate, and indeed from the very villages which I hoped to visit before long. Whenever I noticed that my informants realized that in talking of their marriage relations they were displaying familiarity with the country ahead, I turned the conversation to such neutral subjects as the cult of the gods and the phases and ceremonies of the agricultural year. In this way I filled many pages in my notebooks with ethnographic material, while yet using every opportunity to elicit information on the populations closer to the snow-ranges.

In the house of Dame Tame, the leading man of Rute-Hate, I paused one day to admire the large collection of mithan shoulder blades hanging up on the walls close to the hearth. Tame explained his exceptionally large collection by saying that as a priest he was entitled to the left shoulder of every sacrificial animal slaughtered at the rites he performed. This led me to a discussion of Miri gods, of whom there are many. The greatest of all deities are Kir, Moru, Kite and Mote. They are male gods and were described to me as four brothers, tall like the mountains.

While these great gods never approach the villages of man, priests and seers go in dreams to their habitations, which are said to stand on high ground twelve days' journey to the east of the Miri country. It is because of the length and difficult nature of this journey that they accept the sacrifice of only fully grown mithan, the hardiest of the Miri's domesticated animals. On these dream journeys the priests and seers climb several high mountains and cross two large rivers by raft. Normally the four gods are benevolently disposed towards man, and people invoke them with prayers for prosperity and good health ; but whosoever arouses their wrath is doomed and his whole household perishes with him.

Doni the sun-god and Sü the earth-goddess are the messengers of the big four and act on their orders. Animals sacrificed to Doni and Sü must be white or at least partially white. Those men who regularly worship Doni and Sü are believed to live to a ripe old age, and whoever sacrifices white animals will have children who are handsome and light of skin. Some priests have also the power to harness the forces of evil spirits and send them out to kill people just as a war leader orders his warriors to attack his enemies. But Doni and Sü dislike such black magic and may cause the death of a priest who uses dangerous spirits to further his own ends.

I cannot claim that during the few weeks among the Miris I penetrated very deeply into the realm of their religious ideas, but I learnt enough of their ritual practices to assess the place of Miri religion among the religious systems of the other hill-tribes on Assam's borders.

In some of the houses we met slaves or people captured in war whose original home was in distant villages, and from them I heard of areas never visited by the ordinary villagers of Rute-Hate. A young woman whose light skin and pronouncedly mongoloid features aroused my interest, came from a village which, she said, lay high up near the snows, close to the land of the Tibetans. There men and women wore warm Tibetan clothes, but their houses were not very different from those of Rute-Hate. They bought their clothes from 'Agla Nime', the Tibet on this side of the main snow-ranges, but none of them ever went to 'Erü Nime', the Tibet beyond the land of eternal snow. She herself had been captured in war and sold and resold until she reached Rute-Hate. Now she was married to a man of Rute-Hate and she was happy with her husband and her children.

On the fourth day of our stay in Rute-Hate, when we had made friends with many of the villagers and were no longer a continuous focus of attention, we watched a ceremony connected with the conclusion of a solemn friendship pact. The tribesmen of the Kamla area, like the Daflas of the Panior and Kiyi valleys, set great store on certain very precious Tibetan bells and the exchange of such bells for mithan and other valuables forges a bond of friendship between the two partners second not even to the ties created by a marriage alliance.

Chugdu Tani, a young man of Mingö who had but recently come to live in Rute-Hate after a quarrel with several men of his home-village, had told me he was expecting the visit of a friend to whom he was selling a famous bell. Like other famous bells it had a name, Rusi, and Tani had originally acquired it from a man in the Khru valley. Tani's friend had made an initial payment of two mithan and some pigs, cloths and salt : he was now to bring two more mithan and receive possession of the bell.

This was a solemn moment, and the ceremonies we were to watch emphasized the great importance of the pact of friendship resulting from the transfer of the bell Rusi. It was late in the afternoon, and the sun was just disappearing behind Mount Domku, when a procession of some thirty men and women were seen climbing the hill slope below the village. Ahead walked two men leading a mithan, whose horns were adorned with long streamers of bamboo shavings, as well as a half-grown mithan calf. Next came a priest in ceremonial robes and a line of women, each of whom carried a basket of provisions. They were followed by Boki Tari, the purchaser of the bell and the prospective partner in the pact of friendship. He wore an impressive head-dress of yak's hair and he, as well as the men walking behind him, carried long spears in addition to the usual Tibetan swords. A priest, chanting prayers, brought up the rear of the procession.

The mithan were tied up outside Tani's house and the visitors went inside, sitting down by the hearths without any formality, the men in one group and the women in another. The two priests paced up and down the long room, chanting and swinging their bamboo whisks. Their song was in praise of the bell Rusi, moulded by gods and cherished by generations of proud possessors. They called on the spirits of the house and the locality begging them to show favour to the guests. Then they purified the food, sprinkling it with beer, and prayed, " May the food and drink be wholesome, may none who partake of the feast suffer pains in the stomach or belly ; may all eat and drink and part happily." Not until the priests had touched the vessels of millet beer with their whisks, and using gourd ladles, had poured a few drops on the mithan and on the floor of the house, was the beer served.

On the first evening of such a feast, I was told, it is customary for guests and hosts to drink beer brewed by the seller of the bell. On the following day the assembly would consume the beer brought by the purchaser.

In buying a Tibetan bell from young Chugdu Tani, Boko Tari forged another link in a net of ritual friendship pacts which covered a large part of the surrounding country. His home village lay in the hills beyond the Kamla some eight miles south-west of Rute-Hate and his friendship pacts and marriage alliance extended over nine villages situated in a roughly circular area with a diameter of some twenty-five miles.

The numerous visits which precede the transfer of a bell serve an important purpose. During these visits, each of which involves lavish entertainment, the families of the two prospective allies become acquainted and individual attachments spring up under the mantle of ceremonial friendship.

It is difficult to explain how these small bronze bells, which in Tibet rank among the paraphernalia of lamaistic ritual, came to be regarded as the supreme symbols of wealth and prestige. Fitted with silver or brass handles and tongue-like clapper, such bells are found in the possession of nearly every Tibetan lama and are rung in the course of prayers and incantations. The Daflas and Miris, however, are unaware of their character as musical instruments, and none of the *maje* I saw in the Subansiri area had clapper or handle. To the Daflas and Miris they are the work of gods, and as such they are cherished and handed down from generation to generation. Each *maje* is believed to be unique ; it has a distinctive name and is attributed with male or female sex.

Thus a complete change of function and significance seems to have accompanied the transfer of these bells from the sphere of Buddhist ritual to that of the tribal value system. Indeed the present rôle of *maje* among

199

the Miris recalls the use of Chinese porcelain jars and plates as symbols of wealth and currency for ritual payments among the Dayaks of Borneo and various hill-tribes of the Philippine Islands and the Moluccas. There too the use for which the ceramics were manufactured has been obliterated by the new values attributed to them in a different cultural milieu, and their attraction lies almost solely in the prestige which their possession lends to the owner. Similarly a Dafla values a *maje* not because it is useful or beautiful, but because as the owner of a certain well-known *maje* he gains in social status.

The anthropologist may point to the great rôle which the transfer of such Tibetan bells plays in establishing ritual friendships, but he cannot explain the change of significance without data from the area of contact between Tibetan and tribal culture. Were it possible to extend enquiries to the region where Daflas are in touch with populations practising lamaistic ritual, we might be able to trace the chain of associations which led the Subansiri tribesmen to consider Tibetan prayer bells as sacred objects fashioned by gods, the ceremonial transfer of which creates between seller and buyer a bond similar to that established by a marriage alliance. But this contact zone lay still far ahead and we began to doubt whether we would ever reach the sphere of direct Tibetan influence which seemed to hold the answer to so many problems.

14

LEGACY OF THE PAST

IN RUTE-HATE we were only on the threshold of the unexplored tract of country south of the Great Himalayan Range which all that season had been our ultimate objective, and now it looked as though we, like the Miri Mission thirty years earlier, would have to turn back at the very gateway to the promised land. Both our time and our barter goods were running short and the Miris never tired of telling us that when the waters of the Kamla rose with the spring floods crossing by raft would become impracticable. To be marooned north of the Kamla was a risk which personally I would have taken, but which neither Gocham Tapak nor any of our other interpreters, anxious to return to their families and fields, were prepared even to contemplate. And the shortage of supplies and exchange goods meant that wherever they ran out, we would be immobilized and unable to pay for either porters or food.

We had therefore to reconcile ourselves to the unpalatable fact that any further move would have to be limited to a very short reconnaissance into the area beyond the Indo-Tibetan trade divide. If this season it was impossible to reach the villages regularly visited by Tibetan traders, I wanted at least to gain an impression of the tribesmen who relied on trade with Tibet and were entirely independent of Assamese supplies, so that any subsequent touring could be planned with a greater knowledge of conditions in the country ahead.

After their initial reticence had worn off the Miris of Rute-Hate talked freely of their numerous connections with the people of the northern regions and particularly those of the Sipi valley. One of the main routes to the valley of the Upper Subansiri seemed to follow the valley of the Selu, an important tributary of the Kamla, and then to cross the snow-ranges which we could clearly see from a point above Rute-Hate. Another route ran from the Sipi valley across high ranges to Marra in the Subansiri valley and from there into Tibet.

Whether I wanted to visit the Selu, or the Sipi valley I had to pass through Göba, the nearest village north of Rute-Hate. For Göba lying at no great distance from the confluence of Selu and Kamla controlled the paths to Sartam and Tali, as well as to Nöyi in the Selu valley and Nilö on the banks of the Sipi. The friendliness of the people of Rute-Hate led us to believe that the time had now come to make plans for a forward move. So I asked Chaglo Tara to take a present of salt to his friends in Göba and invite them to my camp to discuss the prospects of a visit to their village. Late on the evening of his departure, however, Temi and Tapak came to my tent with news that quickly dispelled my optimism. Drinking beer in the house of Dame Tame they had been told of the panic that our approach had caused. When the news of our arrival in Mingö reached Rute-Hate all the villagers had fled taking their cattle and belongings to the forest, lest like the Nagas at the time of the Miri Mission, we speared and ate their mithan, pigs and fowls.

The people of Rute-Hate now recognized the difference between the Miri Mission and our small party that brought no foreign porters or armed escort and paid for all supplies in such valued commodities as cloth and salt. The Miris of the villages north of Rute-Hate, however, were still panicky and maintained that they would do all in their power to prevent any Government party from entering their territory.

Moreover, there were various families in Sibing-pa, a settlement near Rute-Hate, in Göba, and in Sartam and Tali who were greatly disturbed by our presence, because according to the tribal code of honour they were bound to avenge their kinsmen who had died at the hands of the Miri Mission.

Tapak and Temi had argued that I could not be held responsible for events that had occurred more than a generation ago. But could I disclaim all connection with the Miri Mission, which in the eyes of the tribesmen represented the power still ruling in the plains of Assam? I felt that it was better to lay the ghosts of 1912 and restore friendly relations between the North Kamla Miris and Government in a manner that satisfied the conscience of the tribesmen. Even if the majority of the villagers were ready to let bygones be bygones, embarrassing situations were bound to arise as long as blood remained between them and Government. It would have been awkward, for instance, if I had unwittingly tried to call at the house of one of the deceased's kinsmen. According to tribal law he could not have offered me hospitality and my behaviour would not only have given great offence but might well have led to a serious situation.

Convinced that it was no longer possible to ignore this difficulty, I broached the subject myself and appealed to Dame Tage, in whose hospitable house I had spent many hours, to help me to heal the old sores. I asked him to arrange for a meeting with the aggrieved parties so that matters could be settled in accordance with tribal custom.

That evening a dignified old man in a Tibetan style coat arrived in our camp. He was Haman Tabli of Sibing-pa. At the time of the Miri Mission, he said, the wife of his paternal uncle had gone to Mingö to visit her daughter. She was seen leaving Mingö with the presents she had received from her son-in-law, but she never reached Sibing-pa. Her relations searched for her everywhere, and she was eventually found dead near the Mingö–Rute-Hate path with her head severed from her body. That day Naga porters had passed along the path going south-wards, and there was no doubt in the minds of the Miris that on their way they had indulged in a little private head-hunting. Gocham Tapak, who as a boy had been with the Miri Mission, remembered the incident and told me that Captain Kerwood had only heard of the woman's death after he had left Rute-Hate. It is not mentioned in either of the printed reports, which only say that the discipline of the Nagas left much to be desired.

From what was remembered after thirty-three years it appears that these Naga porters were an absolute terror to the countryside. The Miris of all the villages I visited told of the indiscriminate killing of mithan, goat, pig and fowl; the Naga porters, they said, were quite uncontrolled, their camps being usually at some distance from those of the officers and sepoys, and moving in large convoys, they threw the villagers into a panic so that all fled from their houses. Against this background the suspicion and ultimate hostility of the villages of Sartam, Tali and Rugi which led to the abandonment of the Mission's plans was not altogether surprising, and I realized that a great deal of tact would be required to remove the latent resentment against Government and turn the Miris of the Upper Kamla valley into friends.

I began my campaign of reconciliation by telling Haman Tabli that I greatly regretted the murder of his aunt, which had certainly been committed without the orders and knowledge of the officers. As I was anxious that there should be no more blood between him and the men of Government, I was willing to compensate him for the death of his kinswoman. I had no mithan or Tibetan bells, for these I was unable to carry on the long journey I had made, but I would give him a silk cloth for the skin of his kinswoman, a brass bowl for her head, a string of beads for her intestines, and a quantity of salt to assuage his grief. I had learnt this way of specifying articles paid as compensation in the negotiations I had witnessed between Likha Teji and Nabum Epo, and Haman Tabli expressed no surprise at my assessment of his kinswoman's worth. Yet he did not seem satisfied and—rather surprisingly—asked for an additional twenty rupees. Whether he felt that these coins from the plains were more suitable reparation for a deed committed by men of Government, or whether he was acting on the suggestion of some member of my camp I do not know. But I was only too pleased to remove this cause of embarrassment, and gladly added twenty silver rupees to the other gifts. We sealed the peace with much rice-beer, and I felt that I had advanced in the esteem of a village that lay astride what was probably one of the most important routes towards Tibetan controlled territory.

On March 28th, my messengers returned from Göba. When I saw them coming up the hill with two unfamiliar figures, I thought this must mean that the Göba people would receive us with friendliness. But alas! Chaglo Tara, who had taken my message, and the two envoys from Göba explained dramatically that my going to that village would certainly lead to disaster. Göba's immediate neighbours, the men of Tumr, Sartam and Tali, had voiced their determination to kill us if we dared enter their country, and in Göba itself there was fierce opposition to my coming. The population of Göba consisted largely of two clans, Tungam and Tagro, and while the Tungam people had no strong feelings in the matter, the Tagro men still looked to revenge the death of their clansmen who had been killed when the first ' sahibs ' from India entered their country.

In Göba, Chaglo Tara had incidentally met two men of Nilö and their reaction too was anything but encouraging. They said that if I tried to come to their village, they would sew the paths with *panji* and fell the trees to block all approaches to the Sipi valley.

I used all the tact and persuasion I could command to make the two Göba men change their attitude. They were perfectly polite, and indeed had brought me gifts of beer and chickens, but they kept on repeating that they had come in order to save me from walking into danger. They and their clansmen had no quarrel with me, but the

Tagro men would not tolerate my visit, and even if I avoided Göba and went to Nilö, the Sartam warriors were likely to waylay me on the return journey.

There was nothing to do but to suggest that the visitors should rest in the house of one of their friends in Rute-Hate and come and see me again before they returned to their village. Perhaps, I thought, they might change their minds if they heard that we had in no way inconvenienced the people of Rute-Hate and paid for every service in salt and cloth. This assumption was correct. Next morning the envoys' attitude had noticeably softened. They would return to Göba, they said, and tell the villagers what manner of people we were. Two prominent men of Rute-Hate volunteered to accompany them and help in negotiating a brief trip to Göba and Nilö.

Hardly had the party left, when bringers of evil tidings arrived from the opposite direction. They were men of Mingö, Bidak and Güte, and the stories they brought threw Gocham Tapak and my other interpreters into a state little short of panic. The new arrivals besought me not to go any further. They claimed to have heard on excellent authority that the men of Sartam, Rugi and Tali—the villages that had clashed with the Miri Mission—were planning to avenge their losses of thirty-three years ago. If we ventured as far as Göba, they would certainly attack and kill us, and even if we went to Nilö, we might be ambushed.

Most disturbing, however, was the news that the Tali and Sartam men had heard of Gocham Tapak's presence in our camp. His father Kojum had been the principal interpreter of the Miri Mission and local rumour declared that on one occasion Kojum had taken part in the fighting ; they blamed Kojum for the misfortune that the Miri Mission had brought upon their fathers and sought to revenge themselves upon his son.

So far Tapak's familiarity with the country had been of considerable advantage, but his childhood association with the Miri Mission now proved anything but propitious. According to tribal custom a son is responsible for the deeds of his father, and in the area where hostilities had occurred Tapak was in enemy territory. He had been somewhat nervous ever since we had crosssed the Kamla, but the news brought by the messengers from Mingö and Bidak threw him into panic and I was seriously afraid that he might refuse to go any further. Such a defection would have been little short of a disaster for he was the only man in our party who had full mastery of the local dialect. While Temi and my other interpreter Nakr Mado, a Hill Miri settled near North Lakhimpur, experienced no difficulty in conversing with the Miris of the Lower Kamla, they had found it progressively harder to understand the tribesmen the further we moved up the valley, and here in Rute-Hate they could no longer be relied on for effective interpretation. In an atmosphere of latent suspicions and old grievances inexact translating can lead to fatal misunderstandings ; everything depended on Gocham Tapak and I devoted myself to bolstering up his morale and playing on his vanity as Government's principal go-between in all dealings with the Miris north of the Kamla.

The delay caused by the protracted negotiations with Göba was all the more deplorable as after a period of bad weather, the days were once more sunny and warm. No rain had fallen for two days and the felled trees and undergrowth on the newly cleared fields were sufficiently dry for firing. On many slopes the *jhum* were burning and the smoke from these field fires drifted over the landscape reducing visibility to a few miles and veiling the brilliance of the sun even at midday.

On the morning of Good Friday Dangme Tame and his picturesque son Tekin returned disgruntled from Göba. For reasons which a delegation of Göba men who, they said, were close behind them would explain, they had failed to persuade the villagers to agree to our visit. A few hours later a large party came over the hill, and as they filed down the wide open slope above our camp we were relieved to see that there were men as well as women and that all carried gifts of chickens and long bamboo vessels of beer.

With the help of our friends of Rute-Hate we soon got a conversation going, and I gave generous presents of salt and matches in return for the beer and the fowls they had brought. From the clan names of the men I gathered that all the settlements of Göba were represented in the party, and when their spokesman began to speak it was obvious that he was delivering a prepared statement. The long and the short of this lengthy speech was that though the people of Göba would like to be friends and welcome us to their village, they feared the men of Sartam and Tali would attack while we were in the village, and Göba would then get a bad name for failing to protect their guests. Göba was not on good terms with either Sartam or Tali, but if I postponed my visit until next year they would try to settle the dispute and arrange a *dapo*, which would also provide security to Göba's visitors.

206

I replied that I was not afraid for myself, but that I appreciated their difficulties and would not insist on a visit which might embarrass them. But if I could not go to Göba I would like to go to Nilö and it was for them and the men of Rute-Hate, many of whom had connections of marriage and friendship with the Nilö people, to help me find porters for that trip.

Shouts of protest followed these words. But when I added that I only wanted to visit the Sipi valley and could not spend more than two days in Nilö because I must hasten back to the Apa Tani country before the floods made the Kamla impassable, they fell to arguing anew among themselves. The astonishing outcome of the debate was the offer to take me not only to Nilö but also to Göba provided I was content with a brief visit, and did not make demands for porters which would interfere with their agricultural operations.

If I stayed only one night in Göba, the men of Sartam would have no chance of making trouble, and in Nilö they had sufficient friends to assure our safety.

I could hardly believe my ears, and accepted the offer with alacrity. Lest they change their minds I said we would start the day after to-morrow. We would travel with only the lightest of loads and leave the rest of the baggage in Rute-Hate where we would return after our visit to Göba and Nilö. Happy with this arrangement, everyone became very merry on the rice-beer that was passed round and the Göba people chatted animatedly to our Miri interpreters and the Apa Tanis, who understood about one word in three.

The Göba men left next morning promising to send porters to fetch us. Yet there was still another obstacle ahead. That same evening another group of Göba men, consisting of the relatives of a man killed by the Miri Mission, arrived in Rute-Hate and I feared that unless I succeeded in reconciling them, they might agitate against our visit. So, taking the bull by the horns, I sent word to the aggrieved men that I would like to meet them and talk over their complaints.

It was already dark when four elderly men appeared in camp. Their spokesman, Niktor Tasser, explained that at the time of the Miri Mission the people of Göba had been on friendly terms with the sahibs, and had even carried some of their loads. When the fighting broke out in Tali, the Sartam men called upon their friends in Göba to assist them in bringing hostilities to a close. Accordingly several Göba men, one of whom was Niktor Tasser's brother, went to Sartam in broad daylight and passed quite close to the camp. They could easily have made a detour, but thinking that the sahibs, with whom they had no quarrel, would do them no harm, they took the shortest route and were surprised when the sepoys opened fire. Two men were killed, one of whom was Tasser's brother. Later on, one of the sahibs called out to them to remove the bodies.

Gocham Tapak, who had been present at the incident, corroborated the story and told me that the sepoys had fired without orders and that the commanding officer had been furious at their lack of discipline.

However this may have been, the indignation of the victims' kinsmen was understandable, and I saw no other alternative but to make amends for the ill-judged and panicky actions of my forerunners. In taking this decision I realized that I might be blamed for admitting that even Government might have to pay compensation for losses inflicted in a military action. But I argued that in unadministered territory there was no code of law other than that of the tribesmen and that by their standards it was entirely honourable to end old feuds by paying compensation. Indeed, there seemed to be no better way of utilizing ' political presents ' than by putting an end to old grievances and turning potential enemies into the friends of Government.

I explained to the men that although I could not accept any personal responsibility for those past events I would be happy to set their minds at rest, and was prepared to give presents to the heirs and relatives of the men killed at Sartam. According to Miri custom, they replied, they should get one Tibetan bell, one mithan, one bronze plate, one string of beads of mithan value and various smaller items. This was the minimum price for a man's life and without such a payment it was impossible to restore friendly relations. I knew only too well that these demands were by no means excessive, but any payment on that scale would have placed an unbearable strain on my dwindling resources in barter goods. I said therefore that I was not going to pay blood-money for their deceased kinsmen, but that as gifts of good-will I would give the man's brother an Assamese silk cloth, a brass cup, some beads and a quantity of salt, and to each of the other three close kinsmen one cotton cloth and some salt.

This was such a windfall for Niktor Tasser and his cousins, that they accepted my gifts of reconciliation after only as much hesitation as dignity demanded. No one could now blame them for failing in their duty towards their kinsmen.

The Ghosts of the Miri Mission

A round of rice-beer sealed our friendship and it seemed that the ghosts of the Miri Mission had at last been laid. The last hurdle to our progress was removed and it appeared that only a catastrophic change in the weather or some other unforeseeable misfortune could frustrate our hopes of getting at least as far as Nilö.

15

UNFINISHED EXPLORATION

THE PORTERS from Göba arrived at the appointed time and early in the morning of April 2nd we set out for the Sipi valley. The heat was damp and oppressive, and the landscape so shadowed in haze, that on the whole journey we never saw more than a few hundred yards ahead. The day's march seemed long and tedious, and although the Miris showed great solicitude for our well-being, lending us their little plaited fans with which to stir the heavy atmosphere, we were glad when we climbed out of the last gulley.

In general lay-out the village of Göba was very similar to Mingö and Rute-Hate, but the people's style of dress clearly indicated that we had crossed the trade divide between Assam and Tibet. Tibetan woollen cloth and ornaments were in common use ; I did not see a single cloth of Assamese origin and salt, I was told, came from Tibet.

While the friendliness of our reception in Göba left little to be desired, disturbing news came from Nilö, whose inhabitants, it appeared, were divided on the desirability of our visit. They were reported to have argued that as no one from India and no one from Tibet had ever before visited their village, they saw no reason to break their age-old seclusion. They blamed the people of Rute-Hate for telling us of Nilö's existence, and threatened that if any harm resulted from our visit they would revenge themselves upon those who had shown us the way. Disheartening though this was, the reference to Tibet was interesting, for surely they would not have coupled visitors from Tibet with those from India if no Tibetans had ever been known to visit the villages within the orbit of their experience.

The Göba people asked me to defer our departure until the return of the men they had sent to Nilö to prepare the ground. In other circumstances, I would have acquiesced in this matter, and a few days' stay in Göba would not have been a waste of time. But we had rations

210

32. Chugdu Tagla, the leading man of Bidak village.

33. Miri woman of Rute-Hate village smoking a bamboo pipe.

34. A young Dafla man held prisoner in the Apa Tani village of Haja.

35. Miri woman of Dobom village with grass skirt.

for only a week, and the oppressive heat forebode a change in the weather, which the Göba people would almost certainly have used as an excuse to get out of the Nilö trip.

We were discussing matters round the fire in Chugdu Char's house, when a man burst into the room shouting that his daughter was dying. The child had just been shot in the chest by an arrow loosed by an infuriated neighbour from whom her father had stolen a pig, and he begged us to try and save her life. While I continued my negotiations, Betty collected her first-aid bag and followed two men to a house at the far end of the village. There she found a girl, perhaps eight years old, with a fresh arrow wound just above the chest-bone. Fortunately there was no immediate danger and the wound was soon disinfected and dressed. As doctor's fees, Betty was offered part of the disputed pig, but she considered it wiser not to share in such controversial meat. Even the most succulent cutlet did not seem worth the risk of an arrow from the bow of the pig's enraged owner.

Nevertheless I was sorry. I felt that we had deserved a better dinner than a plate of sticky red rice and some spiced *dhal*, for that 2nd of April happened to be our seventh wedding anniversary. After an unusually strenuous march, hours of exhausting argument in smoky houses and the treatment of a casualty thrown in for good measure, a juicy piece of fresh pork would have helped to make the celebration a happier occasion. It was the sixth year in succession that we had celebrated our wedding anniversary in jungle camps, sometimes in tents and sometimes in bamboo huts, and if such occasions did nothing else, they served to remind us of the delights of civilization which, as long as we had enjoyed them, we had accepted so casually. Dinner in the ballroom of the Berkeley seemed a curious contrast to this unappetizing fare, eaten off tin plates, in a village where an arrow quickly avenges the craving for ill-gotten pork.

Next morning we were up before dawn, anxious to start for the Sipi valley. Though this journey fell far short of our earlier ambitions, it marked a distinct advance into territory of which literally nothing was known. It took us two hours of argument to assemble sufficient porters ; the Göba men were reluctant to leave their beds, and there was so much discussion as to which particular men should accompany us that it was eight-thirty before we could start. Heading north-east, we climbed easily through old *jhum* and secondary jungle, but as soon as we entered the region of high forest the path deteriorated, and at one point we found ourselves feeling our way across a landslide which had torn the hill-side open for hundreds of feet. Looking up there was nothing to see but a wide channel of rubble, and looking down we gazed into a' disquietingly abrupt gorge. Even Gocham Tapak was worried and, clinging to an upturned root beside me, remarked that he had really hoped to live a few more years.

After a steady ascent of three hours, the path turned due north and we entered a narrow upland valley where storm-wrought confusion reigned amidst the giant trees, bamboos and bananas. Dungu Char begged us to make no noise while passing through this high country lest the deities of the mountain-tops were offended and showed their displeasure at the intrusion by sending bad weather. His warning must have come too late ; thunder soon proclaimed an approaching storm and the first heavy drops quickly turned to driving rain.

Laboriously we picked our way through the débris of broken branches, thick undergrowth and scattered rocks until, as evening drew near, we looked for a suitable camp site. It was growing dark when our guides pointed to a bamboo-covered slope not far from a small waterfall, and here at a crazy angle we set up our tent. The Miris put down offerings for the spirits of the mountain-tops and a fowl was sacrificed with a prayer for our safety. Then they set to work with swords and knives and quickly made excellent shelters, which were far more rain-proof than our battered tent.

We woke next morning stiff and sore from the night on the knobbly ground ; the forest was blotted out by mountain mist and for most of the morning we struggled along a path that was smothered in snow-broken jungle growth. Towards midday we came to a resting-place known as Ogu-Lutu, but instead of the view of the Sipi valley we had been promised, there was nothing but a bank of mist. The way improved, however, when we came to the area in which the people of Nilö are accustomed to hunt and graze their mithan, and for an hour we walked briskly down the back of a narrow spur where the path was good and the incline not too steep. Suddenly we heard voices. Our guides stopped and listened. We were close to the next resting-place, and the voices could only be those of Nilö men.

" The sahib should put on his hat," whispered Dungu Char to Tapak, " it would not look well if he met the Nilö men bareheaded like a slave or a young boy." Tapak quickly translated these instructions, and putting on our battered felt hats we escaped the embarrassment of entering on relations with Nilö with a social *faux pas.*

That there were loud and animated voices to be heard was, in itself, reassuring, for hostile Nilö warriors would have crouched in silence beside the path. In a few moments we came on a group of men sitting round a fire. They rose as we approached and among them I recognized the two young men from Rute-Hate and Göba, who had gone ahead to announce our coming. The others—there were perhaps six or seven —looked different from the tribesmen I had so far encountered. They wore round cane-hats with the narrowest of brims ; most of them were dressed in strip-sewn woollen clothes of Tibetan origin and wore necklaces of outsize beads made from white conch shell and pale blue porcelain.

They welcomed us in a calm and dignified manner. Nilö Takhe bade us sit down and we fell at once into easy conversation. He was a powerfully built man with a broad, massive face and disorderly short hair ; his clansman, the elderly Tedu, was taller and sparer with a longish face and small slit eyes. Through Tapak I explained that my only purpose in coming to Nilö was to pay them a friendly visit and to see the Sipi valley. Nilö Takhe replied that as long as we came alone and were free of contagious disease we were welcome, but of sepoys and foreign porters they would have none. I assured them that no porters other than their own Göba friends were with me. Then we drank millet beer together, and the Nilö men smoked their first cigarettes and learnt the magic of matches.

After a brief and friendly talk we left for the village. The path dropped rapidly through dense forest, and it was not until we reached an abandoned *jhum* that we had our first view of the Sipi valley.

So far our Miri companions had referred to our destination as Nilö ; now we discovered that just as the terms Likha and Licha are clan names used to denote localities inhabited by these clans, the name Nilö is that of a clan whose members are spread out over a number of separate villages, that include Rilu-Aio on the north bank and Linkü-Rangpu on the south bank of the Sipi river. The latter village lay just below us and we climbed down through fields and scraggy forest. It consisted of a small cluster of seven unusually broad houses built on high piles and roofed with palm leaves. I remarked on the different thatching material used here and in the Kamla valley and was told that in the villages of this area grass is not much used for roofing work.

We were taken to a level place beside Nilö Takhe's house, and within a few moments the entire population of the village had assembled. All were clad in Tibetan cloth, dyed deep shades of purple and red, and many women wore red woollen caps. None of the men, however, tied their hair in the front knot customary among the Apa Tanis, the Daflas and the Kamla Miris, and not only men, but even some women had their hair clipped in a short bob, so that it was often difficult to distinguish between the sexes.

Our first call was at the house of Nilö Takhe. The interior looked very much like the great halls of Miri houses with which we were familiar, and the etiquette of hospitality followed the same pattern. The beer was fortunately good, and though on the whole Miri beer seldom comes up to the standard of the best Dafla brews, and the connoisseur of Naga beverages has to forget the delicious Ao rice-beer to appreciate either, we were too thankful for the enthusiastic reception to pay much attention to the quality of the drink.

Nilö Takhe struck us at once as a man of character, and it was clear that he spoke not only for himself but also for the community. He was pleased, he said, that we had come to his village to make friends and establish contacts where previously none had been. He had heard of Assam, and of the events in the Kamla valley at the time of the Miri Mission. His own trade connections, however, lay to the north and from tribal neighbours in touch with Tibetans he and the people of Nilö were able to obtain salt, cloth, swords and beads. In exchange they gave skins and furs and, pointing to several deer skins hanging under the rafters, he showed us the type of goods the Sipi people sell. No, he said, in answer to my question, he himself had not been to Tibet. Once a year he went to a village known as Raba in the Möngö valley where he had a friend from whom he obtained all those commodities which he required. The path to Raba lay across the hills, and was so difficult that men without loads took three days to make the journey, while women and children could not complete it in under five. It was impossible to drive mithan along this path, and ceremonial exchanges of valuables between the people of Nilö and Raba were confined to Tibetan bells and beads.

The entries in my notebook jotted down during this first visit to Nilö Takhe's house are short and barren, for most of the conversation aimed at establishing confidence. A pleasant relaxed atmosphere can in such circumstances only be induced by chatter on ordinary topics and it would have been unwise as well as impolite to subject Nilö Takhe to a lengthy cross-examination at this stage of our acquaintance. Then, as so often on this tour, I found it difficult to combine exploration with detailed enquiries, and there can be no doubt that unless one has sufficient time to follow up the atmosphere of confidence established by such initial contacts, much of the energy and resources expended on rapid exploratory trips yields little in the way of detailed anthropological data.

The friendly tone of the conversation, punctuated with innumerable gulps of millet beer, greatly reassured my interpreters, who were at last convinced that we were in no danger of losing our lives. The risk of losing our sanity in the face of the people's unbridled curiosity, however, remained. Our cook-shed and our tent were the venue of all the villagers and both old and young never seemed to tire of handling our belongings and fingering our persons.

Since leaving Rute-Hate we had been constantly surrounded by people, and after three hard marches we were worn out. One would think that the thrill of entering a geographically and ethnographically unknown region would have proved sufficiently stimulating to banish all fatigue, but there is a limit to the capacity for enjoyment of even the most novel of experiences. Overwhelmed by the smothering attentions of the people of Nilö, we longed for nothing so much as sleep.

Khuike, our Naga boy, and our plucky low-caste cook were working under an equal strain. For days they had been regaled with stories of the savage and warlike spirit of the Sipi people and now their cook-shed was invaded by crowds of fierce looking men who frightened as well as exasperated them.

Next morning we were still in bed when Tapak announced the arrival of a large delegation of men and women from Rilu-Aio, the settlement on the slope opposite Linkü-Rangpu. I dressed hurriedly and went out to meet them. They brought gifts of chicken and beer and I presented them with salt, which they received with many expressions of appreciation, remarking on the excellence of the taste, and the whiteness and fineness of the grain.

The people from this settlement of the Nilö clan confirmed the impressions of the Sipi population I had had on the previous day. Not only in dress and general appearance, but also in physical type they differed from the tribesmen of the Kamla valley. Many of the men appeared to be round headed and had narrow slit eyes quite unlike those of the Kamla Miris and Daflas, which are on the whole large and deep set. They struck me as representing a developed Mongoloid type comparable perhaps to that found among certain Chinese populations, whereas most of the Assamese hillmen belong to the less highly specialized Palæo-Mongoloid group.

A little after the main crowd of visitors came Nilö Terü of Rilu-Aio. He waited for me on the path outside the village and explained his aloofness by saying that he had a new-born son at home. He was anxious to avoid the turmoil which surrounded the tents, for it seems that the slightest misadventure which befalls a father in the days following a son's birth, would automatically affect the new-born child. I admired Terü's cloth, which consisted of strips of woollen fabric woven in a pleasing pattern of colours. Within a few minutes he began to talk quite freely and showed no hesitation in telling me of routes that lead from the Sipi valley to the focal points of trade in Tibetan goods from where he had procured the clothes he was wearing.

The Nilö people, and presumably also the inhabitants of other villages in the Sipi valley, obtain most of their Tibetan goods by way of the Möngö valley, which lies on one of the trade routes linking the Sipi and the Upper Subansiri. On the Survey of India map the Möngö river, described as Menga, is tentatively sketched as flowing into the Subansiri. But all my informants were agreed that the Möngö is a tributary of the Sipi, and they pointed out the ridge behind which lies the confluence of the two rivers.

The Nilö people reach the Möngö valley by a path which traverses the hills to the north of the Sipi and leads to Tamin, a village on the right bank of the Möngö. Then, crossing the river by a suspension bridge, they come to Tamro ; from Tamro the route runs over the mountains that separates the Möngö and the Subansiri, and, passing through the villages of Moye, Doyam, Bakti and Moso, reaches Marra, a region in the Upper Subansiri valley, and the big village of Sheke which is often visited by Tibetans. None of the men I talked to had ever been as far as Marra, but they said that from the Sipi valley Sheke could be reached in six or seven days.

Through their trading partners in the Möngö valley they obtained supplies of Tibetan goods, and there was for them no need to proceed further into the country, where they would lack the protection which only trusted friends can afford the traveller.

Here it is mainly the lack of security which stands in the way of long-distance trading. In the Central Himalaya, and particularly in Nepal, the trader who journeys to Tibet to buy salt and other goods will also visit villages in the lower ranges, and some travel even as far as the plains of India, so that in the course of the year the same man is likely to traverse the entire breadth of the Himalaya. There is no comparable flow of trade in the Subansiri area. Tibetans do not venture any great distance into the country of tribesmen who are a law unto themselves, nor is there any trading community comparable to Sherpas or Bhutias who could serve as middlemen between Tibet and the sphere of Indian economic influence. The absence of good communications alone would be no obstacle, for many of the paths in the Kamla region are no worse, though much less frequented, than the paths over which the Sherpas and other Himalayan trading communities maintain a regular traffic of porter-borne goods.

When the last visitor from Rilu-Aio had disappeared down the hill-side we climbed up to Nilö Takhe's house and sat down at his fire-side ; over the first mug of rice-beer he suggested that he and I should conclude a *dapo*, a treaty of friendship. He offered to provide a mithan for sacrifice, if I for my part would reciprocate with a comparable present. Nothing could have suited me better than to have a ceremonial friend on one of the main routes to the Upper Subansiri, but I feared that the conclusion of such a pact would strain my already meagre resources. The exchange of gifts of equal value is an essential part of every treaty of friendship and what could I give Nilö Takhe to match the mithan he had proffered ? Lest I be put under too great an obligation, I gave my present first. I chose a very good green woollen blanket, which I had bought in Shillong and added a string of large red beads. But the blanket did not meet with Takhe's approval. It was suggested that he would prefer an Assamese silk cloth, and accordingly I made the necessary replacement.

Shortly afterwards Takhe brought a smallish mithan and tied it up near my tent. Then everyone sat about waiting. I sent Tapak to Takhe's house to see what had happened, and he returned saying that Takhe expected me to make my gift up to the value of the mithan. This put me in a dilemma. I could not exhaust my dwindling supply of exchange goods for the sake of a *dapo* pact with Nilö Takhe, but on the other hand, it would have been foolish to reject an offer of friendship in a new and perhaps vital area.

My hesitation created great embarrassment and the tension grew with every minute of indecision. Tapak was alarmed at the prospect of offending Takhe, who had retired to his house and awaited a new offer. His attitude was not unreasonable, for the prestige of a man depends not

217

only on the value of the gifts he is able to give, but also on the value of those gifts he is thus entitled to receive. Judged by tribal standards my gifts were paltry. They compared unfavourably with the substantial valuables customarily exchanged when establishing a formal alliance and in accepting so meagre a gift Takhe would, under ordinary circumstances, suffer a great loss of face.

In the end I decided to discuss matters with Takhe. I explained to him the impossibility of carrying numerous valuables with me on far-flung journeys. But friendship with the representatives of the rulers of the Indian plains, I pointed out, would add to his fame and if in the following year we came through his village on our way northwards, he and his villagers would benefit from friendly co-operation with Government.

Gocham Tapak added his persuasions to my argument and finally Takhe agreed to sacrifice the mithan and leave the question of further gifts to me.

Everyone was pleased. The elders gathered round with smiles on their faces and the young men of the village began to dig two holes in front of my tent. In one they planted a *tage*, a thorny tree with fire-red blossoms, which easily takes root. The *dapo* mithan was tied to it, and a priest recited incantations, praying that this pact of friendship would endure in future generations. A man of Takhe's house then beheaded the mithan ; and the blood was allowed to flow over the second hole into which I was presently invited to erect an upright stone. This stone was set up for Takhe. Nearby, two more stones were set up at right angles : the upright stone was for myself and the flat one for my wife. Takhe then declared before the assembled villagers that henceforth my enemies would be his enemies, and that on my next visit he would accompany me to his friends in the Möngö valley : no one in that area would harm me when it became known that I had concluded a *dapo* with Nilö Takhe.

To end the ceremony I presented Takhe with a brass bowl, a fairly lasting symbol of friendship, and gave him a cotton cloth for his young son, who, in case of Takhe's death, would automatically take over the *dapo* obligations.

The rest of the day was spent in visiting other prominent villagers. In one house I met Nilö Tasso, who as a young boy had been captured while visiting Mingö and had subsequently been sold to the father of our friend Chugdu Tagla of Bidak. He had grown up as Tagla's slave, married a slave-girl, who though not of Nilö clan was like himself from Linkü-Rangpu. Two years ago, however, he had killed Tagla's brother in a drunken brawl, and fearful of Tagla's wrath he had fled to his home village. There, sheltered by Nilö Takhe and his other kinsmen, he thought himself safe as long as he did not venture into the Kamla valley.

An interesting point in this story is the comparative ease with which Tasso and his wife escaped from Bidak. If even after the excitement that followed the murder of Tagla's brother, both the offender and his wife could leave Bidak, why had they not taken an earlier opportunity to return to their home village? It seems that like so many other 'slaves' Tasso had never tried to leave his owner, and had it not been for the drunken quarrel, he might have continued to live in Bidak with no thought of ever rejoining his clansmen.

It was late in the afternoon of our last day in Nilö that three men from Nöyi village came to see us. Nöyi lies in the Selu valley, and the visitors had crossed the hills separating the Selu from the Sipi on hearing of our arrival. Curiosity seems to have been the main incentive for this long journey, but I gave them some salt to take back to their village as an offering of good-will. One of the three, a youth in his teens, was the most beautiful creature I had seen for a long time. Among the crowd of grimy, coarse-featured tribesmen and squat unattractive women, the beauty of this slim graceful youth seemed almost miraculous. I could not take my eyes from the symmetrical oval face, the fine narrow nose, and the perfectly modelled mouth which broke into an irresistible smile when he received my gift of salt.

But there were other things to do than to indulge in the admiration of a beautiful face. The Göba men who had carried our luggage clamoured for a speedy return. They had exhausted the provisions which they had brought with them, and as food was scarce that year in Linkü-Rangpu they were given only grudging hospitality in the houses of their Nilö friends.

That night they could gorge themselves on the meat of Takhe's sacrificial mithan, but next day they would be without food. Moreover, they were anxious to get back to their fields, where much had to be done during these days of beneficial rain.

The entire population of Linkü-Rangpu, with additions of curious villagers of the neighbourhood, came to watch our departure. There was no difficulty over the number or weight of the loads and no real reason for any argument or discussion, but adding their voices to those of our porters, the onlookers produced a noise extraordinary even for these hills, where the habit of shouting across valleys has invested the human voice with unusual power.

In the midst of this vocal pandemonium we took a most cordial farewell of Nilö Takhe and the elders of the village, and set off with many assurances of everlasting friendship. To retrace one's steps is an anti-climax on every exploratory trip, and that day we knew that we were turning back from the furthest point we would reach that season. To add discomfort to melancholy it rained steadily for the first twenty-four hours, and we spent the night in the dripping forest with leeches attacking from every side.

When next day we reached Göba, we would have been glad to rest, but the crowds who gathered before the porters even put down their loads included envoys from several neighbouring villages. While we had been in Nilö, it appeared, the Miris of the Upper Kamla and the Selu had come to the conclusion that good relations with Government could only be to their advantage. Everybody seemed anxious to give me information and to encourage me to come to their villages. Morbem Takhio of Tumr, a village which a week ago had declared itself hostile to Government, gave me a detailed account of the way to Agla Marra, which he himself had visited several times. From Tumr, a village close to the confluence of Kamla and Selu, it was three days to Soreng, which was the home village of Takhio's wife. From Soreng, he said, one must follow a northward path to Hai, the last major settlement before the snow-range that separates the Kamla basin from the valley of the Upper Subansiri. It takes about three days to cross this range, but although there is often snow on the passes, this route is usually closed only during one month of the year.

Beyond lies Agla Marra, also known as Agla Nime or ' Near Tibet '. Coming from Soreng and Hai one first reaches Tachi, a village on the right bank of the Subansiri, and from Tachi one crosses the river by a suspension bridge, and thus reaches Tape, a village on the left bank. The people of Agla Marra were akin to the tribesmen of the Selu valley and cultivated in much the same way, growing millet and maize on hill-fields. In addition to cattle they kept yak and sheep and large fierce dogs. They dressed in clothes made of wool, and some even had iron armour and guns which had been imported from Tibet.

When in 1953 I travelled in Eastern Nepal, it struck me that Agla Nime might be an area comparable to the Sherpa area of Khumbu, which though lying to the south of the Great Himalayan Range, is essentially Tibetan in character and could well be described as 'Near Tibet'. If it is true that yak are kept and yet millet is grown, the altitude of Agla Nime must be between 8,000 and 10,000 feet, for yak do not thrive below this altitude and maize and millet cannot be grown much above it. There is, of course, the possibility that these crops are cultivated only in the valley area of the Subansiri, whereas yak and sheep are bred in side valleys, high above the course of the river.

Tibetans from Erü Nime (Far Tibet) are said to come to Agla Marra at all times of the year and from this it would seem that there is a route which does not entail crossing the Great Himalayan Range. It may follow the valley of the Subansiri in the same way that some of the trade routes between Tibet and Nepal avoid snowbound passes by leading along the banks of such rivers as the Rongshar and the Sun Kosi.

Morbam Takhio offered to take me to Agla Marra, if I wanted to go there after the rains, and this offer was repeated by men from Nöyi who promised to provide the necessary porters. Just when my stock of trade goods was nearly exhausted, all difficulties vanished and the road to the north and the mythical McMahon Line seemed clear. At that time I was confident that the Government of India would continue the policy of exploration in that part of the Himalaya, and during the return journey to the Apa Tani country I spent a great deal of time and energy on consolidating our lines of communications by gathering information on personal relationships and forging ties of friendship with the villages *en route*.

The return to Rute-Hate was uneventful. The Göba people, though eager to start work on their fields, carried our loads without protest and our friend and guide Dungu Char was as charming and courteous as he had been on the way up. At every difficult place he pointed out the easiest steps to take and the best creepers to afford a handhold. His behaviour towards Betty was of a gallantry surprising in a people among whom women are not considered in need of specially solicitous treatment. Even though Betty is rather more agile than I, and much more sure-footed, Char helped her over every obstacle and watched carefully lest she slipped on the steeper slopes.

We often wondered how it was that the members of the Miri Mission had arrived at so different an impression of the tribesmen. Their official report implies that the Miris are inclined to be arrogant and truculent, and the statement that only 'the presence of a large force draws out the latent affections of the hillman ' is only one of several hastily drawn conclusions. My own experience is entirely to the contrary. Although I went about unarmed and with so small a party that even self-protection would have been impossible, I never encountered the slightest sign of arrogance ; everywhere I was treated with courtesy and friendliness, and even when I was told that it would be impossible to arrange for any particular journey I wanted to make, the excuses put forward were couched in the politest of terms. Far from being the treacherous savages of popular belief in Assam, the Miris of these hills struck me as cheerful companions, and the most warm-hearted of friends.

Offers of future co-operation multiplied as we retraced our steps down the Kamla valley. Dungu Tamin of Rute-Hate proposed to conclude a *dapo* rite, and the sacrifice of a goat accompanied by the planting of a *tage* tree and the setting up of stones sealed the pact of friendship. In my opinion such *dapo* pacts are a more dependable guarantee of personal safety than the largest practical escort. For the breach of *dapo* obligations draws supernatural sanctions upon the head of the culprit, whom the god Potor-Met, as the guardian of such pacts, afflicts with a paralysis resulting ultimately in death.

On the day we left Rute-Hate another visitor from Nöyi arrived. He was reported to be an important man, and he invited me to his village, saying that a mithan was being held in readiness for the *dapo* rites, and that next year his clansmen would take me to Soreng and across the snows to Agla Marra. There was no doubt that the amount of cloth and salt earned by Göba and other villagers as porters' wages had impressed the people of the Selu valley. They obviously thought that they too might make friends with travellers dispensing such useful commodities.

The news from Sartam, Rugi and Tali was no less encouraging. These villages, which had opposed the progress of the Miri Mission, and had at first announced their intention of fighting rather than allow me to enter their territories, had now changed their tune. They sent envoys to Göba with a message that they were willing to end the old feud by making a *dapo* ; they would provide the necessary mithan, if I in turn would free them from the obligation to revenge their dead by paying nominal compensation, as I had done in the case of Rute-Hate and Göba. Once peace was restored, they would give me porters and all the help I required to reach the snow-ranges and Agla Marra.

It was tragic that in the face of all these promising offers we had to turn south instead of north. Had we had sufficient supplies we might have braved the monsoon, and even so late in the season have made a dash for Agla Marra. But our barter goods were running out and the necessity to return to Duta seemed inexorable.

The only difficulty that complicated our departure from Rute-Hate was Bhattachariya's inability to walk. He had sprained an ankle on the day before we left for Nilö, and we had had to leave him behind in Rute-Hate in the care of Temi. Even after a week's rest his foot was still extremely painful and it was obvious that he could not walk back to the Apa Tani country. A stretcher or a carrying chair was out of the question on the paths by which we were to travel, but fortunately he was light enough for our two Apa Tanis and one stout Miri to take turns in carrying him pick-a-back. I am afraid he had a very uncomfortable journey ; at the end of a march he often arrived cramped and sore, but throughout this ordeal he retained his good spirits and never uttered a word of complaint.

After a night in Mingö we went on to Bidak, where Chugdu Tagla had prepared an excellent camp. He insisted on one day's halt in his village, and though my interpreters were impatient to recross the Kamla as long as the good weather lasted, I did not have the heart to refuse.

Ever since our first meeting Chugdu Tagla had talked of providing a mithan for a *dapo* pact. The news that I had concluded such a pact with Nilö Takhe, however, upset his plans. There had been blood between Tagla and the Nilö clan from the day that Nilö Tasso, whom I had met in Linkü-Rangpu, had speared Tagla's younger brother. He told me quite frankly that for a long time he had been planning to raid the house that sheltered his brother's murderer. Would I object to such a raid now that I had concluded a *dapo* with Nilö Takhe ?

The question put me in an awkward position, for it was obvious that for years to come Government would have no power to prevent raiding in areas as remote as the Sipi valley. Yet, to declare myself disinterested would, in the eyes of the Miris, have devalued all the *dapo* pacts I had so far concluded. So I replied that I would certainly disapprove of a raid undertaken against a village with which I had formally made friends, and that Tagla's legitimate claims should be settled by negotiation. I pointed out that as both the Chugdu and the Nilö clans were now friends of Government, they should avoid fighting amongst themselves, and I suggested that as Dangme Tame of Rute-Hate, whom I had invested with the red mantle of a Government

223

headman, was on good terms with both parties, he should act as go-between and negotiate a settlement. Dangme Tame, who had accompanied me as far as Bidak, promised to do his best, and Tagla agreed to go ahead with the *dapo* ceremonies.

The rite was performed. A *tage* tree was planted, stones were erected, and Dangme Tame, acting in his priestly capacity, invoked the immortals, praying Potor-Met and all the great gods to witness the rite and guarantee the eternal friendship between Tagla's clan and all the sahibs who ever came to Bidak.

To seal the *dapo*, I gave Tagla an Assamese silk cloth and three large cornelian beads, which I had bought in an antique shop in Hyderabad. Tagla was renowned as a collector of beads, and delighted with my gift, he emphasized that it was such beads that the Miris valued and not the red and blue bazaar beads which we had been using as exchange goods.

Later in the day he invited us to his house and showed us his large collection. From strongly made baskets hidden in the attic, Tagla drew string after string of valuable beads. Some were white and as large as pigeons' eggs, others were made of turquoise matrix and deep blue lapis lazuli, some were of sky blue porcelain and yet others were fashioned from conch shell. The pride of Tagla's collection was a necklace of large cornelian beads, which he had collected one by one over a period of years; well matched and of a wonderful rich colour they were a delight to look upon.

Tagla was not only one of the richest, but he was also one of the most married men among my Miri acquaintances. The list of his wives comprised ten names, and I am not sure whether it was complete. He had married only one of these ladies with ' great rites ', eight he had married with minor rites and one he had abducted. As they came from seven different villages in the valleys of Kamla and Khru, Tagla's ' in-laws ' were scattered over a very wide area.

Among Miris as among the Daflas of the Panior and Kiyi areas a man's status and influence depends largely on his position in a net-work of alliances, and marriages as well as the ceremonial transfer of Tibetan bells are indispensable devices in extending this network. But it would seem that in the Kamla region clan memberships is also an important factor in determining social alignments. While in the Panior and Kiyi regions two men of the same clan think nothing of disrupting the solidarity of their clan by raiding each other, such Miri clans as the

224

Kabak group present, despite internal jealousies, a united front to the outside world.

Long ago the ancestors of the Kabak clan are believed to have lived in the Upper Kamla valley ; from there they migrated southwards, and establishing themselves in the locality now known as Mingö, experienced a period of rapid growth which resulted in the founding of three sub-clans known as Ragchak, Rogum and Rogrom. While the Rogrom branch settled in the hills to the east where, centred on the village of Hova, it now forms the bulk of the population, the Rogum people crossed the Kamla and founded the village of Lapchi-Lapche. The Ragchak branch, on the other hand, remained in Mingö and, spreading over the surrounding villages of Bidak, Gope and Balu, put out new shoots now known under the names of Chugdu, Changmo, Chaglo, Chagia, Chagrak and Chagdo. The dynamic character of the Kabak clan is a good example of the growth of clan communities in the Subansiri area. It is remarkable that within the span of a few generations an immigrant clan, settled originally in a single village, was able to extend its dominance over a large tract of country, and to retain its political cohesion and its character as an exogamous unit, despite a process of progressive fission resulting in the emergence of individual lineages identified by separate clan names.

From Bidak to Dobom we followed the route on which we had come. Then, instead of returning to Chemir, we dropped into the valley of the Kamla and crossed the river immediately below Rakhe. The Dobom men were doubtful whether we could still cross the river by raft and they had prepared two long canes in case it should be necessary to improvise a *sole*, a single-rope bridge across which one hauls oneself hand over hand. Such bridges are common in these hills, but fortunately I was never compelled to drag myself across some gaping valley, hanging several hundred feet above the level of the water, for I fear that the only way I could have made the passage would have been bundled up like a piece of luggage and propelled by porters on either bank. When we reached the river bank, however, we found the water still shallow enough for the use of rafts and I was saved from the ignominious experience of a *sole* crossing.

In Rakhe, Guch Tamar and his men as well as a large delegation of Apa Tanis were gathered together for the final negotiations between Hari and the Miris of Chemir. After two days' discussion, a compromise was reached, and I had the satisfaction of seeing the end of the long drawn-out feud, which for more than a year had paralysed all trade between Miris and Apa Tanis.

From Rakhe it was only three days to Duta, but these last three marches were fraught with more difficulties and annoyances than the six weeks of the North Kamla tour. The agricultural season had just begun, and in Rakhe we had to leave behind several loads to be dispatched as soon as transport was available. When we came to the Dafla village of Taplo, we realized at once that so small a settlement could not furnish sufficient men to replace the porters recruited in Rakhe. Some of them agreed to accompany us to Duta, but several men changed their minds during the night and, abandoning a day's wages, ran off home. The few men who had enlisted at Taplo, soon regretted their decision, and dropping their loads on the path, faded away into the forest. In the end it was the Apa Tani delegates returning from the *mel*, the Government interpreters and our Naga boy Khuike who pocketed their pride, and staggering under the unaccustomed weights, brought all the loads safely back to Pape.

This sudden breakdown of the transport arrangements was only partly due to the pressure of work at the opening of the agricultural season. The main reason was my inability to pay for services in kind. Rupee coins were to the tribesmen north of the Apa Tani valley of little value; I had exhausted my supplies of barter goods and I could not even promise payment in salt and cloth on arrival in Duta, for I did not know whether the store held sufficient stocks to meet such commitments.

Fortunately our return coincided with the arrival of a consignment of cloth from Joyhing and I was able to reward the men who had carried my loads to the Apa Tani country.

Once more established in our house at Pape, I enjoyed a few days' anthropological work among the Apa Tanis. Government had decided to suspend all operations in the hills during the rains; the Political Officer and all the Assam Rifles had left the Apa Tani country more than a month before, and I began winding up the store at Pape and making arrangements for the return of the staff to Joyhing. I sent them off in relays and, leaving with the last party, allowed myself the longest possible time in which to round off my investigations.

The political scene was, however, still confused, for no settlement between the Licha Daflas and the Apa Tanis had yet been achieved. In the course of his stay in Kirum the Political Officer had taken several prisoners by way of reprisal for Licha's behaviour, and these he had handed over to the Apa Tanis as hostages when he and the Assam Rifles withdrew to Joyhing.

On my first visit to Haja I found one of these prisoners sitting on the low railing of a verandah animatedly chatting with several Apa Tani girls. His left foot was encased in a massive block of wood, which whenever he wanted to move he lifted with the help of a string. A young man with a jolly full-moon face, he did not look at all like the renowned warrior who had achieved a certain notoriety among Apa Tanis (Pl. 34). He seemed well fed, and he told me in great detail of his brother's attempts to collect the mithan which would pay for his ransom. His only complaint was of the dullness of his life, but his boredom was undoubtedly relieved by flirtations with the Apa Tani girls who came to dally round his prison and by the frequent visits of Dafla friends from Talo and Nielom.

Licha Saha, who was one of the men who had come forward to negotiate with us at Kirum, was in the custody of another patrician of Haja. Being old and decrepit he was not fettered, but lived in the house of his gaoler more like a guest than a prisoner. He was allowed a good deal of freedom and more than once he came to see me at Pape to discuss the possibilities of a settlement with Licha.

The unresolved problems the Political Officer had had to leave behind him underline very clearly the pitfalls that attend executive action in an area in which the machinery for a full and permanent administration has still to be set up. To arrange for negotiations between disputing parties in Talo and Likha, and watch the ensuing *mel* as an interested and potentially powerful observer was one thing. But to try and enforce decisions and arrest—or rather capture—Daflas who had ultimately to be handed over to their opponents as hostages was another. Little had been gained by such drastic action, and while doing their best to establish a rule of law the officers of Government had against their will become deeply involved in tribal politics.

Looking back on the experience of our two seasons in the Subansiri I am convinced that exploration and a thorough study of political, social and economic conditions of an area must under all circumstances precede any active interference in the inhabitants' affairs. It is impracticable to explore an area, and to claim at the same time the right to administer justice or to enforce settlements on disputing parties. Mediation may sometimes be feasible and acceptable, but without a fair knowledge of tribal custom even mediation is rarely successful. The idea that tribesmen proudly conscious of their age-old independence will easily concede to newcomers the right to lay down the law is utterly unrealistic, and while, in order to avoid trouble, they may at times comply with the wishes of a party displaying superior strength, they will consider such compliance only as a temporary necessity.

Our return to the plains through Mai and Potin was favoured by unseasonably dry weather and we lingered in these villages long enough to allow me to check my notes on Dafla agriculture. On May 22nd we reached Joyhing and in the steaming heat of the Assam plains began work on the plans for next season's touring. To reach Agla Marra and the Tibetan border seemed only a matter of organizing supplies and barter goods, for the ceremonial friendships we had concluded and the contacts we had made seemed to assure us safety of passage. Indeed I was convinced that with a small party a northward move through the Kamla and Selu valley could now be completed with little difficulty and no great expenditure.

But it was not to be. The Government of India decided not to send out an expedition in the winter of 1945–46, and to postpone indefinitely the exploration of the tribal country along the Tibetan border. In 1948 political work in the Apa Tani and Dafla country was resumed by Lt.-Col. Betts, whose wife, writing under her maiden name Ursula Graham-Bower, has given us a brilliant account of the gradual extension of Government's control over part of the Subansiri area.[1] They were the first to enter the Palin valley, but circumstances prevented them from following up the exploration of the regions north of the Kamla, and the valley of the Upper Subansiri, the Agla Marra of the Miri tribesmen, remains to this day *terra incognita*.

[1] Cf. *The Hidden Land*, London, 1953.

EPILOGUE

A<small>T THE</small> end of our peregrinations through the hills and valleys
of the Subansiri we may well have asked ourselves whether the
results of the enterprise were at all proportionate to the exertions
and expenditure, and to the large apparatus of staff and porters involved.
The anthropologist who goes to live among a tribe for a year or two
with no preoccupation other than the study of its social and cultural
life returns with notebooks full of detailed information and—if he is
at all worth his salt—with a well-rounded and integrated picture of the
society he has investigated. For him there is a direct and a fairly stable
correlation between the energy and ingenuity expended, and the value
of the material contained in his records.

When anthropological research is combined with political under-
takings and the geographical exploration of a large tract of country
inhabited by a number of different tribes, tangible results are not necessarily
commensurate with the effort and material resources expended. The thrill
of entering new country and of turning the tribesmen's suspicion to
friendship, and the satisfaction of overcoming difficulties of transport or
supply are not fully reflected in the bare entries in notebooks and diaries.
Indeed it may often appear that many days' effort have resulted in only
minute additions to the investigator's ethnographic knowledge. Too
many hours may have been spent in negotiation and argument, too many
days in trudging through sodden jungles and climbing over uninhabited
hills, to allow of a great accumulation of systematized knowledge. The
concrete information obtained in the ten days of an exhausting trek may
be less than the outcome of a few mornings' anthropological enquiry
with intelligent informants.

In evaluating the outcome of our two seasons' travel in the Subansiri
area, one must distinguish between the anthropological results, and those
more practical achievements which were of immediate interest to the
Government of India. These practical achievements stood throughout in
the forefront of official policy, and it is they which in the eyes of Government justified the considerable expenditure on transport and barter goods.

229

Epilogue

At the beginning of 1944 the influence of the Government of India reached no further than a few miles beyond the 'Inner Line' and the Apa Tanis as well as the majority of Daflas in the region of Panior and Kiyi had no contact with representatives of Government. Indeed, the Miri *posa*-holders, those 'pensioners of Government', were virtually the only hillmen with whom Political Officers had regular, though infrequent, official dealings.

By May 1945 the picture had completely changed. In a large area, including the densely populated Apa Tani valley, representatives of Government were on friendly terms with the tribesmen, and hundreds of Apa Tanis, Daflas and Miris had worked for Government as porters. A trade depot established at Pape had brought Indian goods into the heart of the Apa Tani country, whence they had found their way to many neighbouring villages, and the advantages of economic co-operation with Government had impressed itself on a wide circle of tribesmen who had previously had little or no contact with the Plains.

At the same time, the scanty knowledge of conditions in tribal country, which even in 1944 had been mainly based on the reports of the Miri Mission of 1912, had been augmented by the results of systematic observation among Apa Tanis as well as Daflas and Miris, and a body of knowledge on inter-tribal relations, agriculture, tribal economics and trade made it possible to formulate future policy in the light of factual information. Further investigations in the field, moreover, such as those carried out by Lt.-Col. and Mrs. Betts in 1948 and 1949, were facilitated by the existence of a core of trained interpreters as well as by the good-will of a number of prominent men well disposed to the officers of Government.

These achievements, though not inconsiderable, nevertheless fell far short of the effective control established by the Government of India in such areas as the Naga hills. True, the operations in the Kiyi valley had taught the tribesmen that Government officers intervening in an inter-tribal dispute might, in attempting to achieve a settlement, exert considerable pressure on one or both parties. The methods which had been employed resembled procedures familiar to Daflas and Apa Tanis : an arrest was in their eyes indistinguishable from a capture, and the punitive burning of a village appeared only as a variation of a raid. It did not take the tribesmen long to discover, however, that Government's intervention in tribal disputes could be countered by a policy of procrastination, elusion and temporary withdrawal. The superiority of

230

arms of the Assam Rifles was recognized, and at times even over-rated, but the tribesmen's awe of fire-arms was largely offset by the realization that the narrowest screen of forest provided protection from a passing column, and that Government parties could not maintain themselves in forward camps without the help of tribal porters.

It was only the Apa Tanis, the most settled and most civilized of the Subansiri tribes, whose attitude towards Government could not be guided by such considerations. Dwelling in large permanent villages and dependent on the uninterrupted cultivation of their carefully tended land, they had—and always will have—to come to a *modus vivendi* with any power strong enough to establish itself for any length of time in their valley. Peaceful cultivators and resourceful traders, the Apa Tanis can, however, only profit from a policy of pacification, and a clash of interests is likely to arise only in the event of outside interference with the traditional social and economic order and the customary laws of the tribe.

The Daflas and the Miris, on the other hand, shifting cultivators without attachment to permanent village sites, warlike, independent and scattered in relatively small groups over a vast mountain country, pose innumerable problems for any administration that attempts to establish a measure of regular control.

The first of these problems is the difficulty of communications. The tracks linking Dafla and Miri villages with the plains of Assam cannot be negotiated by pack animals and all loads have to be transported on the backs of porters. Many of these tracks become impassable during the rains, and swollen streams often interrupt even village to village communications.

To build roads and bridges suitable for wheeled traffic would require such enormous resources that it can hardly be considered a practical solution. If even the Ledo Road, built during the war to link Assam with Burma and China, had to be abandoned soon after completion because the cost of maintenance would have vastly exceeded its economic value, there is little likelihood that the limited commerce of small tribal populations would justify the construction of motorable roads in one of the world's most difficult mountain countries. With torrential rain and periodic earth tremors often causing large land-slides, even the maintenance of bridle-paths would prove an expensive undertaking. Yet, without a network of bridle-paths, linked by iron suspension bridges spanning unfordable rivers, it would be impossible to extend effective

231

political control over the hills. Air-droppings and the use of helicopters could ease the problem of supplying advanced outposts, but the potentialities of airborne transport are limited by the character of the country which, with the one exception of the Apa Tani valley, offers no terrain suitable for landing strips.

Porters, and in some areas perhaps pack animals, will therefore be the main means of transport for a long time to come, and there is no doubt that improved communications will result in an increase in traffic and that this will make for greater security on the more frequented highways.

When I first arrived in the Subansiri area no Apa Tani dared to use the path through the Dafla villages of Selsemchi and Potin, but as soon as large porter convoys began to pass along this route, it was considered safe even for small parties of Apa Tanis travelling on private business. The same phenomenon was observable in the Miri country south of the Kamla, where individual Apa Tanis could safely travel and trade in the wake of my porter column, even though at that time I would have been quite unable to afford them protection.

Improved communications, however, will not of themselves lead to the pacification of a country in which for countless generations armed force has been the conventional means of settling disputes. Contemplating the future of these hill-tracts, suddenly thrown into prominence by the recent political changes in Tibet, one may well wonder how it will be possible to replace feuds and recourse to raiding by a rule of law under which even the inhabitants of small hamlets can enjoy security of property and person. Short of policing the country with large military forces—an impracticable and hardly a desirable solution—I cannot see any way of changing Dafla habits and attitudes overnight. The best chance for bringing about a *slow* change, on the other hand, lies in the development and encouragement of the existing indigenous institutions providing for the settlement of disputes and the conclusion of peace treaties. It may be possible, for instance, to arrange for periodic *mel* or tribal councils organized on a regional basis as an alternative to the cumbersome machinery of negotiation by go-betweens which is usually only set in motion after a dispute between two parties has resulted in violence ; and the principle of *dapo* treaties could be so developed as to link an ever increasing number of villages in non-aggression and security pacts and thus gradually extend the rule of law within the framework of the recognized tribal code.

Soil Erosion and Agricultural Techniques

It is certain, however, that whatever methods the Government of India adopts in order to extend its influence over the Subansiri region, thereby reinforcing its political claim to the whole territory south of the McMahon Line, penetration can only be achieved by slow stages.

The romantics may feel satisfaction that somewhere in the world there are still unsophisticated and picturesque peoples who persist in their traditional ways of life, ignorant of the 'blessings' of a civilization which threatens to eliminate the cultural individuality of small groups and to spread mass produced mediocrity to the remotest Asian village. Security of life and property, they may argue, can be too high a price to pay for the disintegration of a people's culture, and for the decline of those social and æsthetic values which stimulate economic effort and lend zest to the striving for wealth and prestige.

The recognition of all that is inherently valuable in tribal cultures, however, must not blind us to the fact that in many respects the tribesmen of the Subansiri area could derive great benefit from closer contact with the outside world, and particularly the introduction of such basic measures as fundamental education, medical aid and above all instruction in improved agricultural methods.

The progressive deterioration of the soil in many parts of the Dafla and Miri country might be halted by the introduction of terrace-cultivation in place of the present wasteful slash-and-burn methods, which tend to exhaust soil fertility, and sometimes necessitate the abandonment of despoiled land. Anyone who has seen the extensive terracing of hillsides, no less steep than those of the Kamla and Panior valleys, whereby the people of eastern Nepal have turned their rugged mountain country into a land of plenty, must realize that in the Subansiri area too agricultural output could be greatly increased. What the Rais have done in the Dudh Kosi valley, where flights of terraces reaching from altitudes of 4,000 feet up to over 7,500 feet bear rich crops of rice, millet and maize in the lower altitudes, and wheat, barley and potatoes in the higher, could presumably be repeated in the Kamla valley. To introduce such terracing even in a small area would certainly require prodigious effort, considerable expenditure and skilful social engineering, but the adoption of rice cultivation on irrigated terraces by the Mai and Jorum Daflas, who have profited from the example of the Apa Tanis, shows that the Daflas are not inherently averse to learning new methods of husbandry.

233

Epilogue

The nature of the terrain, however, sets limits to the development of agricultural techniques. Narrow terraces on steep slopes offer little scope for the use of plough and draft animals, and hoe and digging stick will continue to be the main instruments of tillage.

The quality of implements wielded by hand, however, could be greatly improved. Spades made from mithan shoulder blades will undoubtedly be replaced by a more effective instrument as soon as the villages along the trade divide between Assam and Tibet can obtain adequate supplies of iron.

It is in this middle zone, furthest removed from both Indian and Tibetan sources of supply, that the scarcity of salt and iron as well as of textiles is most acute. The eagerness with which the inhabitants of this zone seized the chance of earning a cotton cloth or a pound of salt by carrying our loads is proof of the great demand for such goods. But, however great the need of more adequate clothing and better implements, what are these populations to give in exchange for the goods which improved communications with India would enable them to buy? The vegetable dyes, cane-ropes, roughly cured skins and furs, and minor jungle produce which are eagerly sought by Tibetans, are not in demand in Assam, and it is therefore not merely a question of opening the country to Indian trade, but of helping the tribes to develop the production of goods for which there is a market among the plains populations of Assam, or providing them with new sources of income which would provide a basis for the intensification of trade.

The outlines of a plan providing for the gradual pacification and economic development of the area, which I submitted to the Government of India, have been printed as part of my report *Ethnographic Notes on the Tribes of the Subansiri Region* (Assam Government Press, Shillong, 1947) and some of my suggestions have since been implemented. The recent establishment of Chinese military bases in Tibet must increase the urgency of extending effective control over the no man's land that stretches between the two great powers. For however cordial the new Republic's relations with China may be, no Indian government can contemplate with any degree of complacency the continued existence of unadministered and unexplored hill tracts inside the line claimed as its international frontier.

Another season's exploration might have closed the gap between the Sipi valley which we reached in April 1945 and the Tibetan frontier villages on the Chayal Chu and the Tsari Chu visited by Kingdon

Ward [1] and F. Ludlow. [2] Both these explorers approached the upper course of the Subansiri from the Tibetan side, but neither of them succeeded in descending along the Chayal Chu or the Tsari Chu into the area known to us as Agla Marra, the country of 'savage and war-like' Lobas. Such Loba tribesmen as they encountered at Lung on the Chayul Chu and at Migyitun on the Tsari Chu were to all outward appearances indistinguishable from the people we met in the valleys of the Kamla and Sipi. A Loba photographed by F. Ludlow at Migyitun [3] resembles in every detail of dress and appearance the tribesmen of the Sipi valley, and the Lobas whom he met near the Kashong La show all the typical characteristics of the Miris of the Upper Kamla valley. [4]

These photographs, of whose existence I was unaware until after I had left the Subansiri area, are convincing proof that populations very similar to those we came to know in the Kamla and Sipi valleys extend as far north as the Great Himalayan Range, and that some of them occasionally cross the high passes into Tibet. While there remains a stretch of unexplored country between the points reached by Kingdon Ward and Ludlow on the Tibetan side and the northernmost part of the area which we visited in 1945, the ethnographical gap seems to have been closed. People of practically identical appearance have now been encountered and photographed both north and south of Agla Marra, and it is permissible to assume that they form at least an important part of the intervening population. Doubtful only is the identity of the people known to the Daflas as Borus and Ngas.

It is possible, and even probable, that in some high valleys south of the Great Himalayan Range, there live populations corresponding to the Sherpas of Nepal or the Bhutias of other Himalayan areas, populations more nearly akin to the Tibetans than to the tribesmen described as Lobas. The Nga shepherds of whom the Mengo people spoke may be such high altitude dwellers, and so may the yak breeders of whom I heard in Nilö. Neither Kingdon Ward nor Ludlow make any mention of such people, but it is doubtful whether they would have struck a traveller, not particularly concerned with ethnographic classifications, as significantly different from the Tibetan peasantry of the border areas. Just

[1] *Assam Adventure*, London, 1941, p. 74.

[2] 'The Sources of the Subansiri and Siyom', *The Himalayan Journal*, Vol. X, 1938.

[3] F. Ludlow, *op. cit.*, illustration 5.

[4] *Ibidem*, illustration 6.

as nine out of ten travellers meeting a group of Sherpas on the road between Tingri and the Nangpa La would take them for Tibetans, so people from Agla Marra other than Lobas may have passed unrecognized even if seen by one of the few explorers who approached the Subansiri area from the Tibetan side.

What then are the prospects of closing the geographical gap and visiting the area immediately south of the Great Himalayan Range ? For the officers of the Government of India or a scientific expedition approved and assisted by the Indian authorities, there should be no unsurmountable difficulty of reaching Agla Marra by the route follow-ing the Selu river or by that which passes through the Sipi and Möngö valleys. Even a fraction of the resources spent year after year on Himalayan mountaineering ventures would suffice to put these unknown borderlands on the ethnographic map and acquaint us with populations living in complete seclusion from the modern world.

INDEX

AUTHOR'S PUBLICATIONS ON THE
SUBANSIRI REGION

Ethnographic Notes on the Tribes of the Subansiri Region, Assam Government Press, Shillong, 1947.

Exploration in the Eastern Himalayas, Diaries of Travel in the Subansiri Region 1944 and 1945, Shillong 1947.

'Agriculture and Land Tenure among the Apa Tanis', *Man in India*, Vol. XXVI, 1946, No. 1.

'Notes on Tribal Justice among the Apa Tanis', *Man in India*, Vol. XXVI, 1946, Nos. 3 and 4.

'Culture Types in the Assam Himalayas', *The Indian Geographical Journal*, Vol. XXI, 1946, No. 2.

'Anthropology and Administration in the Tribal Areas of the North-East Frontier', *Eastern Anthropologist*, Vol. III, 1949, No. 1.

'The After-Life in Indian Tribal Belief', *Journal of the Royal Anthropological Institute*, Vol. 83, 1953, Part I, pp. 37–49.

INDEX

Index